Management Decision-Making, Big Data & Analytics

Sara Miller McCune founded SAGE Publishing in 1965 to support the dissemination of usable knowledge and educate a global community. SAGE publishes more than 1000 journals and over 800 new books each year, spanning a wide range of subject areas. Our growing selection of library products includes archives, data, case studies and video. SAGE remains majority owned by our founder and after her lifetime will become owned by a charitable trust that secures the company's continued independence.

Los Angeles | London | New Delhi | Singapore | Washington DC | Melbourne

Management Decision-Making, Big Data & Analytics

Simone Gressel, David J. Pauleen & Nazim Taskin

Los Angeles | London | New Delhi
Singapore | Washington DC | Melbourne

Los Angeles | London | New Delhi
Singapore | Washington DC | Melbourne

SAGE Publications Ltd
1 Oliver's Yard
55 City Road
London EC1Y 1SP

SAGE Publications Inc.
2455 Teller Road
Thousand Oaks, California 91320

SAGE Publications India Pvt Ltd
B 1/I 1 Mohan Cooperative Industrial Area
Mathura Road
New Delhi 110 044

SAGE Publications Asia-Pacific Pte Ltd
3 Church Street
#10-04 Samsung Hub
Singapore 049483

Editor: Ruth Stitt
Assistant editor: Jessica Moran
Assistant editor, digital: Sunita Patel
Production editor: Sarah Cooke
Copyeditor: Gemma Marren
Proofreader: Katie Forsythe
Indexer: Silvia Benvenuto
Marketing manager: Abigail Sparks
Cover design: Francis Kenney
Typeset by: C&M Digitals (P) Ltd, Chennai, India

Library of Congress Control Number: 2020934797

British Library Cataloguing in Publication data

A catalogue record for this book is available from the
British Library

ISBN 978-1-5264-9201-2
ISBN 978-1-5264-9200-5 (pbk)

CONTENTS

DETAILED CONTENTS

LIST OF FIGURES

LIST OF TABLES

ONLINE RESOURCES

Management Decision-Making, Big Data and Analytics is supported by online resources. Visit **https://study.sagepub.com/gressel** to take advantage of the learning resources for students and lecturers.

FOR STUDENTS

Free **SAGE Journal Articles** to extend your knowledge and support your assignments.

Weblinks highlighting real-world examples.

FOR LECTURERS

An **Instructor's Manual** providing tutor's notes and answers to chapter questions and exercises to support your teaching.

PowerPoint Slides which can be adapted and edited to suit your own teaching needs.

ABOUT THE AUTHORS

SIMONE GRESSEL

Simone Gressel (PhD) is a lecturer at The Hague University of Applied Sciences in the Netherlands. She has studied in Germany, the Netherlands, the United States, and completed her doctoral studies in Management and Information Systems in New Zealand. As part of the Management Analytics Decision-Making group, her research aims at exploring the role of analytics and big data as well as human factors such as intuition and experience in the managerial decision-making process, and how a balance between both can be established. She has also held Director positions in the IT industry.

DAVID J. PAULEEN

David J. Pauleen (PhD) is professor of Technology Management at Massey University, New Zealand. His current research revolves around wisdom in management, personal knowledge management, knowledge management, cross-cultural management, emerging work practices, and virtual team leadership dynamics, communication and technology. His work has appeared in numerous journals including: *Information Systems Journal* (2018), *Decision Sciences Journal* (2018), *Journal of Business Ethics* (2019, 2013), *Journal of Management Information Systems* (2003–4), and *Journal of Information Technology* (2001). He is editor of the book, *Cross-Cultural Perspectives on Knowledge Management* (2007), and co-editor of *Personal Knowledge Management: Individual, Organizational and Social Perspectives* (2010) and the *Handbook of Practical Wisdom: Leadership, Organization and Integral Business Practice* (2013). He co-authored the book, *Wisdom, Analytics and Wicked Problems: Integral Decision-Making in the Information Age* (2019), and is the co-editor of the *Routledge Practical Wisdom in Leadership and Organization Series*.

NAZIM TASKIN

Nazim Taskin is a senior lecturer at the School of Management, Massey University, New Zealand. He holds a PhD in Interdisciplinary Studies from the University of British Columbia, Okanagan, Canada. His research interests include enterprise systems, strategic IS/IT alignment, big data and analytics, decision-making and knowledge management.

Nazim has published in various journals and conferences including *Australasian Journal of Information Systems*, *Journal of Knowledge Management*, *Journal of Electronic Commerce*, *Journal of Enterprise Information Management*, *Business Strategy and the Environment*, Hawaii International Conference on System Sciences (HICSS), Australasian Conference on Information Systems (ACIS), Americas Conference on Information Systems (AMCIS), and European Conference on Information Systems (ECIS). He has also co-authored a book chapter.

ABBREVIATIONS

AaaS	Analytics as a Service
AI	artificial intelligence
BDAC	big data analytics capability
BDAKM	Big Data, Analytics, Knowledge Management model
BI	business intelligence
BI&A	business intelligence and analytics
DaaS	Data as a Service
DAO	Decentralized Autonomous Organization
DBMS	database management systems
DJAMM	Data Journey to Analytics Maturity Model
DL	deep learning
DM	decision-making
DSS	Decision Support Systems
EDW	enterprise data warehouses
ERP	enterprise resource planning
ES	enterprise system
GDPR	General Data Protection Regulation
HTML	Hypertext Markup Language
HTTP	Hypertext Transfer Protocol
IoT	Internet of Things
IS	information systems
KM	knowledge management
KMS	knowledge management system
KPI	key performance indicator
KSAs	knowledge, skills and abilities
MEC	Mobile Edge Computing
MIS	management information system
ML	machine learning
RDBMS	Relational Database Management Systems
RFID	radio-frequency identification
ROI	return on investment
SaaS	Software as a Service
STEM	Science, Technology, Engineering and Mathematics
URI	Uniform Resource Identifiers

FOREWORD

This is a book for real people who have to make decisions and who want to use the best technology and data analytics available today. A distinguishing feature of the book is its care to place the human element at the centre. Human judgment, the collective knowledge of management teams, interpersonal communication, the cultural divide between managers and information technologists, as well as the propensity for people to get caught up in the hype and inflated expectations around new technologies at the expense of reality are all examples of the kind of care that I mention. Similarly, big data, analytics, AI, deep learning technology, and augmented intelligence technology are also carefully explained in accessible language in relation to management decision-making. You do not need to be a technologist to make sense of this book. The many useful charts and diagrams, the recommended additional readings, insightful quotations that give voice to managers' experiences in working with big data to make decisions, and summaries of key learning for each chapter all lend themselves to making the learning experience easier and more applicable. Most importantly, I think it is a book that will make you want to learn and read more on this critically important topic.

Professor (Honorary) David Rooney, Macquarie Business School – Macquarie University, Australia

1
PROFESSIONAL MINDSETS

Contents

Highlight Box 1.1

Professional Mindsets: Who Is Thinking What?

What do managers think when they hear about big data and analytics? Do they understand these technologies and how they can be used in decision-making? And what about those who work with data and analytics, the information technologists ... do they know what managers need to make better decisions? The following observations by working professionals, based on recent research (Gressel, 2020), hint at what's on managers' and technologists' minds:

Head of Data/Analytics Department: 'Some people absolutely get it, but the level of engagement varies. And largely, business people feel that actually data is hard, and analytics is hard, and they need help. And until we get them help, and get them data and analytics, there is no point really thinking about where they fit into the business.'

(Continued)

CEO of a Small Company: 'I think a lot of the challenges come down to education. To a lot of people, data can mean – at an extreme level, "That's what I use to top up on my phone," to "Oh, I absolutely understand the power of data and I know the distinction between the management of data, using tools to analyze it, and extracting insights."'

Business Analyst: 'If the CEO is telling me to go back and look at the data again, sometimes I feel this is coming from someone who has a fear, a mistrust or a misunderstanding of what this data actually represents. And in that case, I may need to reemphasize or sell the point a little bit better and maybe do a better job at explaining what the data represents. But then on the other hand, if the CEO comes from an analytic background, then he understands the business and he understands the data. So if he wants it, it's not just because he's the CEO, but because he understands both sides.'

Head of Data/Analytics Department: 'The real challenge is knowing the right questions, and those questions should be driven from understanding how data can create value in your business. So in a lot of cases I meet business people who say "I've got a need or an issue, and I believe that data can help" – and I say "Cool, let's talk, articulate your need."'

CHAPTER 1 KEY LESSONS

1. Data-based decision-making is now a critical tool in management decision-making and organizational success.
2. Managers must have enough knowledge of data and analytics to ask the right questions about how they can be used in decision-making.
3. Managers need to bridge the current divide between themselves and information technologists.

INTRODUCTION

Managers and technologists are educated and trained to think and speak differently about technology and business. In an age where data-driven decision-making is becoming the new norm, where technology and business overlap, the gap resulting from the differences between technologists and managers needs to be bridged. In this first chapter, we want to set the stage for the book by delving deeper into these differences, their origins and how to bridge the gap. In essence, managers and technologists perceive the world differently and think about problems differently. This often results in them having difficulty finding common ground when it comes to making decisions about business or technology-based problems. In Highlight Box 1.1 we underscore these issues by using some of the quotes we have collected during our research. Of course, we must point out that managers, particularly in IT-related departments, can have technology-based backgrounds – however, in most organizations, these are a minority.

In this book, when we speak of managers we refer to those working in organizations from line managers to C-level (CEO, CFO, CIO, etc) executives. Decision-making is at the core of what these managers do (Intezari and Pauleen, 2019). Indeed, Herbert Simon (1960) considers 'decision-making' and the whole process of management to be synonymous. When managers engage in decision-making, they need to weigh up choices and consider consequences. They have to consider how stakeholders will respond. In this sense, managers see the world as a set of competing interests in which they must seek mutually acceptable solutions. Management decision-making will be explored in greater detail in Chapter 4.

Information technologists is the term we use in this book to describe as a group all for those in the organization who work primarily with technology, particularly data and information systems. Over the years, and as technology has developed, they have included systems analysts, software engineers, network engineers, IT specialists, web designers, mobile app developers and so on. More recently, in the age of big data and analytics, they are often referred to as data scientists, data analysts, data engineers, data architects and the like. Highlight Box 1.2 lists some of these positions and describes their responsibilities. It is probably safe to say that in general, information technologists tend to be more immediate and hands-on, putting their focus on engineering solutions to the problems they encounter. This is different from managers on the business side who tend to engage in more conjectural thinking when approaching problems as they consider the relationships between people, context and the problem.

Highlight Box 1.2

Table 1.1   Information technologists' roles

Role	Key Knowledge	Selected Responsibilities	Selected Tools/Languages
Statistician	• Statistical theories, methods, techniques • Mathematics	• Design surveys and experiments • Apply statistical methods, theories, techniques, analysis • Visualize findings in a report	• SPSS • SAS • R • RATS • E-Views • MPlus • STAT, • HLM • Minitab • MLWin • PLS • Lisrel • AMOS • Shazam • Statistica

(Continued)

Table 1.1   (Continued)

Role	Key Knowledge	Selected Responsibilities	Selected Tools/Languages
Data Architect	• Databases and data warehouses	• Develop architecture for data and data warehouse • ETL	• SQL • XML • Pig • Spark
Data Engineer	• Databases and data warehouses • Software engineering	• Develop architecture and infrastructure for data and data warehouse • ETL • Data modeling • Data management	• SQL • NoSQL • MySQL • R • SAS • MatLab • Hadoop • Java • Python • Perl • Pig
Data Analyst	• Statistics • Mathematics • Visualization • Data wrangling	• Answering the business question given to them using different techniques, methods, tools to analyze collected data	• SQL • NoSQL • MySQL • SAS • R • Python • Java Script • Perl • Pig • Hive • Tableau
Data Scientist	• Mathematics • Statistics • Modeling • Computer science or software engineering • Machine learning • Visualization	• Data cleansing • Data processing • Finding answers to the business questions they developed • Communicating results to business manager and relevant IT staff	• R • Python • SAS • Hive • MatLab • SQL • Perl • Ruby • Pig • Spark • Hadoop • Bayesian Networks • Microsoft Azure AI • Microsoft Azure ML
Business Analyst	• Business processes • BI tools	• Database design • ROI assessment • Budget management • Risk management • Producing reports for decision-makers • Marketing and finance activities	• Jira • Toad • Trello • Microsoft Axure • Tableau

Source: Granville, 2013, 2014a, 2014b, 2014c; Mazenko, 2016; Schmarzo, 2018; DataFlair, 2019

Data science can be defined as a field possessing attributes from other fields such as computer science, software engineering, statistics, mathematics, data mining, machine learning (ML), management science and operations research/industrial engineering. With recent advances in technology, data collection and analysis, new roles have emerged, such as: data scientist, data analyst, data engineer and data architect. *Data scientists* normally excel in statistics, mathematics, data engineering, machine learning, business, software engineering, visualization and spatial data. They explore data collected from different sources, gain insights and look for patterns to predict future events. *Statisticians* generally design surveys or conduct experiments to collect data, then analyze and interpret the data by applying statistical theories, methods, techniques and analysis, before applying visualization techniques to present the results. *Data architects* and *data engineers* possess extensive knowledge of databases and data warehouses and focus on developing the architecture for the data or data warehousing and data integration. Data engineers may also possess deep knowledge of software engineering. *Data analysts* usually work with structured or organized data. They convert the collected data, usually from enterprise systems, into different formats before conducting their analysis and creating visual representations of them to address business issues. *Business analysts* manage business processes and produce scheduled as well as ad hoc reports for decision-makers. They are often responsible for database design, ROI assessment, managing budgets and risks, and planning marketing and finance activities. They work closely with business managers.

Key organizational actors perceive decision situations differently and think differently about how to solve problems; this can have significant implications for interpersonal and organizational effectiveness. In this chapter we will look at what has changed for management in the age of big data and how these changes can be addressed. We also look in more depth at the mindsets of managers and information technologists, how these can be understood and how they can be bridged through the building of shared mental models and other strategies. Finally, we highlight that there is currently a shortage of managers and information technologists with the knowledge and skills to effectively fuse business decision-making with big data and analytics. We explain how this book can help develop essential skills necessary to address this shortage.

MANAGEMENT IN THE AGE OF BIG DATA

Google, Facebook and Amazon are examples of successful companies that were started in and have thrived since the Dot-Com age. The founders of these Internet-based companies grew up and were educated and socialized with computers and the early Internet. Their experiences, education and interests allowed them to see the potential of Internet-based technology, including the promise of big data and analytics, and made it possible for them to design and engineer technical platforms that could create and address business and social needs. In the early days of these companies, the founders would hire like-minded employees, who all spoke the same 'language'.

The Dot-Com bubble of 2000 changed everything. It laid bare the fact that while technologists had great ideas and could develop technology, they were not always the most suitable people to manage businesses. Examples of companies that failed due to bad management abound and include Boo.com – an online fashion company, Pets.com – an online pet supplies company, and WebVan – an online grocery service. The founders of the companies that survived realized that they needed to bring in business-oriented managers and executives – people trained to run businesses. For example, Apple brought in Tim Cook in 1998 and Google hired Eric Schmidt in 2001 to help manage their business operations.

Businesses that existed before the Dot-Com era, so-called 'bricks and mortar' companies, saw the changes being wrought by emerging technologies and realized that they needed to incorporate them into their operations. The evolution of data and analytics-based technologies and their impact on management decision-making are covered in more detail in Chapters 2 and 3, but through the early Dot-Com era and certainly by the time social media and mobile technologies became ascendant it became clear to most businesses that big data and analytics could provide significant business opportunities (Bholat, 2015).

While Dot-Com companies evolved in tandem with these technologies, traditional businesses were always trying to incorporate the latest technology into their operations, from computers in the 1960s to enterprise systems in the 1990s (see Chapter 2 – Technological Evolution of Data and Its Management). These technologies usually required significant changes in organizational processes and culture. Not only did they have to develop their technological infrastructure, but they needed to reconsider their human resources. Of course, they needed information technologists to develop, implement and operate the new technologies and business analysts to help make the data more relevant to the business, but they also needed managers and executives who understood the potential of technology and knew the right questions to ask about what technology was needed and how it could be used to greatest advantage. In cases where the business side did not understand the technology, money was wasted, opportunities were missed and businesses often failed. With the advent of the Internet, mobile applications, social media and other recent technologies, the pace of change, the sophistication of these technologies, and their effects on business have all accelerated. Even companies that started in the Dot-Com age may have trouble evolving at current rates of change. Facebook, the most dominant social media site for a generation, is now confronting social, technical and political challenges that may very well spell the beginning of the end for it.

In the age of big data, business managers will need to be able to work with business analysts, who will need to be able to work with data scientists: ideally, they will all be able to work together (Davenport and Dyché, 2013). It will be challenging to integrate these people and technologies into a seamless whole that will be able to exchange relevant information and knowledge in an effective decision-making process. Let's look more closely at how technology might be integrated in management decision-making.

A decision situation, or decision-demanding situation, refers to a situation when decision-making is required (Intezari and Pauleen, 2019). There are all kinds of decisions made in business from operational to strategic, each with its own set of challenges. In this book we tend to focus on strategic decision-making, because strategic decisions are usually the most complex and challenging kinds of decisions managers must make. Because of the considerable ambiguity, uncertainty and risk associated with strategic decisions, the effective use of big data and analytics requires high levels of human judgment, experience, expertise and knowledge to judge the value of the data and understand the implications of the analysis for the decision situation (Pauleen and Wang, 2017). Human knowledge can bring focus to the complex environments that global business must grapple with today, while analyzing and integrating data can inform and illuminate in great detail many areas of the global environment. In the field of marketing, for example, multinational consumer data and multi-source marketing data can be generated through the integration of population censuses, product types and regional industrial profiles. The use of big data at these levels will require data scientists and analysts who can collect data from different sources, extract meaning from the data through sophisticated analysis, combine analyzed data in ways that add value to the business, and present it in ways that managers can understand and use.

Information technologists bring different perspectives and kinds of knowledge and experience when they analyze big data with either a specific purpose in mind or when exploring new opportunities (Pauleen and Wang, 2017). In such cases, a data scientist would apply their knowledge to extract relevant information from big data but also when choosing the analytic tools to be used in analyzing the data. For example, key search words via text mining may be presented by data attributes of frequency, region and gender. The data scientist will decide which key words will be analyzed. This combination of data analysis and human input can generate new knowledge, which can provide insight into how to address previously defined problems or to initiate new organizational initiatives. A good example of creating knowledge based on big data and analytics to initiate new actions is Amazon's recommender system, which uses customer data and dedicated analytics to suggest products to customers.

Finally, the information and knowledge derived from the data need to be acted on in the form of management decisions. Managers should have the perspective, training and knowledge to make the best use of whatever advantages the data and analytics have to offer.

The key question, however, is 'do they?' Do managers know enough about big data and analytics to know the right questions to ask – what data is needed, what kinds of analysis can be done, how to make best use of the data? Can managers understand what the information technologists are telling them? And just to even the scales a bit, do the information technologists understand the kind of data and analysis that the managers need to make decisions that benefit the organization?

THE DIFFERENT MINDSETS OF MANAGERS AND INFORMATION TECHNOLOGISTS

As discussed above and illustrated in Highlight Box 1.1, managers and information technologists have different mindsets – different ways of understanding and approaching problems – due to different education, training and experiences. These differing mindsets bring diverse strengths; to capitalise on this, it is important to understand the differences.

One approach is to think about these differences is in terms of computational knowledge and contextual knowledge (Intezari and Pauleen, 2019). Information technologists will tend to have high levels of computational knowledge, which, for the purpose of this book, focuses on knowing how to collect, analyze and interpret data. Managers, on the other hand, will tend to have higher levels of contextual knowledge, which based on their education (for example, an MBA) might include knowledge in finance, human resources, economics and marketing, as well as their particular areas of domain experience and expertise. Unless a manager worked or was educated as an information technologist, they are unlikely to have deep levels of computational knowledge. These human resources of computational and contextual knowledge make for a potentially powerful combination when it comes to solving problems and making decisions, but they must be in sync and complement each other. If they are not, the result will be confusion and the inefficient use of resources.

Consider This Box 1.3

Getting on the Same Page

Data-based decisions may pose significant communication challenges if the data analyst (who is mainly involved in the data collection and data analysis phases) and the decision-maker (who interprets and uses the results of the analysis) are not the same person. The data analyst's lack of contextual knowledge as well as the decision-maker's lack of computational knowledge may cause problems. For example, if the decision-maker's data needs are miscommunicated to the big data and analytics experts, inaccurate or insufficient data may be collected and inaccurate analysis may be applied to the data by the analytics expert. Similarly, if the decision-maker does not have a certain level of computational knowledge, he or she is likely to misunderstand the complexity involved in data collection and analysis, and also to misinterpret the results of the data analysis.

Questions to think about

1. How can decision-makers and analysts ensure that they are on the same page in regard to data needs and analytics objectives?
2. How can both parties be more sensitized to understanding each other's perspectives?
3. With which group do you identify? Discuss your perspective and approach to decision-making with other students that identify with the opposite group.

Let's take a more detailed look at the kinds of knowledge managers and information technologists possess and how they apply it when it comes to linking data, analytics and decision-making into a single process (Figures 1.1 and 1.2).

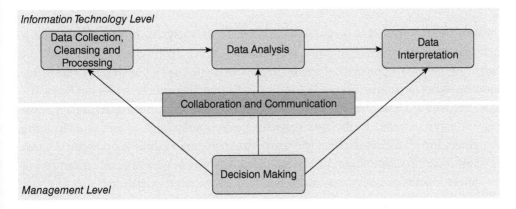

Figure 1.1   Data-based decision-making

The data collection phase encompasses three activities: data identification, data collection and data evaluation (Intezari and Pauleen, 2019). Before the manager is able to make a data-based decision, the required data needs to be identified and collected from credible sources and stored in reliable data storage. Credibility of the data sources is essential to ensure data correctness and accuracy (Sathi, 2012). The data collection phase also includes cleansing data and processing it for future use. Then the relevance and accuracy of the data must be evaluated in relation to the decision situation (for more on data veracity, see Chapter 2). The data collection phase requires high levels of

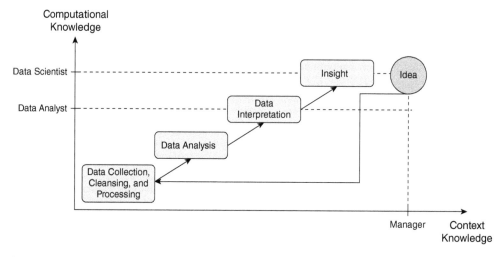

Figure 1.2   Roles of information technologists and managers

computational knowledge, but also requires high levels of contextual knowledge, usually as an input from managers. The decision-maker and data analyst should collaborate to determine what data is required in a given decision situation, what data sources should be used, and how to collect the data.

Once the required data is retrieved, it needs to be analyzed. In this phase, data is analyzed using analytics techniques, tools and statistical algorithms. To have a reliable output from the data preparation process, it is necessary to have a high level of knowledge about analytics techniques and tools to ensure selecting the correct ones for analyzing the data. The data analysis phase in particular requires a high level of computational knowledge, which here refers to the data specialist's expert knowledge of and skills in using computers and statistical software packages. Although data analysis is primarily the task of an information technologist, ideally managers will have at least basic understanding of the different kinds of analytics available and why and when they are used.

In the data interpretation phase the output of the data analysis can be visualized as numbers, charts or statements, and (as discussed in Chapters 2 and 3) can be descriptive, diagnostic, predictive, prescriptive or autonomous in nature. The formatting of the data may be done by a data analyst, but the interpretation is likely to be done by a business analyst or ideally by the manager who is using the data as an input into their decision-making. In interpreting data, contextual knowledge is essential as it is the manager's knowledge of and experience with the decision situation (including the problem, motivations and objectives) that will draw insight and ideas from the data.

As can be surmised from the above discussion, even within the two groups there will be specialized knowledge bases, with varying mixes of computational and contextual knowledge.

The information technologists may specialize in any or all of the three phases of data and analytics and may be classed as data engineers, data architects, data scientists or data analysts (see Highlight Box 1.2). Managers from line managers to CEOS, as well as business analysts, will also bring different levels of experience and specialist domain knowledge which will strongly shape the levels of contextual knowledge they bring to bear in a decision situation. Ultimately, the quality of a data-based decision depends on the manager's contextual knowledge to transform the data into knowledge and to apply the results of the analytics to the decision situation.

It is important to keep in mind that data-based decisions, especially decisions driven by big data and analytics, are technology bound. Due to the volume, variety and velocity of big data (see Chapter 2), it is almost impossible to perform data collection and data analysis without implementing appropriate technologies such as advanced database management systems and complex statistical software packages. Organizations must keep in mind that they need highly trained and knowledgeable employees to successfully use these technologies. Since it is unlikely that any single individual will possess all the technical and managerial knowledge to go from data to decisions, it is imperative that the various experts in the organization be able to work together effectively. This requires communication and shared mental models.

THE IMPORTANCE OF COMMUNICATION AND SHARED MENTAL MODELS BETWEEN MANAGERS AND INFORMATION TECHNOLOGISTS

Knowledge guides us in how we live and work. This guidance works in the form of often habitual patterns of assumptions, cognitions and feelings (Pauleen et al., 2010): what we call mental models. Our individual mental models are formed by our upbringing and education and are fundamental in shaping the way we understand and act in the world. When we choose to study a particular major at university we are often following our natural proclivities or interests. University education often strengthens these inclinations and begins a process of systematic enculturation in ways of understanding and responding to oneself and the world around us. We are in a sense enculturated into a select form of knowledge (Holden, 2002). It is safe to say that three years or more of university education in STEM subjects (Science, Technology, Engineering and Mathematics) is going to result in the acquisition of a distinct body of knowledge and the development of mental models quite different from those educated in other areas such as arts, humanities and business.

These mental models are then further reinforced in our careers. Newly hired computer engineers work closely with and are taught and mentored by more senior computer engineers, while new hires in business learn the ropes by watching and listening to their more experienced colleagues. It is worth pointing out that even within these broad groups there are distinct subcultures. For example, those working in marketing have different mental models from accountants and human resource professionals, and software programmers will see and approach problems differently from computer engineers. Within an organization, these differing mental models create function-based silos of knowledge, but because knowledge also communicates and signals social meanings (McCarthy, 1996), these silos also become social silos. In other words, technologists and managers tend to hang out with their own kind.

Working across both functional knowledge silos and social silos is a huge organizational challenge, especially when these different functional groups need to work together when dealing with complex problems. Different groups bring their own ways of knowing: their own ways of 'seeing' a problem and their own approaches for solving it. And they tend to communicate with and understand only each other. How can we marshal an organization's diverse intellectual resources into an instrument of collective organizational action (Rooney and Schneider, 2005)?

The different mental models exist and the only way to effectively share knowledge is through communication. Through communication we develop social relationships, and through social relationships we build shared mental models (Pauleen et al., 2010). Shared mental models occur when we begin to understand the language and thinking of others and combine them with our own. In a sense we seek to merge Mental Model 1 (information technologists) and Mental Model 2 (business managers) and create Mental Model 3 (shared technologists-managers). This book addresses this issue in part through sharing relevant information and knowledge of both management decision-making and technology-based data. By studying and internalizing this knowledge, one can become more confident in communicating with colleagues in the IT or management functions. Computational or contextual knowledge of course will not be enough to develop shared mental models. A whole range of knowledge, skills and abilities (KSAs), many outside the scope of this book, but hopefully within the scope of a university education, might include interpersonal and intergroup communication skills, management skills, and even political and diplomatic skills. Add to this the capacities for foresight, insight, empathetic understanding, tolerance of ambiguity, emotional intelligence and so on and you begin to build the KSAs necessary to foster genuine knowledge sharing (Pauleen et al., 2010).

Beyond aspects dealing with human KSAs it's worth organizations considering how they can build organizational culture (Chapter 7) that supports knowledge sharing and integration. The right kinds of information systems are also critical. Intezari and Gressel (2017) suggest that big data information systems supporting decision-making should be social, cross-lingual, integrative, simple and understandable as well as dynamic and agile.

The social system has been covered above, but closely linked to it, they say, is the need for multi-language processing; that is, the systems need to be *cross-lingual*, supporting natural language processing to effectively capture, process and disseminate the knowledge required for interpreting big data analysis, and incorporate the analytics into strategic decision-making. By doing this, big data systems become a force for integrating the collection, consolidation and connection of fragmented and scattered, as well as structured and unstructured, data. To this end, the systems should be *simple and understandable*, designed in such a way that the decision-maker and all other participants involved in the system can understand and have confidence in using them. Data and information systems must also be dynamic and agile, and systems that are social, cross-lingual, integrative, simple and understandable will tend to support agility and dynamism. Being able to easily access and understand user-friendly data, will enable people to make more timely, relevant and viable decisions.

As pointed out above, Internet-based companies that have emerged in the Internet age and the following age of big data and analytics have tended to address these issues by employing staff with multiple knowledge sets. More traditional companies, however, are finding these issues challenging to resolve. We suggest that both the management decision-makers and information technologists should have a certain level of both computational and contextual knowledge, as well as the communication skills and other KSAs that will allow them to their work together to build shared mental models.

ADDRESSING THE TALENT SHORTAGE

Specialists in big data and analytics are a sought-after commodity crucial for big data success; however, they are in short supply, which poses a major challenge for organizations (Janssen et al., 2017): 'According to the U.S. Department of Labor, the shortage of people with big data skills in the U.S. alone was predicted to be between 120,000 and 190,000 by 2018' (Alharthi et al., 2017: 288). Managers with the ability to understand and apply big data and analytics in their work in general, and decision-making in particular, also appear to be in short supply.

Highlight Box 1.4

Managers, Analytics and Decision-Making

A 2018 survey of New Zealand managers (from directors and board members to supervisory-level managers) found that 95.7 per cent of these managers were familiar with the term 'analytics'

(Continued)

and 89.6 per cent were at least moderately familiar with the term 'big data' (Taskin et al., 2019). The study also found that almost 60 per cent of managers often or always relied on outputs from data analytics for decision-making. All of the managers mentioned that they at least sometimes incorporate their own intuition and experience into their decision-making. At the same time, however, the study found that a quarter of the managers said they value or trust their intuition and experience more than analytics, while about the same number of participants (28.4 per cent) said just the opposite. The study also found that those who favored analytics over intuition were more often mid-level managers who were not in a position to use big data insights for strategic company decisions. Top executives were generally not as competent as they could be in using analytic tools and techniques and seemed to rely on other managers within the organization to generate big data insights, and those insights are then used to confirm their own intuition or are ignored if they conflict with their gut feeling.

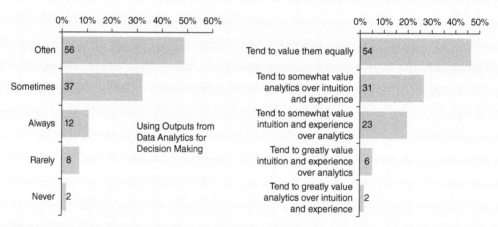

Figure 1.3   Using outputs from data analytics for decision-making

One way this skills shortage can be addressed on a larger scale is through university–industry collaboration to provide the KSAs needed to develop a more adept and adaptable workforce. This book along with university classes and professional training programs are all resources in educating the kinds of managers and information technologists that are needed for organizations to survive and thrive in environments that are rapidly evolving due to technological innovation. To integrate new technologies, traditional businesses and even companies that began in the Internet age will need to evolve as well by not only making changes in their technological infrastructure, but also in their organizational culture and human resources. Data scientists will be needed and they will have to be able to work together with business analysts (Davenport and Dyché, 2013) and of course, business managers. It will be challenging to integrate these people and technologies into a seamless whole that will be able to exchange relevant information and knowledge in an effective decision-making process. It will require people with special talents.

When it comes to the successful adoption of big data technologies, human resources will be critical. A major challenge that organizations face is the lack of analytics skills in existing employees, particularly managers on the business side, as well as a shortage of trained specialized analytics talent, such as data scientists. As pointed out throughout this chapter, organizations require managers who can 'do' or at least understand data and analytics, and information technologists who can 'do' or at least understand business. These people are in short supply and hot demand.

The rapidly spreading use of big data and analytics has prompted increased attention to *talent management* to acquire, secure and train employees in order to develop the necessary skills to exploit the potential of big data and analytics (McAfee and Brynjolfsson, 2012; Shah et al., 2012; Watson, 2016; Bumblauskas et al., 2017). In Chapter 7, we will look in depth at necessary organizational prerequisites for integrating big data and management decision-making, but here will just summarize some of the key responses to address the talent shortage.

Skills gap analysis is one effective tool to assess which big data and analytics skills are lacking in an organization (Watson and Marjanovic, 2013). When the gap is identified, appropriate and tailored measures such as new hires, consulting services or training efforts can be employed to elevate necessary skill levels. Turning data into meaningful insights requires scientific rigor, solid knowledge of statistics, and expertise in the respective empirical methodology, but it also requires the ability and maturity to understand the limitations of data – the ways in which it may be flawed or badly analyzed or misconstrued (Wirth and Wirth, 2017).

After identifying gaps, specific data and analytics needs for each department must be determined. New hires should be selected to match specific department cultures in order to avoid culture clashes or communication problems. Another option is to establish a centralized analytics and data unit that all departments can use as a shared resource. Centralized units allow for the hiring of specialist people, as not every information technologist needs to have the same well-rounded set of skills to adapt to the business managers of the department. The decision to centralize or decentralize should be made before hiring individuals to ensure the best fit and combination of talent.

In addition to externally trained new hires and consultants, internal development and training programs can be designed by HR departments. This allows for a more customized approach that meets the needs of the organizations and specific departments. The training can target business managers and facilitate a basic understanding of analytics and its use for decision-making, reducing fears and distrust around data. Training can also be addressed to information technologists to help them understand business needs and priorities. In particular, workshops that bring together information technologists and business managers within organizations can lead to good results, not only to facilitate knowledge transfer, but also to form the basis for further and future collaboration.

CHAPTER SUMMARY

In this chapter, we have introduced the case for this book. In the age of big data, management decision-making takes on new challenges. These stem from the new technologies of big data and analytics and the changes they bring to decision-making. While these technologies have the potential to better inform decision-making, they will also challenge traditional ways of doing things. Some of the challenges are technological, involving, for example, infrastructure and knowledge of emerging trends and technology, and some concern getting the right human resources and the necessary KSAs on board with new hires or proper training programs. With regard to management decision-making, arguably, the biggest challenge is how to manage the changes in practices and processes that will allow these new technologies and human resources to work together to produce the best possible decision outcomes. This chapter sets the scene and the rest of the book will complete the picture. For now, we can sum up this chapter's key lessons as follows:

KEY LESSONS

In this chapter we have set out the reasons for this book, which can be summarized as:

1. Data-based decision-making is now a critical tool in management decision-making and organizational success. To make the most effective use of data-based decision-making ...
2. ... the management side of the organization must have enough collective knowledge to ask the questions that matter concerning most, if not all, aspects of data-based decision-making, including everything from setting up organizational data systems to questioning data collection, analysis, presentation and use in single decision situations. To accomplish this ...
3. ... managers must learn about big data and analytics and how they can be used and they must be able to bridge the current divide between themselves and information technologists.

2
INTRODUCTION TO BIG DATA

Contents

Highlight Box 2.1

How Much Data Is Out There?

Statista (2019) reports that the number of emails sent and received per day will increase from 281.1 billion in 2018 to 333.2 billion in 2022. According to Domo's *Data Never Sleeps 6.0* report (2018), each minute, in 2018, Snapchat users shared 2,083,333 snaps and watched 4.2 million videos; YouTube users watched 4,333,560 videos and uploaded 400 hours of video; 12,986,111 text messages were sent; 3,138,420GB data were used in the USA; and users sent 159,362,760 emails. Furthermore, according to the recent predictions of IDC (Reinsel et al., 2018) the size of the Global Datasphere (including data on data towers, cloud,

(Continued)

PCs, mobile devices, vehicles, Internet of Things (IoT), etc.), i.e. the amount of data in the world, will reach 175 ZB by 2025.

Source: Domo, 2018; Reinsel et al., 2018; Statista, 2019

Table 2.1   How much is a Yottabyte?

1,024MB	1 Gigabyte (GB)	10^9	2^{30} bytes
1,024GB	1 Terabyte (TB)	10^{12}	2^{40} bytes
1,024TB	1 Petabyte (PB)	10^{15}	2^{50} bytes
1,024PB	1 Exabyte (EB)	10^{18}	2^{60} bytes
1,024EB	1 Zettabyte (ZB)	10^{21}	2^{70} bytes
1,024ZB	1 Yottabyte (YB)	10^{24}	2^{80} bytes

Questions to think about

1. Assume that a 10-second video you shot with your camera takes up 50MB in your smartphone. How many videos taken with your smartphone camera can you store in a device with 200 Petabytes?
2. If around one million books are published in your country per year, how many years would it take to fill 1 ZettaByte of disk storage?

   Hint 1: One character is 1 byte. Assume that each page has 500 words with an average length of 5 characters per word, and each book has 200 pages.

   Hint 2: Assume that same number of books are published each year.

CHAPTER 2 KEY LESSONS

1. Data has always been important to organizations and management decision-making.
2. Big data is evolving and growing rapidly based on new technologies.
3. In combination with new and more powerful analytics, big data has the potential to revolutionize the ways organizations operate and managers make decisions.
4. This potential will be tempered by serious challenges in the utilization of big data that will need to be carefully managed by organizations.

INTRODUCTION

The age of big data and advanced analytics offers new opportunities for management decision-making, but also entails diverse challenges because of its technological novelty and many managers' general lack of experience with the technology and its potential capabilities. Even the term 'big data' is not universally defined or understood, and other management knowledge gaps, such as how to effectively use big data, have not yet been fully identified (Gandomi and Haider, 2015). These gaps lead to misunderstandings of big data's opportunities, limitations and challenges. To comprehend all aspects of big data decision-making, it is essential not only to understand the evolution of big data and advanced analytics, but also what is currently understood by these terms.

This chapter provides readers with a comprehensive introduction to data and big data, including its historical evolution and current use in organizations. This includes a thorough overview of all key terms and concepts. The relationship between data, information, knowledge and wisdom is explored to form an appreciation of context. A critical appraisal of big data and its uses is offered, including organizational best practices and various challenges to implementing big data, such as limited budgets, lack of trained personnel, and managing risk, privacy and legal concerns. Examples and cases from our recent research are presented to illustrate key points.

TECHNOLOGICAL EVOLUTION OF DATA AND ITS MANAGEMENT

Big data and analytics are often perceived and marketed as a new phenomenon, but in fact they are built upon established technologies such as data warehouses and database management systems (DBMS). Data has been used since the 1950s to support decisions and business processes through the early forms of data management and analytics.

Going back even further in time, we can see that Taylor's scientific management techniques in the early 1900s were the first trigger to store and analyze data albeit limited by the technological capabilities of that time. From the 1930s, digital computers were introduced and eventually led to the data processing era in the 1950s and 1960s, in which managers of financial and military institutions relied on information systems to complete subtasks and automate processes. The increasing use of information systems from the 1960s to 1980s enabled managers to use data for routine decision-making in the management information systems (MIS) era. In this era, the main challenges were about defining success for an information system and ensuring the quality and reliability of the information systems in the organization.

With increasing amounts of data becoming available during this time, new tools and techniques were needed. This was the formative age of information systems (IS), when the discipline began to actively develop theories and methods to manage and use data in management and organizational contexts. Large quantities of collected data often resulted in information overload, which led to new approaches to decision-making

(Niesen et al., 2016). Although the systems helped managers and organizations with decision-making and improving the accuracy and efficiency of operations, there were still questions about whether systems were improving productivity. The challenge organizations faced was not about the data but whether the amount of data was overloading decision-makers with too much information.

In the 1980s, organizations came to recognize the value of IS when developing their strategic goals. This led to a further increase in the use of IS, including the development of the networked organization and to the development of more user-friendly interfaces such as client–server interfaces and eventually the personal computing era. This brought data to the manager's desk. Wider accessibility to computers and information systems helped improve decision-making and individual performance. However, the increasing number of systems raised the question of alignment: are our information systems aligned with our organizational goals and with each other? This question also made managers look more carefully at whether the systems were improving the organization and its performance.

At the beginning of the 1990s, in the enterprise system (ES) and networking era, enterprise resource planning (ERP) systems made data available across organizations, which allowed data to be accessed and shared between managers and applications. Enterprise systems and supply chain management systems allowed data to be shared between organizations on a global scale. These advances enabled more sophisticated group decision support systems. ERP systems provided real time and accurate information by integrating different functional areas in one system. The challenge with these systems was their high cost to the organizations. Managers questioned return on investment (ROI) with these systems as well as whether they resulted in significant strategic value.

While private telecommunications networks made data sharing available in multi-office and multi-national organizations since the 1980s, it was the advent and expansion of the Internet in the mid-1990s that greatly expanded the capabilities of information sharing beyond organizational borders, and made information accessible instantaneously across the world. While enterprise systems could improve decision-making, connectivity through networks, such as the Internet, encouraged and enabled collaboration. This also marked the beginning of the customer-focused era (2000 and beyond), as organizations began collecting IP-specific information about their customers through cookies and server logs, which enabled a customized experience for individuals (Chen et al., 2012). Amazon's recommendation engine as well as Google's search algorithms were pioneering examples of these sophisticated IS applications. The challenge in this era was to develop a system that was 'acceptable' to the end user and valuable to the company. Table 2.2, modified from Petter et al. (2012), illustrates the different information systems eras and the main challenges of those eras.

Table 2.2 The evolution of data and information systems

	Data Processing Era	MIS Era	DSS Era (Information Age)	Personal Computing Era	Enterprise System and Networking Era	Customer-Focused Era (Internet Era)	Big Data and Analytics Era	Autonomous Systems/Computing Era
(Digital Transformation Age)	Data Processing Era		DSS Era		EDW Era	Real-time DW Era	Big Data Era	Autonomous Systems Era
Timeline	1950	1960	1970	1980	1990	2000	2010	2020
Motivating factors		• Realizing the benefits of IS in • Managerial decision-making • Accuracy in operations • Speed of operations • Reduction in cost		• Availability and wider us of PCs and information systems	• Accessibility of integrated, real time, accurate data • Internet	• Availability of customized systems	• Rise of technology systems and devices • Increasing power of computers and sophistication of software development	• Advancement in ML and AI
Objective/ Use		• Routine decision-making • Management reporting		• Improving decision-making and personal performance	Improve • Decision support • Access to real time and accurate data • Collaboration inter-personal/ organizations	• Provide customized experience for individuals	• Prediction, optimized decision outcome and insight	• Limiting human input into analytics
Challenges/ Issues	• Technical quality of the system • Lack of consensus on definition of success of the system	• Information overload • Human factors • Productivity		• Alignment of IS with organizational goals • Questionable impact of IS on organization and performance	• ROI on IT investment • Strategic value of the systems	• Developing technology 'acceptable' to user and beneficial to the company	• 'Identifying appropriate Opportunities' • 'Selecting the right Platform' to store and analyze data • 'Integrating the Platforms' of big data with others • 'Providing governance' around big data • 'Getting the right people' with required skills	• Minimizing biases around ML and AI

Source: adapted from Petter et al., 2012: 353; Watson and Marjanovic, 2013; Davenport and Harris, 2017; Davenport, 2018

As can be seen from this brief history, there were challenges in developing, using and managing data and information systems in support of organizational and management processes, including decision-making. These challenges included issues of sufficient technological and human resources, cost–value proposition and ROI, business-technology alignment, finding appropriate uses for the data (for example, management decision-making), creating user-friendly interfaces, and dealing with information overload. These problems are to some extent comparable to the ones that organizations are now facing with big data.

In Table 2.3, adapted from Watson and Marjanovic (2013: 6), the focus is on the grounding of big data in the field of data management and the use of management tools, especially for decision-making. Big data is depicted as the fourth generation of data management, which rooted big data in the database management field. In the pre-big data ages the focus was on the development and use of single user Decision Support Systems (DSS), which are characterized by a single decision-maker relying on a DSS that is populated by only one or a small number of internal, structured data sources: the use was limited to strategic and tactical decisions and by the limited technology available at the time.

Table 2.3 Evolution of data management and decision-making

Data Management Age	Description	Application	Decision Type	Data Type
1970s – First Generation	A single decision-maker using data and analytic aids to support decision-making Single data source, mostly from a few operational systems	Decision Support Systems (DSS)	Tactical and strategic	Structured Batch mode update Low in volume
1990s – Second Generation	Data-focused approach to data management Data received from several systems	Enterprise data warehouses (EDW)	Strategic, tactical, and operational (first steps in some organizations)	Structured Batch mode update
2000s – Third Generation	Operational decisions and processes are supported by real-time data	Real-time data warehouses	Strategic, tactical, and operational	Mostly structured Real time

Data Management Age	Description	Application	Decision Type	Data Type
2010s – Fourth Generation	New ways of using data, such as deeper understanding, better predictions or greater context Relatively new data sources are utilized	Big data for all organizations Mobile and sensor data	Strategic, tactical, and operational	Structured and unstructured Real time
2020s – Fifth Generation	Data generated by devices, stored and processed in the cloud and analyzed at the edge High use of AI	Edge computing Systems supported with AI applications	Strategic, tactical, and operational	Structured and unstructured Real time, visual and audio

Source: adapted from Watson and Marjanovic, 2013: 6; Davenport and Harris, 2017; Duan et al., 2019

The second generation of enterprise data warehouses (EDW) was led by an increase in reporting needs, which resulted in a larger number of systems providing data, and led to increased use that also extended beyond organizational boundaries. These systems helped managers with tactical and strategic decision-making. Some organizations also used these systems with some real-time data capability for operational decision-making. During the first two ages of data management, the data was usually structured and updates were handled with batch mode. In addition, the technology was still primitive and finding experienced information technologists was a challenge.

Real-time data warehousing is considered the third generation. Still mostly structured data was being captured in real time, enabling managers to extend their use of data to operational decision-making as well, which led to another increase in users. This increase was supported by business intelligence (BI) systems. Organizations developed and used BI systems with their real-time data to gain more business insights and make more effective decisions. This eventually made companies dependent on BI in order to compete or keep their share in the market (Watson and Marjanovic, 2013).

The current big data generation offers new data sources (3Vs, see below) that exceed the capabilities of relational database management systems (RDBMS). New technologies enable the use of big data to create a richer context for improved decision-making, particularly when combined with traditional data. The 3V characteristics of big data have led to challenges including: identifying opportunities, selecting among different platforms for storing data and for integrating big data platforms with other available platforms, providing governance and finally human resources (Watson and Marjanovic, 2013). This most recent and evolved stage is evident in the wide range of organizations utilizing big data for various purposes, incorporating unstructured and diverse data sources into their decision-making. Finally, the fifth generation is beginning to emerge. This will involve an array of new technologies that are now being developed (see Chapter 10). To increasingly greater degrees over time, this generation of data management and decision-making will be managed by artificial intelligence (AI).

Arguably big data is not a new phenomenon but rather part of the technological evolution of data and its applications (Intezari and Gressel, 2017). Big data can be seen as an extension of traditional data, and big data solutions as an extension of traditional data warehouses and analytics. Whether the age of big data and analytics is evolutionary or revolutionary remains to be seen, but it is clear that today's organizations have a wide spectrum of sophisticated analytics techniques and tools available to choose from, which are rooted in the field of data management.

BIG DATA AND ANALYTICS

In business, big data and analytics have always been linked. As we have just seen above, data and analytics are not new to business. They have been used in traditional functions such as business intelligence since the 1950s. While big data and analytics are often linked with each other and the terms used interchangeably, they are in fact two separate things. Big data refers to the huge volumes of data that are continuously produced in different forms and by numerous data sources. Analytics refers to the techniques for exploring and investigating data using statistical and operations analyses to gain insight, usually to improve decision-making. Although big data and analytics are two different things, they each derive their value from the other. Without analytics, big data has little or no value. Analytics without big data is similar to traditional data analysis; it has value, but not to the degree that big data would confer. In this book we acknowledge this joining of the two technologies by generally linking them together through the term 'big data and analytics'. Big data is discussed in detail in this chapter. Analytics is introduced in Chapter 3, and its role in management decision-making is covered in Chapter 5. While describing the two technologies separately, it is important to keep in mind just how interlinked they are.

Two trends are driving the growth of big data and analytics. The first is the rise of technology systems and devices that drive the production and collection of data. These include the Internet (and related networks), mobile devices, satellites, radio-frequency identification (RFID), sensors, cameras and a host of other new and emergent technologies. The second is the ever-increasing power of computers and sophistication of software development. Together these two sets of technologies have made available both vast amounts of data and the ability to analyze that data in real or near-real time (see Highlight Box 2.1). The reach of big data and analytic knowledge is impressive and pervasive.

WHAT IS BIG DATA?

First used in a publication on the visualization of large data sets by Cox and Ellsworth in 1997, big data has surged to the forefront of public discourse. Its uses and the consequences of its use are being explored by academia, industry and government. These uses and consequences will be explored later in this chapter and throughout the rest of this book.

In 2001, big data was characterized in a way that served to distinguish it from traditional data and this characterization has taken hold in academia and industry. Gartner's Doug Laney established three defining dimensions, which are now commonly known as the 3Vs (Laney, 2001): *volume, velocity* and *variety*. Since then, fourth and fifth dimensions have been added by some researchers: *veracity* (Jagadish et al., 2014), and *value* (Mishra et al., 2017). An overview of these dimensions can be seen in Table 2.4.

Table 2.4 Big data dimensions, descriptions and challenges

Dimension	Description	Challenges
Volume	Data sets exceed the capacity of DBMS and traditional analytics tools	Storing data
		Processing power
	Data is expressed in terabytes, petabytes, and more	
Velocity	Data is processed in (near) real time	Data stream or transfer from various devices
	Data collection, analysis and interpretation are continuous processes	Heterogeneous structure of data
Variety	Type of data from diverse data sources – often unstructured – from social media, sensors, text, audio or video files	Some of these formats pose problems for data analysis because converting the formats, understanding the content of the data, and making them readable to everyone accessing it is a challenge – this is related to the problem of compatibility of devices
		Comprehension of data
Veracity	Data sources must be credible and suitable for the organization to provide reliable results	Assuring accuracy of the data and reducing ambiguity
	Involves data sourcing and cleaning	
	Veracity is related to the accuracy of the data	

(Continued)

Table 2.4   (Continued)

Dimension	Description	Challenges
Value	Economic and social benefits are derived from the use of big data

Refers to knowledge and value extraction from data in different formats and from different sources | How to measure ROI?

It is costly to extract meaning from big data |

Source: based on the studies of McAfee and Brynjolfsson (2012); Sathi (2012); O'Leary (2013); Tole (2013); Watson and Marjanovic (2013); Jagadish et al. (2014); Colombo and Ferrari (2015); Abbasi et al. (2016); Bumblauskas et al. (2017); Mishra et al. (2017); Sivarajah et al. (2017)

Volume

The *volume* of big data greatly exceeds the size of traditional data sets and creates challenges for DBMS and data warehouses. However, the volume of data that determines big data is hard to pinpoint to a specific number, generally ranging from terabytes to petabytes or even exabytes (Mishra et al., 2017). This results from the continuous growth of data that is produced every second over the Internet, sensors, customer transactions and so forth. Furthermore, as technological capabilities increase, various limitations decrease. Data can now be stored, transmitted, accessed and analyzed more efficiently and effectively than ever. The lower costs of data storage enable organizations to store increasing amounts of customer and production data.

Cloud computing, for example, offers organizations of all sizes tailored solutions and capacities for their data storage. An organization pays for the used capacity and is provided with rapid elasticity and ubiquitous network access. Cloud computing supports data use and provides organizations with ubiquitous information available anywhere at any time. It also provides the possibility of pay as you go analytics-as-a-service. Users not only have the ability to access their data and information from remote devices, but can also use the necessary analytic tools on demand.

Similarly, AI can offer solutions to big data problems; for example it can be used to analyze petabytes of data to generate insights. Regardless of the volume of big data available, it is worth considering the advice found on the SAS website that states that 'what business does with the data is more important than the volume of data they store' (SAS, 2020). One of the major challenges of dealing with huge volumes of data is having adequate processing power to retrieve, process, integrate and analyze it (Sivarajah et al., 2017). Although storing the data was a big challenge, developments in technologies such as Hadoop and cloud have eased this to some extent.

Velocity

The *velocity* of big data is characterized by the speed of data generation (Phillips-Wren et al., 2015), that is, the processing of data in real or near-real time. While traditional data sets were analyzed in days, weeks or months after collection, big data is analyzed in 'continuous flows and processes' (Davenport and Dyché, 2013). Real or near-real-time data access and analysis provide more flexibility and faster organizational responses.

The velocity of data is especially critical in decision-making since real-time data can greatly influence data-based decision-making. Likewise, decisions involving future operations and strategy may influence which data is collected and analyzed. Changes and alterations that result from decision-making therefore have to be immediately implemented and updated in the ongoing data stream (Bumblauskas et al., 2017).

The speed of data creation is at the heart of the expansion of big data and advanced analytics, and techniques that enable the analysis of this vast stream of data are still underutilized in organizations (Bumblauskas et al., 2017). The effects and challenges of data are focused on the non-homogeneity of the data: that is, the different formatting of the data collected from different sources. As velocity refers to gathering and transferring large amounts of data from different sources and processing them in real time, data with different structures will bring additional and significant challenges involving integrating and analyzing multiple forms of data (Sivarajah et al., 2017).

Variety

The *variety* dimension of big data encompasses the different forms of data sources and kinds of information that can be captured and stored. Traditionally data was limited to structured, numerical data, which could be displayed in spreadsheets: such data currently represents just 5 per cent of all available data (Mishra et al., 2017). The variety of big data allows unstructured forms of data to be collected from almost anywhere including from social media to street-mounted security cameras and texts, audio or video files, sensor data, GPS signals, click-streams and so on.

This type of data offers a new spectrum of possibilities for data analysis and insights but also brings challenges that easily exceed the capabilities of traditional DBMS and data analysis because big data will include both structured and unstructured data, with which traditional systems and analysis cannot cope. These different forms of data will need to be converted into a common format before analysis. The major challenge here is to make the data readable to users of the data.

Consider This Box 2.2

Data Veracity and Decision-Making

One of the key aspects of good decision-making is being able to judge what is good and useful data or information for the decision situation at hand and then using it appropriately in the decision-making process. The veracity of the data set that is used in the decision-making process is critical; it is what gives the data set value. If the data is corrupted in any way, there is no value in it and indeed it is likely to harm the decision-making process and output.

An example of a potentially corrupted data set, according to Dave Snowden, founder and chief scientific officer of Cognitive Edge, is one of the key sources of big data: social media (Pauleen, 2017). According to Snowden, social media is an unconstrained system, where a significant percentage (30–40 per cent) of 'tweets' on any given subject are bot-generated. Bot-generated means the data (tweets) is being generated by computer programs, not humans. If organizations are basing decisions, for example on marketing products, on information derived from computer-generated data, they need to be very clear about the veracity and value of such data. As Snowden explains:

> you can't really trust social media within half an hour of a catastrophe, because people start to play games with it; anything explicit will sooner or later be gamed. If an algorithm can interpret it, then an algorithm can be generated to create it. (Pauleen, 2017: 13)

Questions to think about

1. What are consequences of using 'bad' data in management decision-making? Can you think of some examples?
2. Have you had experience with unreliable social media data? Has it affected your decision-making? How can you verify that social media data such as posts are accurate?
3. How might social media data be relevant for management decision-makers?

Veracity and Value

The 3Vs have come to be accepted as the defining characteristics of big data. More recent research is now taking a more considered look at big data. Veracity reflects how credible a data source is and how well the data suits the organization (see Consider This Box 2.2). To benefit decision-making, and analytics in general, the data sources must be credible to ensure data fidelity, truthfulness, correctness and accuracy.

The *veracity* of data has always been an important factor in data management from the earliest times. It was perhaps not so much of an issue when data was collected by an organization, for example customer or production data, for its own use, but it becomes a grave challenge when applied to the volume, velocity and variety of big data. Because big data sources are of varying reliability with some subject to spam, noise and biases, veracity is perhaps the most critically important data quality measure for big data sources. Vetting data sources and cleaning data to assure accuracy and reduce ambiguity related to the data sets are big and often costly challenges for organizations, but absolutely essential if big data is to be used in decision-making. If decisions are made based on bad data, the decisions are like to be faulty and consequences severe (Intezari and Pauleen, 2019).

Value refers to economic benefits that result from the use of big data, and is considered by some sources as the fifth characteristic of big data. It is a concept that originates from practitioner reports on big data by Oracle and market research firm Forrester, and it reflects the necessity to identify value-adding sources of information that are meaningful. We suggest that value is not really a characteristic of big data, but rather the general objective of utilizing big data. The challenge in achieving this objective lies in defining and measuring the value from the data.

While small amounts of data can be stored and analyzed using relatively common programs such as MS Access, Google Docs, Open Office, Numbers and SPSS, the variety and amount of data that managers have available nowadays require more advanced tools. Insights can only be gained by employing analytics and sophisticated tools. Analytics and these tools are introduced in Chapter 3 and the use of analytics in management decision-making is discussed in depth in Chapter 5.

Consider This Box 2.3

Management Perceptions of Big Data

While the literature and industry might disagree about the specific characteristics that categorize data sets as big data, most sources agree on a minimum of 3Vs. Managers, however, who are making decisions based on big data results, might not always have a clear understanding of what big data is, or might even lack the awareness that they are using it. Throughout our research efforts (Gressel, 2020), we have found that only about four out of 25 managers interviewed could list the three main characteristics of big data and these managers were also information technologists. Others were solely focusing on the volume aspect of the data sets' size, with one manager explaining, 'For me, I think that it is just about volume'. This shows a rudimentary understanding at best, but also highlights the gaps in grasping the full extent of big data.

Other managers were critical of big data and considered it to be merely a buzzword, with one explaining, 'Big data I would define as a buzzword to sell stuff to corporates right now [...] And the interesting thing about data today, it's fashion. And a lot of people talk about it. But they don't really understand it'.

(Continued)

However, some managers did not think an understanding of big data was a key requirement for managers. One believed that most of his employees were not aware of the amount of data that flowed into the information they used for their decisions. He also added that they did not need to know, explaining, 'They [my employees] won't be aware. But they don't need to be if everyone is doing their job'. Another manager, in answer to the question of whether he had previous experience with big data, replied, 'Definitely yes, without calling it that. Have always done that – accessing different sources etc.'

Questions to think about

1. What are your perceptions of big data: valuable resource, just hype, or something in between? Explain why.
2. How can managers most effectively use big data?
3. What are the risks of data-driven decisions and how can managers mitigate these risks?

FROM BIG DATA TO USEFUL KNOWLEDGE

'Does big data equal big knowledge?' was a question posed by Pauleen and Wang (2017) in a special issue on big data and knowledge management (KM) in the *Journal of Knowledge Management*. Data only has value if it can be turned into usable information or knowledge. In this textbook we are most interested in knowing whether and how data can be used in management decision-making. In this section we look at ways that the 'data to knowledge' transformation can be conceptualized. We also briefly introduce categorizations of analytics capabilities, which are specific approaches for turning data into useful information for decision-making.

The evolution of big data provides managers with a significant increase in available data. However, raw data alone cannot assist in improving managerial decision-making. To gain insights from data, it has to be processed in a timely manner and put into a form that is useful for users. It is the analysis of big data, or analytics, that turns data into information. Managers can then use this information in combination with their knowledge, experience and insight to improve their decision-making.

Distinguishing between these key terms – namely data, information and knowledge – is vital to understand the key role that analytics tools play in managerial decision-making. These terms are often graphically represented in the form of the DIK pyramid (Figure 2.1). The DIK pyramid, also known as the DIK hierarchy, has been around for many years in the information sciences field and is considered a short-hand representation of the data to knowledge transformation (Wallace, 2007). It suggests that there is an upward movement starting out from the broad base of data that gets transformed into information and then knowledge.

Data is seen as 'a set of discrete, objective facts about events' (Davenport and Prusak, 1998: 2), and therefore 'unprocessed raw representations of reality' (Faucher et al., 2008: 6). Information is understood as data that has been processed to be useful and meaningful for the receiver of the information (Ackoff, 1989). Knowledge can be understood as processed and validated information (Firestone, 2003). Knowledge is processed by individuals: it is the application and personalization of information (Alavi and Leidner, 2001) and it engages one's interpretation and experience. As related to decision-making, information deals mostly with descriptions and answers to questions such as 'who', 'what', 'when', 'where' and 'how many', while knowledge is more prescriptive and deals with 'how-to' and 'why' questions (Ackoff, 1989).

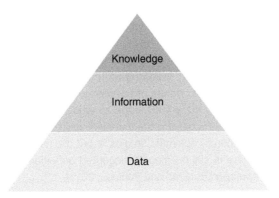

Figure 2.1   DIK pyramid

According to Moore (2017), a data-driven decision-making process begins with the gathering of data, then inferring meaning by setting the data into a context, which produces information. Knowledge is created by synthesizing or combining information, which might involve experience-based judgment calls. Bumblauskas et al. (2017) add an additional level to the DIK pyramid, 'actionable knowledge', explaining 'decision-makers must be able to derive meaning from data or information driving decision-making that can translate into specific action and communication to others' (Bumblauskas et al., 2017: 12f.). This actionable knowledge is required to make effective and timely decisions in the age of big data.

The DIK pyramid has achieved almost meme-like status in academia and industry (Ardolino et al., 2018), particularly in MIS research and practice. The DIK conceptualization draws on the assumption that knowledge can be developed from data and information and that knowledge can be converted back into information and data: this view allows for knowledge to become a storable entity and located in an information or knowledge management system (KMS). It is critically important to understand that this assumption only works insofar as we recognize that what is stored and managed by the systems as knowledge *does not* represent and substitute for the depth and breadth of the knowledge residing in people's minds or bodies (that is, tacit or embodied knowledge). As we see it, management decision-making cannot rely solely on data-derived knowledge: a decision-maker's knowledge, experience and insight are also required.

While the DIK pyramid is regarded by the MIS literature as an efficient way to position knowledge in relation to data and information (Sumbal et al., 2017), the model has received significant criticism. This criticism can be summarized in three ways:

1. Generally, the transformation from one level to the next is not explained (Wognin et al., 2012).
2. The functionality of the pyramid in the real world draws on the assumption of 'pre-emptive acquisition' (Frické, 2009: 135) – which means in practice that data must be collected 'meaninglessly and mindlessly', in the hope that one day it will be turned into information that will answer questions.
3. The ambiguous conceptualization of knowledge, exemplified by terms such as 'processed information', 'information in context', 'validated information' or 'experience in the domain', does not encompass the complex nature of knowledge including implicit or tacit knowledge. This conceptualization limits knowledge to what can be recorded (data) and processed (information). This is despite the extensive discourses and discussions from ancient times to contemporary scientific studies about the nature and the meaning of 'knowledge', that is, there is still no globally accepted definition of the term, nor how knowledge can be developed (Intezari and Pauleen, 2019).

These are valid critiques and have particular resonance in the age of big data and advanced analytics. We will go more deeply into the issues raised by these critiques later in this chapter and in Chapters 3 and 4, but here we can briefly respond:

1. Advanced analytics is quite capable of transforming data into actionable information (see below and Chapter 3), and systematic decision-making can leverage information into integral knowledge-based decisions (Chapters 4 and 5).
2. Pre-emptive acquisition of data (Sivarajah et al., 2017) does seem to be the current fashion. Huge amounts of data are being vacuumed up by industry and government with the expectation or hope that it can or will be useful. We suggest (below) that it will be more efficient and effective to collect data based on likely decisions that (will) need to be made, now or in the future. However, this strategy is likely to be more appropriate for organizations that are advanced in their use of big data and analytics.
3. The complex nature of knowledge and knowing as it relates to rational and non-rational decision-making processes is discussed in depth in Chapter 4.

The DIK pyramid is a convenient, but limited, way to view the relationship between data, information and knowledge and to relate it to management decision-making and organizational pre-requisites regarding systematic approaches to data and analytics (see Chapter 8).

Consider This Box 2.4

Wisdom and the DIK Pyramid

Early scholars added a fourth layer to the DIK pyramid – wisdom – and called it the DIKW pyramid. It was a logical addition, but also simplistic, based on the common (mis-)understanding that wisdom is a higher level of knowledge. As noted above, there is no universally accepted definition of knowledge, so trying to conceptualize wisdom in terms of knowledge cannot result in a clear or appropriate understanding of wisdom. Moreover, it is widely understood in the philosophical, psychological and management literature on wisdom that having knowledge alone does not make one wise (Intezari and Pauleen, 2017). Rather there are other critical qualities involved in practical wisdom beyond knowledge such as experience, cognition, intelligence, beliefs, values and judgment, which are foundational in the development and enactment of wisdom (Ardelt, 2003). Some of these qualities and their role in management decision-making are discussed in Chapter 4.

Questions to think about

1. Do you think the DIK hierarchy is a useful way to think about data, information and knowledge? Can you think of other ways to illustrate and describe the relationship between these concepts?
2. What role, if any, should wisdom play in management decision-making? Should it be part of management education? Why or why not?

Another view of the relationship between data, information and knowledge, one that has more obvious management applications, is the Big Data, Analytics, Knowledge Management model (BDAKM) illustrated in Figure 2.2 (Pauleen and Wang, 2017). In contrast to the DIK model, this model asserts that knowledge plays a fundamental role in the management and use of big data and analytics for simple and obvious reasons: it is human knowledge and experience that decides where to collect data and the analytics for analyzing it, and it is human knowledge that will decide how the information generated from big data and analytics will be used. Pauleen and Wang (2017) termed this 'contextual' knowledge. Contextual knowledge includes the tacit and explicit knowledge of employees, implicit knowledge contained in organizational processes and activities, outputs such as products and services, and stakeholders throughout the supply chain including intended markets. The model illustrates how knowledge mediates the transformation of data into information and then knowledge.

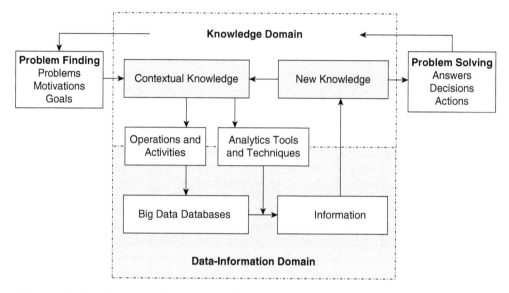

Figure 2.2   Big data, analytics and knowledge management

Source: adapted from Pauleen and Wang, 2017

Although big data may (theoretically) be collected and analyzed without any particular objective in mind (that is, pre-emptive acquisition), in the vast majority of cases, management will initiate the collection and analysis of big data for three main reasons: supporting operations, exploring new business opportunities, and providing up-to-date information for tactical and strategic decision-making (Table 2.5). More detailed examples of uses are given in the last section of this chapter.

Table 2.5   Reasons to collect and analyze data

Purpose of Data Collection	Applications (examples)	Sources of Data (examples)	Types of Analysis (examples)	Required Management Knowledge	Level
Automate and support operation	Warehouse stocking Traffic trends for city planning	Enterprise-wide and inter-organizational information systems	Predictive and prescriptive analytics	Provide expert and domain knowledge when analysts are setting up parameters to establish the environments for data collection and analysis	Operational

Purpose of Data Collection	Applications (examples)	Sources of Data (examples)	Types of Analysis (examples)	Required Management Knowledge	Level
Explore new business opportunities	Identify most profitable customer segments Trend analysis	Web-based Multinational consumers' data and multi-source marketing data	Predictive Amazon Web Services and Google Cloud Platform	Domain knowledge Some technical knowledge to interpret analysis	Tactical/strategic
Support strategic decision-making	Mergers and acquisitions Downsizing/expansion	Simulation data Aggregated internal data External data Experiments	Descriptive and predictive analytics	Expert and domain knowledge Experiment design	Strategic

A CRITICAL LOOK AT BIG DATA: OPPORTUNITIES AND CHALLENGES

Companies that were born in the Internet era – such as Google, Facebook and Amazon – were built around big data (Davenport and Dyché, 2013). These Internet-age companies are exemplars of how big data and analytics can generate business opportunities, but they also serve to illustrate the challenges of big data, such as managing privacy concerns and securing data.

Companies that existed before the Internet age are also looking into opportunities to develop their businesses by effectively using big data and analytics (Bholat, 2015). While big data and analytics offer considerable opportunities for these companies they also present significant challenges (see Chapter 1).

Opportunities and Use Cases

Big data presents a wide range of organizations with significant opportunities in a number of operational and strategic areas. Currently, value-added use of big data is being made in various industries and business areas such as finance, marketing and sales, production and manufacturing, as well as supply chain and logistics. Table 2.6 presents some examples of such organizations.

Table 2.6 Opportunities with big data and analytics

Company	Industry	Data source	Task
Etihad	Airline	Sensor – airplanes	Predict failure of machine parts
Tesco PLC, Great Britain	Retail	Sensor – refrigerator	Predict maintenance and service needs
Daimler, Germany	Automotive	Sensor – cylinder	Predict cylinder head defects
Macy's Inc., USA	Retail	Website, transactions, social media	Real-time price adjustment
Walmart, USA	Retail	Search engine	Anticipate user intent with semantic search
Fonterra, NZ	Primary/Dairy	Sensor, product development	Manage value chain uncertainty modeling, environmental impact analysis, resource management
Australia Post, AU	Postal service	Customer data	Optimize marketing campaigns

Research in a number of areas, for example health care, also benefits from the extended possibilities of big data (Mishra et al., 2017). In the medical field, access to patient data including geographical information, habits and other influencing factors increases the potential to research diseases such as Alzheimer's or diabetes (Agarwal and Dhar, 2014), creating opportunities for new treatments. National and local governments also see opportunities in collecting and using big data in a range of diverse areas from providing national security to better citizen services.

Big data can offer operational benefits in the areas of production, manufacturing and maintenance by employing sensor technology (Kaisler et al., 2013). Sensor-generated data, for example, assists in predicting the failure of machine parts and offers the opportunity to exchange these parts before actual damage or production delays are caused (Watson and Marjanovic, 2013). One of the companies taking advantage of this opportunity is Etihad. By equipping its airplanes with hundreds of sensors, Etihad is able to collect a significant amount of digital data about its fleet, which can then be analyzed and used for predictive maintenance (Alharthi et al., 2017), generating significant savings by pre-empting problems. A similar case is Tesco PLC, which saves on energy costs by analyzing 70 million data points from their refrigerator units to monitor performance and predict maintenance as well as servicing needs (Laskowski, 2013). Daimler is another example of companies relying on sensor data:

During the manufacturing process, Daimler continuously collects more than 500 data attributes of cylinder heads such as physical dimensions and cylinder temperature [...] IBM's SPSS solution helps the company predict errors and correct variances before cylinder head defects can occur. Two years after the initiative began, Daimler cylinder production increased by about 25%. (Alharthi et al., 2017: 287)

Besides the immediate operational advantages afforded manufacturing, big data can also support organizations' short- and medium-term strategies. Data from sensors and such sources as social media can be used in experimental analysis-testing approaches and sentiment analyses, enabling in-depth understanding of customers, improved market segmentation and additional marketing and sales opportunities (Kaisler et al., 2013; Watson and Marjanovic, 2013).

Consider This Box 2.5

Big Data in the Magic Kingdom

A sophisticated example of both operational and strategic benefits from big data are Disney parks' MagicBands, which are bracelets with integrated RFID sensors (Alharthi et al., 2017). The bracelets function as entry passes to the park and offer the benefit of pre-booking and line cutting to the visitors. Most importantly, the RFID chips allow Disney to collect digital information on the bracelet wearer's movement and interaction with the park. The analysis of this data provides Disney with insights into customer behavior, enabling them to improve customer experience by relying on data about waiting times, purchasing history and customer preferences. Besides revenue gains realized by the targeted marketing opportunities and improved customer experience, operational efficiency is also improved (Kuang, 2015). The pre-booking feature, for example, allows for increased crowd control and optimized staffing at rides and restaurants.

Source: The Leadership Network, 2016; Marr, 2017

Questions to think about

1. Discuss which management challenges Disney might have in regard to their bracelets.
2. What kind of challenges would this technology bring to the IT (or analytics) department at Disney?
3. If you were a customer at Disney, what would be your reaction to this new technology?

An example of an organization using big data to drive marketing and sales is Macy's Inc., which relies on real-time pricing, meaning that prices are adjusted by demand

(Laskowski, 2013; Terrific Data, 2016). Up to 73 million products are dynamically price-adjusted based on (near) real-time data from their website and social media, as well as transactions. Walmart Stores Inc. used its big data insights to create a search engine that improves purchase completion by up to 15 per cent, which has increased the company's revenue significantly (Laskowski, 2013). The driver of this improvement is semantic search technology, which anticipates the user's intent through advanced algorithms such as synonym mining and query understanding (Walmart, 2012).

Challenges

While big data's potential is evident, organizations are also confronted with a range of challenges that need to be considered before and while employing big data solutions. Many of these revolve around management: management of the technology, management of the decision-making process, and management of opportunities and risks. These are summarized here and discussed in greater detail in later chapters (see Table 2.7).

Table 2.7 Management challenges with big data and analytics

Type of Challenge	Source of Challenge	Management Challenge	Key Success Factors
Management of Technology	• Rapid rate of data growth (Volume) • Multiple sources and formats of the data (Variety) • Pace of data acquisition (Velocity)	• Investing in new technology • Developing technical and human capabilities • Understanding of the technologies involved in big data	• Corporate culture • HR practices • Legal and public relations
Management of Decision-making Process	• Organizational processes • Time management • People resources	• Transferring findings of big data into action • Distrust in unexpected analytics results • Change Management	

One of the main obstacles recognized in the big data literature is the technological challenges, such as handling the 3Vs of big data: the rapid rate of data growth, the multiple sources and formats of the data, and the pace of data acquisition. Data from different forms and sources needs to be acquired, recorded, stored, integrated, cleaned and analyzed to produce meaningful information. The immediate management challenges include developing the underlying infrastructure, which involves investing in new technologies, and developing the technical and human capabilities to analyze vast amounts of real-time data. Even if an organization decides to store its data in the cloud and analyze it using contracted services, management must at the very least have a thorough understanding of the technologies involved, and the benefits that may be accrued, as well as the potential risks.

Even if organizations go ahead and make the substantial investments to acquire or lease the technology necessary to use big data, they may not see the expected results, as turning data into action is not a simple matter. To a high degree it concerns the management of the decision-making process. To use big data and analytics in decision-making effectively may require major changes in the organization and its personnel and processes.

Many organizations struggle with the information they already have for reasons of poor information management, lack of analysis skills and failure to act on insights (Ross et al., 2013). Advanced technology such as big data is likely to fail in such organizations unless they can manage the fundamental changes necessary to make the best use of such technologies. Such management challenges may include making necessary changes to:

- *Corporate culture*: Culture is an important aspect to consider in this context. If the culture supports, or even insists on, data-based justification for decisions, then adoption and use of big data and analytics is certain to be swift (McAfee and Brynjolfsson, 2012).
- *Human resources and hiring practices*: A major challenge that organizations face is the lack of analytics skills in existing employees as well as a shortage of specialized analytics talent, such as data scientists, on the market (Alharthi et al., 2017). Existing gaps must be filled with either internal training or new hires.
- *Legal and public relations*: One of the most discussed challenges of big data is the concern about legal, ethical and privacy risks of big data use. The legal ramifications are serious and likely to grow as governments begin regulating data collection and use. The public relations issues are easy to observe as companies involved in data breaches or misuse of data scandals deal with falling stock prices and social media outrage.

These management challenges are looked at in greater depth in Chapters 1, 8, 9 and 10.

As we have shown in this chapter, big data involves technology that is complex and emergent. It must be fully understood by managers and organizations before it can be used effectively with managed risk. It is important to separate the hype from the real-world advantages and challenges that big data brings. Adopting and using big data is bound to affect most organizational functions to some degree and sometimes requires significant adjustments throughout the organization. Its use could open the organization up to criticism and legal battles if data is misused or security is compromised (see Chapter 9 for a discussion of these issues). For all the risk and change management required, big data has great potential to significantly enrich management decision-making by providing up-to-date, value-added information and analytically derived insights and predictions.

CHAPTER SUMMARY

In this chapter we have introduced the concept of big data and the opportunities and challenges it presents to organizational management. We began by recounting the history of data, data and information systems, and the relationship between information systems and management, including decision-making. Then we detailed the characteristics of big data that distinguish it from previous understandings of data. These characteristics include the 3Vs of volume, velocity and variety, as well as the important data-related qualities of veracity and value. The value of data lies in its potential to be turned into information through analytics and then into knowledge through human cognition. Two different conceptualizations of how data can be transformed into knowledge, the DIK pyramid and BDKM model, were introduced. Finally, we looked at the kinds of opportunities that big data offers organizations and managers as well the challenges faced when seeking to use big data in organizations. The rest of the book will delve much deeper into the ways data can be turned into information and applied in management decision-making as well as the opportunities and challenges both big data and analytics present to organizations and managers.

KEY LESSONS

In this chapter we have introduced the concept of big data, its evolution and related issues. The most important takeaways can be summarized as:

1. Data has always been important to organizations and management decision-making.
2. Big data is evolving and growing rapidly based on new technologies.
3. In combination with new and more powerful analytics, big data has the potential to revolutionize the ways organizations operate and managers make decisions.
4. This potential will be tempered by serious challenges in the utilization of big data that will need to be carefully managed by organizations.

3

INTRODUCTION TO (ADVANCED) ANALYTICS

Contents

Highlight Box 3.1

Dashboards and Decision-Making

Dashboards are a method for visually representing business intelligence for decision-making. In a dashboard data is presented in a more easily understandable way (see Figure 3.1). The information on the dashboard is created from big data analyzed by analytics programs. These programs can provide descriptive, prescriptive and predictive types of information. The dashboard described below illustrates the kind of information that can be delivered by analytics, in this case information on an online advertising campaign.

In this scenario, a medium-sized organization plans to invest $500,000 for a six-month advertising project that will provide critical information on a strategic decision whether or not to

(Continued)

introduce a new type of product into the market. Before committing this large amount of money, senior executives decide to run a small pilot project. As part of this pilot project, the organization invests $20,000 for advertisements on a new product on a much smaller scale compared to the main project. Managers use a dashboard to help their decision-making on these kinds of projects.

The advertisement will be posted on the company's website and introduced through various media including online newspapers, social media and various other Internet sites. Using the dashboard, managers can select a geographical location where they want to examine the source of web clicks, inquiries and sales. The analysis type list allows managers to choose the type of analysis they want to see on the dashboard, while the calendar box allows them to select a time range for the selected analysis. Additional analysis could allow managers to find out more on visitor behavior, such as the location of the best customers, how much time visitors spend on each page, what time of day visits and sales occur, etc.

Sections on descriptive and predictive analysis give the results on the selected analysis type for the given time range. Finally, the decision section provides a comparison on selected metrics.

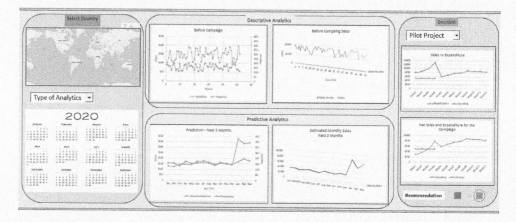

Figure 3.1 Example of a dashboard

Questions

1. A dashboard is a kind of interface between big data inputs and management decision-making. What are the benefits and drawbacks of presenting data this way?
2. Why do certain managers prefer visualizations of data, while others prefer working with source data?
3. Discuss the KSAs a manager needs to have for making a decision using the kinds of analytics presented by a dashboard.
4. What kind of additional information would a manager need for making the investment decision as explained in this scenario?

CHAPTER 3 KEY LESSONS

1.   Analytics have been around for many years, but advanced analytics powered by sophisticated technologies and big data are products of the twenty-first century.
2.   Advanced analytics offer significant new opportunities for organizations to assess environmental conditions and to support data-driven decision-making.
3.   The use of analytics needs to be moderated with human knowledge and judgment.

INTRODUCTION

In Chapter 2, we looked in some depth at big data, including its evolution, its relationship with technology and management decision-making and its very close ties with analytics. In this chapter, we go into some depth about analytics, introducing the evolution of analytics from relatively simple statistics to advanced analytics, explaining in more depth the categories of analytics that exist – i.e. descriptive, prescriptive and predictive analytics. The main concepts related to analysis such as basic data management techniques and basic statistics will be raised. Furthermore, other relevant technologies such as data mining, model building, visualization, reporting, dashboards, cloud computing, artificial intelligence and machine learning are introduced in the context of modern management and management decision-making (see Glossary at the end of this book). This chapter's content is based on current academic and practitioner literature and our own recent empirical findings exploring managers' understanding and use of analytics and related technologies (Taskin et al., 2019; Taskin et al., 2020; Gressel, 2020).

EVOLUTION OF ANALYTICS

Since the 1940s, with the development and introduction of the first electronic and 'general purpose' computers, small amounts of data could be analyzed without the help of relatively sophisticated tools; however, the variety and volume of data that managers have available now require advanced tools. Therefore, advanced analytics is frequently applied in the context of big data. Advanced analytics can be considered a collection of sophisticated tools that primarily serve the discovery and exploration of large and detailed data sets. Kaisler et al. (2013) define analytics and its application to big data as follows:

> We define advanced analytics to be the application of multiple analytic methods that address the diversity of big data – structured or unstructured – to provide estimative results and to yield actionable descriptive, predictive and prescriptive results. (Kaisler et al., 2013: 729)

Insights from big data can only be gained by employing analytics and sophisticated tools. In this section we present four recent frameworks classifying the evolution and capabilities of analytics. These frameworks by Watson and Marjanovic (2013), Chen et al. (2012), Davenport (2013), and Lee (2017) are summarized in Table 3.1. Comprehending the evolution of big data and advanced analytics from its origin in early data management generations fosters a deeper understanding of the status quo. Furthermore, these frameworks provide an overview of applications and tools that managers currently have available for their decision-making.

Table 3.1 Evolution of data and analytics

Evolutionary Step	Chen et al., 2012	Davenport, 2013	Watson and Marjanovic, 2013	Lee, 2017
DSS			*First Generation (of Data Management): The DSS* – a single decision-maker using data and analytic aids to support decision-making. Data sources are single or just a few operational systems.	
EDW	*BI&A 1.0* – data is mostly structured, collected by various legacy systems in RDBMS. Data is mostly used for business reporting functions, statistical analyses and data mining.	*Analytics 1.0: era of business intelligence* – the era of enterprise data warehouse. Data is prepared, stored, queried and reported. Analyses are time-consuming. No explanations or predictions are offered.	*Second Generation: EDW* – data-focused approach to data management. Data is structured and updated in batch mode from several systems.	
DBMS and data warehousing			*Third Generation: Real-Time Data Warehousing* – operational decisions and processes are supported by real-time data. Data volume increased, but data is still mostly structured.	

Evolutionary Step	Chen et al., 2012	Davenport, 2013	Watson and Marjanovic, 2013	Lee, 2017
Big data for first movers		*Analytics 2.0: era of big data –* mostly used by Internet-based firms, changing the role of data and analytics. Use of internal, external and unstructured data. Rise of Hadoop, NoSQL and cloud computing.		*Big Data 1.0 era –* data generated by Web 1.0 with firms having online presence and users searching and clicking through websites.
Big data for all organizations	*BI&A 2.0 –* data is web-based and unstructured. Data is used to analyze customer online behavior, optimize web presences and product recommendations. User-generated content provides feedback and opinions.	*Analytics 3.0: era of data-enriched offerings –* other large organizations from various industries follow the trends of Analytics 2.0.	*Big Data Generation* – new ways of using data, such as deeper understanding, better predictions or greater context. Relatively new data sources are utilized.	*Big Data 2.0 era –* user-generated data on Web 2.0 analyzed with social media analytics (see Table 3.2).
Mobile and sensor data	*BI&A 3.0 –* data is mobile and sensor-based. Data supports highly mobile, location-aware, person-centered and context-relevant operations and transactions.			*Big Data 3.0 era –* increased data with developments in IoT. Tremendous volumes of data from sensors, mobile devices, wearables, etc.
Autonomous systems		*Analytics 4.0: era of autonomous analytics –* the aim is to minimize the (need for) human involvement in model development and instead to learn from data (Pauleen, 2017a).		

Chen et al. (2012) is a widely cited framework, which incorporates business intelligence and analytics capabilities. According to the IT research and advisory firm Gartner (2020b), 'business intelligence (BI) is an umbrella term that includes the applications, infrastructure and tools, and best practices that enable access to and analysis of information to improve and optimize decisions and performance'. Since the 1990s, BI has evolved from a mere IT resource to a strategically important organizational capability. Data analytics is generally understood as the use of hardware and software to extract meaning and patterns from data, and Gartner defines it as a 'catch-all term for a variety of different business intelligence (BI)- and application-related initiatives [...] Increasingly, "analytics" is used to describe statistical and mathematical data analysis that clusters, segments, scores and predicts what scenarios are most likely to happen' (Gartner, 2020a). In the three evolutionary steps that Chen et al. (2012) differentiate, 'business intelligence and analytics' (BI&A) is used as a single term.

The first step, BI&A 1.0, has its foundation in warehousing and data management, the collected data being mostly structured and stored in RDBMS. Managers commonly rely on database queries and reporting tools. Graphics and visualizations are used for exploration and performance metrics. Furthermore, predictive modeling, data segmentation and clustering as well as regression analyses are commonly adopted options in BI&A 1.0. In BI&A 2.0, the collected data is web-based and unstructured. The use of data shifts from business reporting functions to the analysis of customer online behavior, optimization of web presences and product recommendations. Customers' needs can be better understood through the use of cookies, IP addresses and server logs, providing the organization with more insights into the customers' online activities. Text and web mining techniques are also applied to unstructured user-generated content from social networking and multimedia sites, which eventually have to be integrated with organizations' RDBMS. In BI&A 3.0, mobile and Internet/sensor-enabled devices enable operations and transactions that are targeted at individuals and are adapted to a specific context or location. The techniques for capturing and analyzing mobile and sensor data were considered in a developmental stage in the first decade of the 2000s. However, in light of recent technological advancements, the Internet of Things (IoT), which is sensor-based, reached its peak in 2014 and 2015 and is now currently being replaced by the development and use of IoT platforms, which are a multi-layer technology that connects all 'things' in the universe of IoT and enables their management.

Davenport (2013) depicts the evolution of big data with a focus on analytics. The framework suggests there are three eras of analytics; each era being characterized by 'new priorities and technical possibilities' (Davenport, 2013: 65). Analytics 1.0 is set as the first era of analytics, the era of BI. The use of data for business applications is discovered, and data on customers and production is primarily utilized to optimize and support decision-making. Analytics is limited to descriptive capabilities and the process is time-consuming.

It is the era of data warehousing and business intelligence software, which focuses on queries and reporting. This depiction concurs with Chen et al.'s (2012) first evolutionary step, BI&A 1.0. Davenport's Analytics 2.0 is the era of big data, with external data now being available from the Internet, sensors, audio and video (Davenport, 2013). To analyze these additional data sources, new tools are required such as Hadoop, which is open source software that allows faster data processing using parallel servers. DBMS cannot manage the amount and unstructured nature of the data, so companies explore NOSQL options. However, these new possibilities are limited to first movers, i.e. organizations that are Internet-based or in the social networking business. Analytics 3.0 widely coincides with BI&A 2.0, but also incorporates the competencies of BI&A 3.0 as depicted by Chen et al. (2012). To Davenport (2013), Analytics 3.0 is the current era of data-enriched offerings. This era marks the transition from big data being used mainly by Silicon Valley 'information firms and online companies' to it being employed by virtually all industries and companies ranging from start-ups to multinational conglomerates (Davenport, 2013: 67).

In a recent interview (Pauleen, 2017a: 10), Davenport suggested some organizations are at an Analytics 4.0 level, which he describes as 'highly automated and networked environments, in which most or all decisions are made without human intervention'. Industries with organizations at this level are currently found in financial trading and utilities monitoring electricity flow. Davenport comments, 'unfortunately we don't understand these environments very well and they often break down. We need much better insights about how they work before they arrive on a large scale' (Pauleen, 2017a: 10). Chapter 10 introduces emerging technologies that will further support the development of Analytics 4.0.

According to Lee (2017), big data and analytics can be classed into three eras. In the first era, Big Data 1.0, the main drivers were the Internet and development and extensive use of e-commerce by firms. In this era, data was generated by individuals using the Internet and firms with an online presence. Web analytics was restricted to web usage mining, web structure mining and web content mining. In the Big Data 2.0 era, a decade starting from 2005, the main driver was the shift from use of the read-only websites of Web 1.0 to the more interactive and dynamic websites of Web 2.0. Users generated the bulk of data in this era though interactions and sharing of content on social media. With social media analytics firms can collect, monitor, analyze and visualize data collected from social media sites and use it to interpret various human behaviors and develop intelligence and insight based on users'/customers' interests. Going beyond web mining techniques, social media analytics include social network analysis, sentiment analysis, opinion mining, visual analytics, trend analysis and topic modeling (Fan and Gordon, 2014). Table 3.2 details the objectives and methods and provides examples of these types of social media analytics.

Table 3.2 Selected social media analytics

Analytics	Objective	Methods	Example application area
Social network analysis	Understand the underlying structure, connections, and properties of a social network Understand the influence of individuals in a network	Counting number of nodes in a network Computing eigenvectors	Identifying influencers in a social network Identifying subgroups in order to tailor products or services around their needs or preferences
Sentiment analysis Opinion mining	Leverage text analytics to extract user sentiment or opinions from text sources	Word count Polarity lexicons Semantic methods	Stock market prediction, trend and defect identification, managing crises
Visual analytics	Provide summarized information from computational processes through interactive visual interfaces	Dashboard with several metrics and key performance indicators (KPIs)	Detecting events
Trend analysis	Predict future outcomes using archival data	Regression analysis Time series analysis Neural networks Support vector machines	Forecasting sales Predicting marketing campaign outcomes
Topic modeling	Identify main themes of topics	Advanced statistical techniques Machine learning techniques	Identifying important subjects within or between communities Identifying user interest

Source: based on Fan and Gordon, 2014

The main driver of Big Data 3.0, the current era, is the IoT. Sources of data include sensors, wearables, mobile devices, etc. In addition to data types common in Big Data eras 1.0 and 2.0, data in the forms of video, image and audio are also generated in vast amounts through these devices. Streaming analytics to analyze the data from various sources in real time to discover patterns in the analytics is an important feature in this era. This type of analysis is used in a variety of ways including in the healthcare sector, for example to monitor changes in patients' conditions through sensors as well as the finance sector to monitor transactions as part of compliance with regulations.

The stages of these frameworks differ in terms of emphasis and detail: while Davenport (2013) focuses solely on analytics capabilities, Chen et al. (2012) combine analytics and BI developments, Watson and Marjanovic (2013) emphasize big data's data management roots, and Lee (2017) concentrates on the generation of big data and social media analytics and its applications. Nonetheless, the general tendencies and overall developments correspond in all three frameworks, showing a gradual evolution of big data and advanced analytics. The most recent and evolved stage is presented as a wide range of organizations utilizing big data for various purposes, incorporating unstructured and diverse data sources into their decision-making.

FROM DATA TO INFORMATION: ADVANCED ANALYTICS TOOLS AND TECHNIQUES

Big data will only deliver insights and create value if there is a process to tailor it for the user so it is eventually turned into knowledge. Information technology can assist with the transformation from data into information (Davenport and Prusak, 1998). The key question is how do we get from data to information in the age of big data? While organizations have struggled with large volumes of data in the past, the 3Vs are what set big data apart from traditional data sets, and challenge organizations. Modern data sets 'are so large (from terabytes to exabytes), complex and varied (from sensor to social media data) and current (being updated from moment to moment) that they require advanced and unique data storage, management, analysis, and visualization technologies' (Chen et al., 2012: 1166). For big data to be converted into information, advanced analytics tools need to be applied that are capable of handling the 3Vs of big data.

Bose (2009: 156) defines advanced analytics as 'a general term which simply means applying various advanced analytic techniques to data to answer questions or solve problems'. Other tools and techniques, besides the social media analytics highlighted in Table 3.2, that are considered as part of advanced analytics are, for example, complex SQL queries, data mining, text mining, web mining, statistical analysis, data visualization as well as emerging technologies such as artificial intelligence and machine learning (see Chapter 10). Managers mainly employ them for predictive and prescriptive purposes to predict and optimize outcomes, but the techniques can also benefit descriptive analytics. These three types of analytics, namely descriptive, predictive and prescriptive, plus two more recent types of analytics – diagnostic and autonomous – are characterized by their purpose and utilized tools, as highlighted in Table 3.3 and described below.

Table 3.3 Types of analytics

	Descriptive	Predictive	Prescriptive	Diagnostic	Autonomous
Definition	Describing the current situation through reports generated with past and current data	Forecasting and evaluating alternative outcomes given different circumstances on the available data	Developing and assessing the optimized best course of action and solutions to business problems	Developing insights from data to find out root causes of problems	Developing models learning from data to minimize human involvement
Tools/	Scorecards	Mathematical and statistical (descriptive and inferential) techniques including data mining (classification, regression, clustering), machine learning (supervised, unsupervised, and semi-supervised learning model), text mining, etc.	Simulation	Query drills	AI
Methods	Dashboards		Optimization	Agile and spatial visualization	Cognitive technologies, like ML
	Data warehousing		Multi-criteria decision modeling		
	Reporting		Machine learning		
	Simple statistical methods				
	Observations				
	Cases				
Role in Decision-making	Offer insights into business situations and customers (e.g. financial strength of an organization) Identify business opportunities and challenges	Help managers with predicting future conditions	Assessing scenarios to find out optimum solution to business cases to help decision-making	Help managers identify root causes of any problem	Creating models (statistical) with less human input for decision-making

	Descriptive	Predictive	Prescriptive	Diagnostic	Autonomous
Focus	Past and present opportunities, i.e. *What has happened or is happening now?*	Predict future conditions, events by recognizing patterns and relationships, i.e. *What could happen?* *What will happen?*	Optimized solution, cause-and-effect relationships, i.e. *What should happen?* *Why should that happen?*	Root causes, discovery and developing insight. i.e. *Why did something happen?*	Evolution of models based on data with less and less human involvement, i.e. *What can be learned from the data?* *How can the models be improved to learn more from the data?*
Technology and Usage	Analytics powered by humans for humans	Analytics powered by math for processes	Analytics powered by math for processes	Analytics powered by humans for humans	Analytics powered by math for human interaction and autonomous systems
Example	Most business reports using mean, median, mode, frequency, aggregated numbers (i.e. customers, sales, finances, operations, inventories, number of likes or followers on social media), etc.	Airline: sensor data, weather, and flight schedule data used for improving predictions for decision-making Credit score calculation to predict customers' future payment issues	Increasing revenue through optimization of sales force Optimization of production, scheduling and inventory in supply chain	Use of interactive visualization to drill down into the data to find out root causes of any problems and gaining insights in any context, such as supply chain processes or sales	Self-driving cars using advanced algorithms learning from data

Source: McAfee and Brynjolfsson, 2012; Delen and Demirkan, 2013; Elliott, 2013; Banerjee et al, 2013; Tamm et al., 2013; Kawas et al., 2013; Gandomi and Haider, 2015; Rehman et al., 2016; Sivarajah et al, 2017; Davenport and Harris, 2017; Ghosh, 2017; Davenport, 2018; Halo, 2019

Descriptive analytics serves the purpose of determining well-defined past and present opportunities or potential problems. The information gained from business reporting tools such as scorecards and data warehousing enables organizations to alter or adapt their future behavior. Big data can be advantageous in the provision of more extensive and real-time data, offering further insight into business situations and customers.

Predictive analytics enables managers to make more prudent and forward-looking decisions, since the constructed models are designed to predict future conditions. Predictive analytics utilizes qualitative and quantitative techniques and can forecast various scenarios, based on supervised, unsupervised and semi-supervised learning models. Data and mathematical techniques are used to discover explanatory and predictive patterns, which represent the inherent relationships between data inputs and outputs. Big data, in conjunction with predictive analytics, offers increased accuracy for predictions, benefiting different business scenarios from different industries. McAfee and Brynjolfsson (2012) looked at an airline case that improved its prediction of arrival times of airplanes at the airport by using various data sources beyond the pilots' reporting. Using additional sensor, weather and flight schedule data led to a more rigorous predictive model and therefore improved the airline's decision-making. In our research, we observed organizations using analytics to predict consumer behavior in the form of default rates, staffing requirements for customer service departments, and maintenance schedules for regular as well as ad-hoc servicing.

Prescriptive analytics provides the decision-maker with sufficient information about optimal behaviors to clearly determine the best course of action. When analytics is embedded into operational processes, the input of big data will automatically evoke a result, change or decision, and therefore increase the efficiency of day-to-day business activities. Empirical evidence from a study on optimized allocation of an organization's sales force suggests that revenue can be increased marginally if prescriptive analytics are embedded (Kawas et al., 2013).

Diagnostic analytics tries to answer the question of 'why something happened'. Generally, statistical and a variety of visualization techniques are used to answer this question. This type of analysis explores the root causes of incidents using archival data. With diagnostic analytics, managers can drill down into data to find out root causes and gain new insights about any problem before making a decision. This drilling down can be through the use of interactive visualization on most types of reports and in most industries.

Autonomous analytics aims to limit human involvement in model development and analytics. In other analytics types, humans have a significant input in terms of data gathering, identifying the problem, and analysis. Autonomous analytics uses techniques such as artificial intelligence and machine learning to build models that will minimize human involvement. These models learn from previous and current data and improve themselves continuously.

This book refers to the term advanced analytics as a set of advanced tools and techniques that is applied to several or vast data sets, and therefore exceeds the use and outcome of traditional analytics.

Highlight Box 3.2

Powering Up Analytics

How are advanced analytics currently being driven or 'powered'? Elliott (2013) explains this via a range of human intellect and computer algorithms. He outlines four categories of analytics maturity according to how they are 'powered'. While this categorization shows the evolution of analytics maturity from descriptive to autonomous analytics, it allows different interpretations of such technologies and their usage by incorporating how they are powered as part of this evolution to move forward.

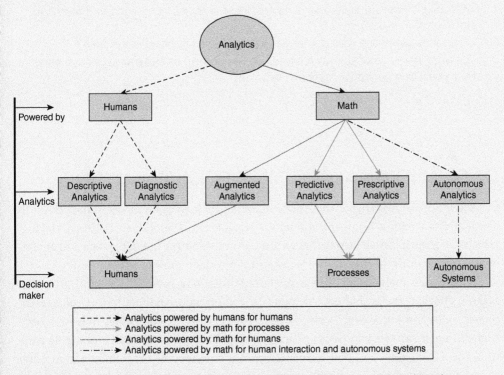

Figure 3.2   Powering analytics for decision-making. Adapted from Elliott (2013)

Analytics powered by humans for humans refers to traditional analytics where a variety of descriptive and diagnostic analytics and related tools are used for improving business decision-making.

(Continued)

Data is aggregated (i.e. OLAP), visualized based on the need (i.e. agile visualization), and reported to support the decision-making.

Analytics powered by math for processes is data prepared by algorithms in order to create predictive models to be applied to forthcoming data. Automatically checking any credit card transaction for fraud by banks is an example for this category where a decision is proposed by a machine. Predictive and prescriptive analytics can be matched to this category.

Analytics powered by math for humans is when humans make decisions through interacting with a machine, using augmented analytics. This form of analytics can help humans with the processes such as data cleansing, clustering, finding patterns in a more 'intelligent' way.

Analytics powered by math for human interaction and autonomous systems is where the need for human input is minimized and mainly machines are capable of making decisions using advanced predictive models. An application of this is the use of advanced algorithms in self-driving cars to navigate (Elliot, 2013).

Questions to think about

1. What are the risks and limitations of each of these analytics types in terms of contributing to decision-making?
2. Discuss the issues and risks of analytics being powered by humans and math?
3. Discuss whether an organization can adopt one or more of these analytics at a time? How would an organization make that decision?

DATA AND ANALYTICS IN DECISION-MAKING

In Chapter 5, we investigate the use of analytics in management decision-making in depth and in Chapter 7, Organizational Prerequisites for Data-driven Decision-Making, we look at organizational factors that encourage or inhibit the use of big data and analytics in organizations. In this section we want to introduce a few of the key issues.

Big data and analytics are 'not a single out-of-the-box product' (Loshin, 2013: 21). Making effective use of big data demands a complicated combination of tools, techniques, skills and knowledge. As we have seen in Chapter 2, companies that were born in the Internet era – such as Google, Facebook and Amazon – were built around big data; thus, these companies and their managers generally possess the capabilities and mindset to manage and make use of it, while companies that existed before the Internet era need to enhance their human and technical capabilities if they want to effectively use big data and analytics.

Due to numerous causes such as globalization and the increasing pace of techno-logical change, the business world is becoming ever more complex and challenging to managers. One response to meeting these challenges is the availability of increasingly greater amounts of data and information (Chapter 2) and the increasing sophistication of information systems (Chapter 2 and Table 3.1). Both big data and advanced analytics can provide reliable, accurate and up-to-the-minute information, which powers increas-ingly sophisticated decision support systems to provide substantial decision support for managers and organizations.

Highlight Box 3.3

Data and Analytics in Decision-Making

Today, advanced analytics and big data are applied to increase efficiency and gain competi-tive advantage. Big data has become a useful source of information for organizations in areas such as customer satisfaction, supply chain risk, competitive intelligence, pricing, as well as discovery and experimentation (Davenport, 2014). The results of a 2011 survey of almost 3,000 executives, managers and analysts show that about half of the top performing organizations employ analytics to gain insights into day-to-day operations but also for guidance regarding future strategies (LaValle et al., 2011). Only about a quarter of the lower performers follow suit. The study also shows that using analytics is preferred to relying on intuition by both top and lower performers in the areas of financial management, operations and production, strategy and business development, as well as sales and marketing. However, lower performers still prefer to rely on their intuition in areas such as customer service, product and research devel-opment, general and risk management.

More recently, a study conducted in New Zealand and Australia in 2018 (Taskin et al., 2020) examined the role of intuition and rationality in strategic decision-making. Data from 654 partici-pants, directorship/board member (16.7 per cent), executive management (34.7 per cent), senior management (32 per cent), middle management (11.5 per cent), first-level management (2.9 per cent), supervisory level (1.1 per cent) and other (1.2 per cent) were collected from New Zealand (46.9 per cent) and Australia (53 per cent). Of these participants, 44.3 per cent had made stra-tegic decisions during their career up to 10 times, while 33.8 per cent were involved in strategic decision-making over 30 times.

Strategic decisions were defined in the study as important non-routine decisions that can enable an organization using required and available resources to achieve or sustain competitive advantage. For such a decision, managers stated that they extensively looked for information (70.4 per cent) and used quantitative techniques (66 per cent) to extensively analyze (71 per cent) the data. Over 66 per cent of the managers defined the process they adopted for decision-making as analytical.

(Continued)

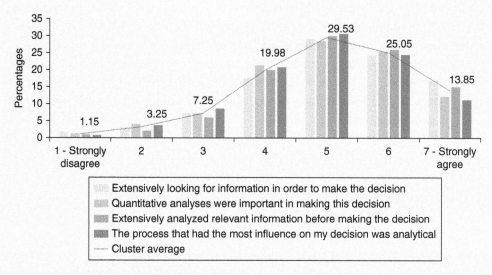

Figure 3.3   Rational decision-making, NZ

Source: Taskin et al., 2020

Questions to think about

1.   How do you see the role of analytics in managerial decision-making?
2.   Considering the trend of organizations' use of analytics, why do you think, as shown in Figure 3.3, that some organizations do not use analytics for decision-making?
3.   If you are currently working or previously worked in a company, how would you describe the extent that your company use(d) analytics?
4.   Based on your experience or previous readings, what type of analysis, methods and tools do companies use for strategic decisions? Please explain with examples.

Empirical work by Brynjolfsson et al. (2011) supports the positive effects of data use on organizational performance. Their findings suggest that data-driven decision-making increases a company's productivity by 5–6 per cent, and furthermore affects asset utilization, return on equity and market value. Another study showed that organizations in the US manufacturing industry that adopted data-driven decision-making had about 3 per cent more added value than non-adopters (Brynjolfsson and McElheran, 2016). These organizations exhibited higher productivity and enhanced performance. These findings are echoed by another empirical study, which finds that business analytics has a positive direct effect on information processing capability and that information processing capability in turn is found to positively affect data-driven decision-making, improving overall decision-making effectiveness (Cao et al., 2015). However, researchers working in the area of big data analytics capability (BDAC), which concerns management, technology and talent capabilities, have found that BDAC's impact on performance is moderated by the alignment between the analytics capability of an organization and its business strategy (Akter et al., 2016) and that organizations need to do more than merely invest in big data analytics: they must also develop capabilities around human resources (Gupta and George, 2016).

Managers, however, are often of three minds when it comes to analytics and decision-making. Many managers believe that data analytics and information systems have a role to play in management decision-making (see Highlight Box 3.3); some, however, believe that data-based decisions are generally superior to human-based decisions. Other managers, however, are of the opinion that because knowledge is embedded in the human mind (Bhatt, 2001) humans will tend to make better decisions than machines. These disparate views echo a prevailing sentiment in decision-making: the potential of analytics and the necessity of human judgment. Bhatt (2001) concludes that while information technologies are capable of organizing data to produce useful information, it is a poor substitute for converting information into knowledge. The conversion of information into knowledge is attributed to human factors and interpretation. Even judgment-based models or decision-making systems, created to substitute for human judgment, require human knowledge as an input in their design. Without this initial human input of expertise, models cannot be effectively designed to optimize decision-making. The question remains, will the knowledge embedded into a system remain current enough to be useful in an emergent decision situation? Knowledge grows as people learn and experience more. This is not true for information systems; at least not until machine learning is perfected.

There may be other reasons to be concerned about whether big data and analytics by themselves can substitute for human experience, knowledge and judgment. The critical research and practitioner literature raise issues around the efficacy of predictive analytics (Pauleen et al. 2016). For example, historical data in the form of data sets are the basis for training algorithms central to predictive analytics, AI and machine learning. One result of this is that 'Judgment and incentive [...] are rendered explicitly in quantitative terms' to 'manufacture the simulation of security' (Danisch, 2011: 246–247). This reliance on analytics-derived knowledge may rob managers of the opportunity to exercise and develop their common sense and the kind of experiential knowledge and resilience they need to manage ambiguity and uncertainty. This danger was demonstrated in the 2007–8 global financial crises (see Highlight Box 3.4), where it was shown that unwise behaviors around information generation and use were contributing factors (Pauleen et al., 2016). Caution is therefore urged when it comes to the use of big data and analytics as these will involve new ways of deciding and managing (Davenport, 2006). Pauleen et al. (2016) suggest that organizations and managers will want to be aware that such use may have the effect of helping to diminish managerial wisdom, resilience and common sense.

Highlight Box 3.4

The Role of Data, Information and Analytics in the Global Financial Crises of 2007–8

In a 2016 study of the global financial crisis, Pauleen et al. explored the role that information played in the crisis. Using textual analysis software they analyzed the semantic structures surrounding the concept 'information' in the 662-page *Financial Crisis Inquiry Report: Final Report of the National Commission on the Causes of the Financial and Economic crisis in the United States* (FCIC, 2011; henceforth, the Report).

Their computer analysis and careful reading of the Report shows that the Commission found that failures related to information were material to the crisis. The researchers' paper highlights: 1) the overwhelming and ever-increasing role of information systems in business and society, 2) the consequences of an over-reliance on data, information and analytics in decision-making, and 3) the lack of governance and risk management in the use of data and information in complex, emergent contexts.

1 The increasing role of information systems in business and society

The researchers note that information systems are evolving both technologically and conceptually and becoming ever more embedded in business and society as they are generating and analyzing ever-increasing amounts of data and information. As this case demonstrates, risk analysis and business intelligence and analytics are particularly popular applications of new technologies. While the finance and banking sectors are data and information driven, and well advised to use advanced data modeling techniques and economic analysis, the Report makes it clear that the reality of working with and managing information in the finance sector is not simple.

Although data is generally plentiful in the finance sector, ironically in the financial crisis, the case shows it is a lack of data and information that is a major problem. The Report notes that although 'The mortgage market is studied constantly by thousands of analysts, academics, regulators, traders and investors', it appears that market participants were unprepared for the destructiveness of this bubble's collapse because of a 'chronic lack of information about the composition of the mortgage market' (465). This lack of information was due to shortcomings in disclosure of information, a lack of reporting requirements, and limited data collection by third parties. In the end 'the lack of information made it difficult to document and describe the various market trading problems that emerged during the crisis' (621). Who has and does not have data mattered in this case. In the Report, data is characterized as not being distributed or integrated well enough to be useful for industry governance, government regulation or academic critique. One result of this lack of information, according to the Report, was that 'During the crises the lack of such basic information created heightened uncertainty' (299).

2 An over-reliance on data, information and analytics in decision-making

According to the Report, 'Financial institutions and credit rating agencies embraced mathematical models as reliable predictors of risks, replacing judgment in too many instances. Too often, risk management became risk justification' (xix). Tens of thousands of loans were approved based on predictive analytics that may not have been programmed to be credibly objective. According to Pauleen et al. (2016), the blind reliance on the data and analysis provided by credit ratings agencies and a serious lack of judgment and an inability to think independently and critically by managers and executives was evident throughout the financial industry. The Report states, 'Financial institutions made, bought, and sold mortgage securities they never examined, did not care to examine, or knew to be defective ... and major firms and investors blindly relied on credit rating agencies as their arbiters of risk' (xvii).

Pauleen et al. (2016) cautioned that independent thinking and sound judgment should not be completely replaced with mechanistic modeling, but used as one of several inputs for a decision. Unfortunately, managers often do not follow this advice, as managers or those working in industries where data and analytics are given precedence over human judgment can use analytics and statistical models to shift accountability in case of failure. No modeling, the authors stated, can ever be assumed to accurately and automatically predict the future and no ethical data scientist would present the results of modeling without relevant caveats about reliability and confidence.

3 Data governance and risk management

Arguably the crisis was caused in large part due to a lack of governance and risk management strategies. This lack of governance was a conscious choice made by government law makers. According to the Report, 'Adequate information about the risks in this market was not available to market participants or government regulators like the Federal Reserve. Because the market had been deregulated by statute in 2000, market participants were not subject to reporting or disclosure requirements and no government agency had oversight responsibility' (299).

Free markets and regulators depend on the free flow of information. Problems may arise if critical information is unavailable to regulators or public scrutiny. In this case many problems arose due to this lack of information directly attributable to largely structural information integration failures. This situation contributed to regulatory failure by, for example, preventing the Federal Reserve from doing its work, as the Report finding regarding hedge funds indicates: 'Some members (of the Federal Reserve) were concerned about the lack of transparency around hedge funds, the consequent lack of market discipline on valuations of hedge fund

(Continued)

holdings, and the fact that the Federal Reserve could not systematically collect information from hedge funds because they were outside its jurisdiction' (241).

Conclusion

Information, along with big data, is becoming ubiquitous. It is a resource that can be used or misused. In the case of the global financial crisis, those in the financial services industries who specialized in the collection of information and who provide analytical and predictive services plainly misused data in the pursuit of profits and to the detriment of many. The lesson to all organizations and industries that are moving into data-driven decision-making is quite clear – data and analytics are useful tools but an incautious reliance on them may result in negative consequences. Sound human judgment, good governance and reliable and accurate data are all essential for the safe and effective use of these technologies.

Questions to think about

1. The global financial crisis took place more than ten years ago. Is it still relevant today? In what way do its lessons regarding the use of data and analytics still apply to organizations today?
2. If you were hiring a manager in the finance sector, what skills and background would you be looking for? What do you think the skills for a successful manager should be to address the problems about decision-making as raised in this case?
3. Algorithmic intelligence is based on the assumption that the world can be fully formalized in a set of rules. Do you feel this is possible? Is the world computable? Discuss your views.

Nevertheless, given advances in technology, software engineering and computer power, the role of data, analytics and IS in decision-making is now significant and growing. Bhidé (2010) depicts the rising importance of analytics as one that will diminish the role of human judgment, explaining, 'The information technology revolution has shifted the balance between judgment and rules, giving a strong economic and psychological boost to judgment-free decision-making' (Bhidé, 2010: 49). The rise of data-driven decision-making, however, does not necessarily entail the absence of human judgment. Data-driven decisions can accommodate big data and analytics as well as the decision-maker's intuition – all depending on the decision-maker's preferences and abilities (Provost and Fawcett, 2013).

Consider This Box 3.5

Big Data, Analytics and Decision-Making: What Do the Experts Think?

In a recent interview Tom Davenport, noted academic and management consultant, commented on important trends and caveats in the use of big data and analytics in support of human decision-making. On the one hand, he thinks cognitive computing or artificial intelligence, which stand at the intersection of big data, analytics and knowledge management, will be able to make sense of massive amounts of data that will not only inform human decision-making but soon be able to make decisions, which will have tremendous implications for how organizations operate. On the other hand, he finds that most companies are still mostly unaware of this potential. Moreover, at a more fundamental level, he believes that most organizations do not even know what their most important decisions are, and have no way of knowing or measuring whether their decisions are getting better or not; probably, he opines, because decision-making is tied up with power, ego and office politics.

Cutting-edge technologies offer great potential in locating emerging decision situations as well as ways of effectively dealing with them. According to Davenport the goal of big data and quantitative analysis is to extract insights (usually prescriptive or predictive) from the analysis of the data and use them to inform decisions. Descriptive analytics, usually done under the rubric of business intelligence, has the same goal. All three forms of analytics should be informing decisions and actions, although according to Davenport there is often a poor connection between the sourcing of data, the analysis thereof, and the decisions being made (Pauleen, 2017a).

Dave Snowden, founder and chief scientific officer at Cognitive Edge, an innovative international consulting firm, is concerned that managers make the dubious assumption that computer algorithms interpret facts the same way that human beings interpret them. While humans have evolved for abductive reasoning, analytics takes a deductive or inductive approach to interpretation. He believes that while analytics is useful, he worries that it might become a substitute for human judgment in complex or wicked decision situations, where problems do not have an enumerable or a well-described set of potential solutions, so analytics may provide only partial help at best. In such situations, he argues, human judgment, experience, knowledge and expertise will be essential.

Source: content derived from interviews with Tom Davenport and Larry Prusak, and Dave Snowden by David Pauleen, 2017b)

Questions to think about

1.   According to Davenport, organizations do not know what their most important decisions are, nor do they know if they are getting better over time. What do you think the implications of this are for the use of big data and analytics in organizations?
2.   Snowden states that humans and computers think differently. In what ways do you think they can work together for maximum effectiveness in complex decision situations?

As investments in and use of big data, analytics and new technologies grow, managers rely more and more on analytics and technical reports to support and legitimize their decisions (Chapter 5). As organizations increasingly invest in and use these technologies, their ability to use them grows and the organizational culture evolves to further encourage, support and set expectations regarding their use (Chapter 7). As a result, managers should, as argued in Chapter 1, have at least a basic understanding of data and analytics, while at the same time developing their own judgment and expertise as these age-old human abilities can even be considered assets in the decision-making process (Lodha et al., 2014).

CHAPTER SUMMARY

In this chapter, we have given a reasonably in-depth introduction to analytics. We have covered the history of analytics and related technologies, the types of analytics in current use, the relationships between big data and analytics, and roles of analytics in management decision-making. We have also discussed why it is reasonable to apply caution when using analytics in management and organizational decision-making.

In Chapter 4 we introduce theoretical and practical decision-making and its place in management and organizations.

KEY LESSONS

In this chapter we have introduced analytics. The most important takeaways can be summarized as:

1. Analytics have been around for a while, but advanced analytics powered by sophisticated technologies and big data are products of the twenty-first century.
2. Advanced analytics offer significant new opportunities for organizations to assess environmental conditions and to support data-driven decision-making.
3. Nevertheless, the use of analytics should be moderated with human input and judgment.

4

MANAGEMENT DECISION-MAKING

Contents

Highlight Box 4.1

Management, Analytics and Decision-Making

Before the age of big data and analytics, managers would tend to rely on their knowledge and experience when making decisions supported by whatever data and information they had at hand or could acquire. These days the 3Vs of big data and advanced analytics would seem to open up a world of possibilities when it comes to management decision-making, and AI and machine learning are predicted to take over decision-making. But perhaps managers and

(Continued)

organizations can learn to incorporate and benefit from a balanced decision-making approach, utilizing analytics as well as their judgment during the decision process as the following quotes would seem to support (Gressel, 2020).

Analytics can provide insight and input into decision-making:

> We're working with our internal analytics team now to develop reports which are much richer for our process, which enable us to make better decisions. (General manager at finance organization)

Data offers objective validation that is particularly valuable when justifying management decisions and making decisions that seem counter-intuitive:

> I've done this profitability statement; I've shown it to the general manager and he said to me: 'How could that be so, they're our biggest customer?'
>
> So I say: 'Here are the reasons ...'
>
> And he turns to the CFO: 'Is this right, are these numbers right?'
>
> And the CFO said: 'Yes, that all reconciles back to our financial statement.'
>
> 'Wow,' exclaimed the general manager, 'I had no idea.' (Executive of IT company)

However, be careful of overusing analytics, which can lead to analysis paralysis:

> Some organizations tend to get consumed by trying to understand why, but actually all they need to do is find out that people like you like to buy a certain type of product. It doesn't really matter at the end of the day, why. And that's an interesting distinction. So a lot of people spend a lot of effort trying to analyze, analyze, analyze, why, why, why – all you need to do is just to have the insight. (Head of department at finance organization)

Analytics have limitations and human judgment plays an important role in the decision-making process:

> You're not going to know everything, and your data is not going to show you everything. So you've always got to have some reliance on your own judgment, and experiences and all that. (Manager at insurance organization)

Questions to think about

1. What issues do these quotes and anecdotes seem to raise about the relationship of data analytics and judgment in management decision-making in business today?
2. If you are currently working, do you use data and analytics in your decision-making? In what ways and to what effect?
3. How would you think the relationship between data analytics and judgment could be affected by experience in a certain role or industry?

CHAPTER 4 KEY LESSONS

1. Management decision-making is as much an art as a science: data, analytics, rational thinking, judgment, intuition and imagination all play a role.
2. Decision-makers need to be acutely aware of the decision situation, contingencies involving the decision situation and their own decision-making style with all its strengths and weaknesses.

INTRODUCTION

In Chapters 2 and 3 we provided an overview of big data and analytics and also introduced their growing influence on business and management decision-making. In this chapter the focus is on management decision-making. In it we review the importance, history and processes of decision-making in the management context. This chapter begins by explaining the importance of effective management decision-making in organizational success and taking a brief look at the history of management decision-making. We then go into some depth looking at a range of decision-making theories: these theories explain the various processes managers might engage in when making decisions. It is important for students to understand decision-making theory and to be able to use it to reflect on their own decision-making styles. Several researchers before us have analyzed the decision-making of countless managers. We want to outline the insights they gained by relaying their decision-making theories here. We then come to the central decision-making theory of this book, dual process theory with its focus on the integral role of both non-rational cognitive processes (which in this study serves as an umbrella term for factors such as intuition, experience, insight and judgment) and rational cognitive processes (which include the use of technology such as analytics and decision support systems) in decision-making.

THE IMPORTANCE OF DECISION-MAKING FOR MANAGERS

> What part does decision-making play in managing? I shall find it convenient to take mild liberties with the English language by using 'decision-making' as though it were synonymous with 'managing'. (Simon, 1960: 1)

Porter (1985) emphasizes that central to the success or failure of a firm is the competitive ability to make decisions. In organizations, decisions are made to solve problems, enhance performance and advance strategy. Decision situations can relate to circumstances either internal or external to the organization (Intezari and Pauleen, 2019) (Figure 4.1). Internal decision situations might involve strategies, procedures and policies, issues around organizational culture including employee satisfaction, commitment and motivation, as well as the organization's physical environment. External decision situations might involve changes in customers' expectations and changes associated with socio-political, environmental and/or economic challenges.

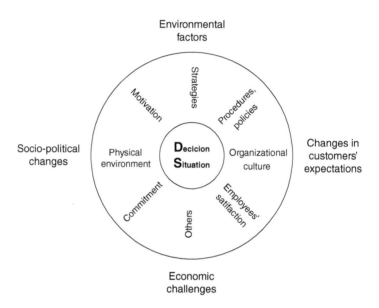

Figure 4.1 Internal and external factors affecting decision situations

The critical importance of decision-making (DM) in management is made crystal clear in Herbert Simon's quote (above) spoken at the opening of his renowned lectures on 'The New Science of Management Decision' in 1960. Decision-making is an integral part of every sort of management activity, and proficiency in decision-making distinguishes an effective manager from an ineffective one (Harrison, 1995). As central to what managers do, decision-making can certainly be considered a key management skill.

Making decisions in the dynamic and uncertain nature of the current business world and making decisions that involve complex problems require managers to possess and utilize a variety of knowledge, skills and abilities and to have access to the latest and most trustworthy information and sources. The KSAs include the contextual, computational, communication and collaboration KSAs discussed in Chapter 1 that we argued today's managers require, while the up-to-date and trustworthy sources of data reflected in the 3Vs, plus veracity and value, were covered in discussions of big data in Chapter 2.

While many situations requiring decisions can be identified by managers (e.g. slow sales, discontent among employees, etc.), other situations requiring decisions and action may not be so obvious. They may be hidden as part of the 'status quo' or they may be buried in the huge volumes of data and information that organizations generate and managers must work through. Given complex and rapidly changing business environments and changing stakeholder expectations, to be effective managers and business analysts must be able to actively search for decision-making occasions, continuously working to meet present and future expectations and conditions. This requires managers to have the KSAs for both finding and solving problems.

In Chapter 1 we suggested that managers need a range of skills to excel at their jobs including interpersonal and intergroup communication skills, management skills, as well as political and diplomatic skills. We also stated that managers will need to have high levels and a wide variety of contextual knowledge that they can gain from both their formal education (e.g. an MBA), from mentors, and from their work and life experience. We also strongly suggested that in the age of big data and analytics, managers will need a fair degree of computational knowledge, the kind of knowledge that will allow them to understand how to apply and direct the use of big data analytics in decision situations. In this chapter we will introduce the need for managers to be aware that both rational and non-rational ways of thinking play important roles in decision-making: that not only critical thinking and logic are essential but also an awareness of how we, as individuals, actually make decisions – based on emotions, insight, experience or best guesses – when confronted with decision situations that may be simple, complex, familiar or unique.

The field of decision-making has been the subject of academic and practitioner interest for years. Understanding all facets of management decision-making is essential. This includes the role and history of decision-making, decision-making processes as well as the effects of technology on decision-making. According to many researchers, the arrival of big data and analytics promises to significantly affect managerial decision-making (e.g. Shah et al., 2012; Davenport et al., 2013). Exploring the effects of big data and advanced analytics on decision-making is therefore also essential to management education and practice.

HISTORY OF DECISION-MAKING

In their *Harvard Business Review* article, 'A brief history of decision-making', Buchanan and O'Connell (2006) give a quick synopsis of decision-making from prehistoric times to the twenty-first century. In this book, we are most interested in management decision-making, which arguably takes root as an academic matter in the 1930s with Chester Bernard's observation that individual managers can be counted on to reliably decide matters in the organization's interest rather than their own (Buchanan and O'Connell, 2006).

Prior to the formal study of management decision-making, philosophers and economists tended to view rationality as the basis of sound decision-making. One of the classic frameworks of rational decision-making is a five-phase model introduced by John Dewey in 1910 (Dewey, 1933: 107): 1) suggestion, 2) intellectualization of the problem, 3) hypotheses, 4) reasoning, and 5) testing the hypotheses. Following in this tradition, management scholars founded what is called the Rational School of decision-making and have been heavily invested in the notion of rational decision-making with the development of numerous models encompassing a number of predetermined steps to be followed to achieve optimal outcomes (See Table 4.1).

However, it was clear to the observant that purely rational management decision-making is a chimera, almost impossible to achieve. When faced with real-world constraints – both contextual and cognitive – decision-makers need to make the best decision they can under the circumstances. Herbert Simon (1957) labeled the sum of these constraints 'bounded rationality': the best decision that decision-makers could make with the resources they have available.

It became clear that decision-making in practice was different from decision-making in theory. In the business world managers had to contend with limitations of time and money, as well as pressures from stakeholders, bosses and organizational norms and culture. In contrast to rational decision-making, the Naturalist School wanted to understand how decisions were actually made in real life (Messick and Bazerman, 2001). In real life, decisions are affected by all the external limitations that the decision situation may present as well as the decision-maker's own emotional and cognitive experiences, such as gut feelings, intuition, insight and judgment, which in this book we term non-rational modes of knowing.

Finally, we come to the role of technology in decision-making. Most technology is explicitly in support of making decision-making more rational. Technologies generally assist in bringing data and information to the decision-maker, in the belief that more data and information will result in more informed and hence better decisions. As we have seen in Chapters 2 and 3, big data and analytics are presented as the means to more, and more timely, data and information, and their role in improving decision-making is touted as one of their most notable benefits. We will investigate in greater detail in Chapter 5 just how these technologies can assist in management decision-making.

In this section, we have given just the briefest history of management decision-making, illustrated in Figure 4.2. In the sections that follow, we present in more detail what we believe are the most important and relevant forms of decision-making for students of management – rational, naturalist, non-rational and dual process decision-making – and how these forms of decision-making influence the outcome of decisions.

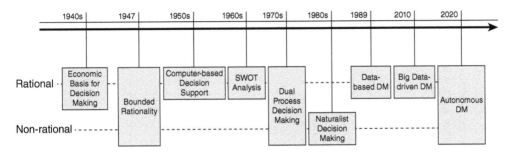

Figure 4.2 Timeline of selected decision-making theories

RATIONAL, NATURALIST AND NON-RATIONAL DECISION-MAKING

As pointed out in the section above, the two main schools of thought on decision-making are the rationalist and the naturalist. The two schools describe different approaches to decision-making and how it occurs or should occur in practice, but also reflect their approaches and views on the use of data, information, knowledge, experience, as well as heuristics, intuition, insight and emotion, which we understand in this book as non-rational elements of decision-making. In this section we look at these two approaches in more detail and how they are reflected in management decision-making.

Rational Decision-Making

Taking a logical approach to decision-making, the rationalist school seeks to identify the steps that a decision-maker should take to achieve optimal outcomes. Rational decision-making is based on a logical and linear step-by-step process. Though the number of steps may vary and be named differently they generally include: defining and diagnosing the causes of the problem, designing possible solutions, and finally deciding on the best solution given whatever constraints may exist (See Highlight Box 4.2). Somewhat optimistically, rationalists generally assume that a decision-maker can 1) perfectly recognize, identify and diagnose the problem, 2) identify and objectively establish all criteria related to the problem, 3) weigh the importance of the criteria according to the business need, 4) perfectly know all the possible alternative solutions, 5) precisely assess all the alternatives against each criterion, and 6) accurately calculate and select the alternative that has the highest value.

Highlight Box 4.2

Management Decision-making Processes

Academics have been researching management decision-making for many years and the result is numerous models and theories of decision-making. Some of these are highlighted in Table 4.1. To reduce the complexity and account for the often significant diversity of the different models, we have listed five stages in this table and the various steps that comprise them. It is a worthwhile exercise to go through the table carefully and look for the commonalities and the few differences that exist and think about these in terms of your own decision-making processes.

Table 4.1 Stages and steps in rational decision-making

Stages / Steps	Defining a problem			Diagnosing the causes of the problem			Designing possible solutions to the problem			Deciding on the best solution within constraints			Implementing the decision		
	Recognize the problem	Identify the problem	Diagnose the problem	Search for criteria related to the problem	Identify criteria related to the problem	Establish criteria related to the problem	Weigh the importance of the criteria according to the business needs and goals	Recognize possible alternative solutions	Identify the possible alternative solutions	Assess all the alternatives against each criterion	Calculate value of the alternatives	Select the alternative that has the highest value	Communicate the decision outcome	Control and monitoring the decision outcome	Feedback and evaluation on the decision outcome
Simon (1960, 1965)	Intelligence: Finding decision-making occasions						Design: Finding possible course of action			Choice: Choosing among courses of action					
Drucker (1967)	Classifying the problem / Defining the problem			Specifying the answer to the problem			Deciding what is 'right'			Putting the decision into action				Feedback	
Mintzberg et al. (1976)	Identification			Development						Selection					
Saaty (1994)			Identifying a problem's key elements	Eliciting judgments		Representing the formed judgments	Prioritizing the elements of the hierarchy			Determining an overall outcome				Analyzing sensitivity to changes in judgment	
Hammond et al. (1999)	Working on the right problem					Specifying objectives		Creating imaginative alternatives		Understanding the consequences	Grappling with trade-offs		Clarifying uncertainties	Thinking about risk tolerance	Considering linked decisions
Harrison (1999)				Setting managerial goals				Searching for alternatives		Comparing and evaluating alternatives		The act of choice	Implementing decisions		Follow-up and control

Stages	Defining a problem	Diagnosing the causes of the problem	Designing possible solutions to the problem	Deciding on the best solution within constraints	Implementing the decision
Galotti (2002)	Setting goals	Gathering information		Decision structuring; Making a final choice	Evaluating
Nutt (2002)		Collecting information	Establishing a systematic search for ideas	Evaluating ideas	Managing barriers
Beach and Connolly (2005)	Diagnosing the decision problem		Selecting an action	Implementing the selected action	
Bazerman (2006)	Defining the problem	Identifying criteria	Weighting the criteria; Generating alternatives	Rate each alternative on each criterion; Compute optimal decision	
Maddalena and Canada (2007)	Assessing		Planning		Implementing; Evaluation
Gibcus et al. (2008)	Recognition; Formulation	Search	Evaluation	Choice	Implementation
Rosanas (2013)	Identifying and defining the problem	Establishing the criteria that any solution must meet	Searching for and generating action alternatives	Analyzing and comparing action alternatives; Choosing an action alternative as the solution to the problem	

Questions to think about

1. What similarities and differences can you spot in the various models presented in the table? What do you think accounts for them?

2. Which of the models (or stages and steps) resemble your own decision-making processes? Do these models introduce ideas that you may want to incorporate into your own processes?

3. Assume that you are required to use a model as shown in the table in your decision-making process. Which model would you use for decision-making? Discuss your rationale.

The rationalist models of decision-making are normative and prescriptive, and expected outcomes and probabilities are evaluated against objective (rather than subjective) criteria. That is, the optimal outcome is logically expected to be achieved if the decision-maker strictly follows specific rules and procedures and precisely assesses the values and risk preferences during the decision-making process (Bazerman and Moore, 2013). Relevant, reliable and sufficient data and information can significantly enhance the accuracy of the objective evaluation and hence play an important role in rationalist decision-making processes. Big data and analytics are therefore being embraced by the rationalist school.

Highlight Box 4.3

Decision Triggers

Decision 'triggers' lead to the identification of decision situations. This is often the first step in the decision-making process. In our research (Gressel, 2020) we found four distinct categories of decision-making triggers: Evaluation, Routine Check, External Trigger and Anecdotal. The differentiation of these triggers as the first decision-making step is important, as they influenced the managers' use of rational and non-rational decision-making processes.

Table 4.2 Decision identification – triggers

Trigger	Description	Illustrative Quote
Evaluation	An internally triggered, intentional review of current practices, or an evaluation of future opportunities.	'So I came in here, and things have always been good at [the company], but I just couldn't get my head around how we seemed to lose so [much business] in a month.'
Routine Check	An ad hoc problem identified during a routine check or review.	'So that was driven by watching the market for all the value of things [...] And once you can spot there's a change, you can then try and capitalize on that.'
External Trigger	An external impulse, i.e. opportunity or problem, prompting a decision.	'Another marketing channel we tried was [...] sort of proposed to us through our creative agency.'
Anecdotal	Concerns, often longstanding, based on employees' perceptions that require a decision.	'So we have been debating this for a long time [...] but we don't seem to be able to get it across the line. And I said, well, in my view, I've validated it just through sitting with people and seeing what happens. And the CEO goes: "Right let's get the data."'

The triggers for decision-making can be based on a manager's feelings, observations and informal canvassing of other employees. However, the use or acquisition of data seems to be central in confirming these preliminary judgments. In our research, data analytics was seen as a valuable tool in the identification step at the beginning of the decision-making process. We found that data analytics can have a direct effect on the problem identification stage of the decision-making process by functioning as an additional trigger point or opportunity to identify a decision situation. The use of data analytics also enabled managers to improve the definition of requirements in this step by providing them with more detail early on in the decision-making process.

Questions to think about

1. In what ways might the type of decision trigger affect the decision-making process that follows?
2. Think about how the initial presentation of a decision situation could affect how the decision will be approached. Give some examples.
3. Discuss the types, roles and importance of decision triggers for rational and non-rational decision-making and give some examples.

The decision-making processes summarized in Highlight Box 4.2 are classified as rational in that they present logical and prescribed steps, but what happens within these steps is not always so clear and simple, or even rational (see Figure 4.3). For example, in one of the classic models of decision-making, Simon (1960, 1965) introduced a three-step decision-making model based on intelligence, design and choice. While Simon explained that the steps are mostly clearly distinct from each other, he also noted that each step contained a self-contained decision-making process. This means that each step of the process might require its own decision-making process, i.e. decisions within decisions. Complexity is also inherent in Mintzberg et al.'s (1976: 263) three-step model, with the authors accounting for the dynamic nature of strategic decisions by proposing a non-sequential nature of the steps, 'subjected to interferences, feedback loops, dead ends, and other factors', which can delay, speed up, stop or restart the decision-making process, and cause cycles within a phase or the circling back to a prior phase. Moreover, the authors state that the selection step consists of either an intuitive approach referred to as judgment, as well as bargaining activities with other stakeholders, or an analysis of previously designed alternatives, which in turn also leads to judgment or bargaining.

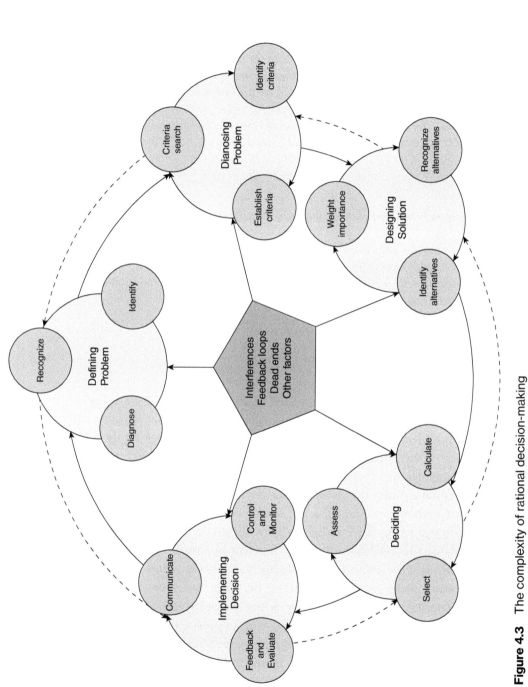

Figure 4.3 The complexity of rational decision-making

As with Mintzberg et al.'s (1976) intuitive approach to judgment, a glance through Table 4.1 indicates a number of steps that arguably challenge the notion of rational decision-making such as *creating imaginative alternatives* (Hammond et al., 1999) and *eliciting judgments* (Saaty, 1994). What these steps are apparently acknowledging is that human decision-making encompasses elements of the non-rational whether desired or not. Non-rational factors, such as intuitive judgment or imagination, in decision-making, we suggest, are part and parcel of being human and we will go on to discuss some of the kinds of non-rational factors that influence decision-making and why they should be acknowledged and consciously incorporated into management decision-making.

Naturalist Decision-Making

In contrast to rational decision-making, the naturalist approach wants to understand how decisions are made in practice, i.e. in the complex, sometimes messy world of the organization (Messick and Bazerman, 2001). While the rationalist models of decision-making are prescriptive, the naturalist models are descriptive in nature. They seek to provide an understanding of the decision-makers' cognitive and behavioral processes as they engage in making different kinds of decisions in their natural environments when faced with complex decision-making situations with limited resources, time and even cognitive abilities (Klein et al., 2010) (Figure 4.4).

Presenting decision-making as a set of straightforward sequential steps simply does not account for the complex nature of decision-making, according to the naturalists. Naturalists do not believe that the functions of decision-making in actual practice follow a set order of tasks. Managers can and often do make decisions without going through a process of ordered phases. Decision-making steps often overlap, some steps can be skipped, and different orders may be followed. These changes may reflect the decision-maker's preferences or biases or may be in response to situational factors (e.g. no time to collect the most appropriate data to inform the relevant step). Moreover, the importance of each step in the whole process of decision-making may vary, depending on the problem situation or other factors.

A manager's preferences or biases may be reflected in the heuristics they apply in their decision-making. Heuristic techniques employ a personal and practical method often unique to the individual decision-maker. Decisions based on heuristics are not likely to be optimal, perfect, logical or rational, but they are used because they are sufficient for addressing an immediate decision situation. As it is often impossible or impractical to find an optimal solution in many business-based decision situations, managers often apply heuristic methods to speed up the process of finding a satisfactory solution.

Heuristics resemble mental shortcuts that ease the cognitive load that rational decision-making often entails. Forms of heuristics include such non-rational approaches as: using a rule of thumb, an educated guess, an intuitive judgment, a guesstimate, profiling or common sense.

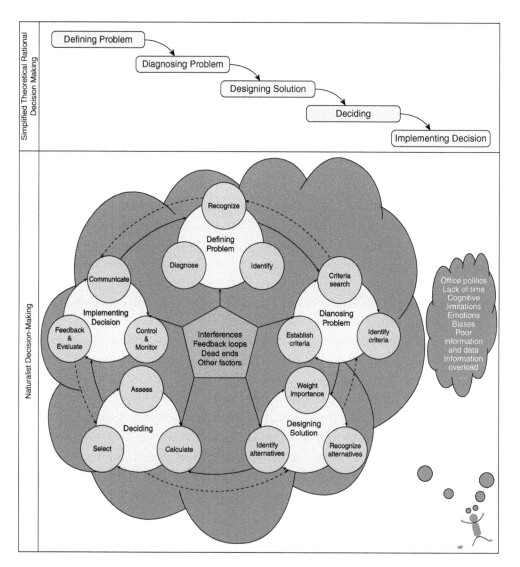

Figure 4.4   Theoretical decision-making vs real-world decision-making

According to naturalist thought, in the real world decision-makers rarely make purely rational decisions even if they understand this as the ideal. Whether consciously or not, managers will deviate from the principles and processes of rational decision-making in the real world due to various reasons (Figure 4.4). These include a whole host of causes from office politics to a lack of time, and from the decision-maker's own cognitive limitations, emotions and biases to poor information and data. Unlike the rational approach that assumes that gathering more data and information can reduce uncertainty, the natural approach opines that too much information does not necessarily reduce uncertainty and may even increase confusion and uncertainty (Intezari and Pauleen, 2019). Figure 4.4 highlights some of these factors that inhibit purely rational decision-making and they are described in more depth in the next section.

Consider This Box 4.4

Does Theory Matter in Real Life?

Kurt Lewin (1951: 169), a pioneer in applied research, stated that 'there is nothing as practical as a good theory' because he concluded 'good theory guides effective action by turning knowledge into wisdom'. In this chapter, we focus on decision-making theory because we believe that with knowledge of relevant theory, students can then begin to reflect on their own decision-making processes. By doing so you can become more aware of how you engage with decision situations and which strategies work and which don't.

How do you make decisions?

Below are a few common strategies that people engage in when faced with challenging decision situations. Which one do you tend to engage in and why? Do these strategies work for you, and if they do, how do they help you make decisions? You may want to discuss strategies with your classmates.

1. Empty my mind and see what pops up.
2. Use my own judgment or intuition.
3. Ask family and friends for advice.
4. Pray for guidance.
5. Find experts/professionals and ask for their help/advice.
6. Search for data or information and weigh the evidence.
7. Write a list of pros and cons and decide.
8. Combinations of the above
9. Something entirely different.

You may want to think of a recent challenging decision you had to make and reflect on the decision-making process you went through. What was helpful and what was not? Perhaps you can begin to develop a personal decision-making style that incorporates your own strategies with those suggested by established theory.

Rational decision-making assumes the strict adherence to a clearly structured process that consists of the clarification of objectives, assessment of alternatives and potential consequences, and a selection of the alternative best suited for obtaining the objectives (Harrison, 1995). In strict rationalist terms, non-rationality consequently is considered a failure to act rationally due to narrow-mindedness or biases attributed to a set of beliefs or prior experience.

Rational decisions when executed correctly will lead to decisions that are verifiable, replicable and backed by data and analytics. While non-rational decisions might have merit and are often based on years of experience, they display a higher level of subjectivity, which may limit their potential to convince other stakeholders. Rational decisions are straightforward when decision situations are relatively simple as with many operational types of decisions. Operational decisions can often be automated with highly rational computer-generated applications (see Table 4.3). These systems are commonly applied in administrative decision-making to make decisions, inform decisions, and in guiding users through decision-making processes. The anticipated growth in the development and growth of such systems is predicated based on increasing sets of big data and self-learning analytics (e.g. machine learning, see Chapter 10).

Table 4.3 Automated types of operational decision-making

Application	Example	Selected Technologies
Product configuration	Matching the customers with appropriate service plan, i.e. mobile customers	• Rule engines to respond to questions in a logical order • Industry specific packages to produce automated decision for specific organizational queries • Statistical or numerical algorithms to produce a decision using quantitative data • Workflow applications to process information and improve business processes • Enterprise systems to connect, automate and process organization-wide information
Yield optimization	Identifying the ticket sale price based on seat availability	
Routing decision	Identifying customers based on records or profiles and managing them for insurance purposes	
Regulatory compliance	Routine decision-making on checking candidates/ customers qualification for a segment, i.e. benefits from a campaign/service	
Fraud detection	Automatic process for checking fraud for transactions	
Operational control	Automatically determining the action to be taken based on changes in environment due to factors like temperature and humidity	

Source: based on Sheshasaayee and Bhargavi, 2017

However, as decision situations become more complex, involving human and environmental factors that are less predictable, purely rational decision-making becomes more difficult, if not impossible. In these situations, managers may involve non-rational processes including heuristics, experience, emotions and gut feelings in their decision-making process. Simon (1987), for example, believed that intuition and analysis are both involved in decision-making as complementary components. Mixing rational and non-rational approaches to decision-making may be done consciously or unconsciously.

Simon also introduced the concept of bounded rationality, which explains that a decision-maker's use of rationality is bounded by the complexity of problems and the decision-maker's mental (in-)capacity to process all available information and alternatives (Simon, 1957). Researchers report that the complexity of the decision situation (the number of alternatives, the number of the attributes and outcomes of each alternative) as well the KSAs of the decision-maker (e.g. deficiencies in reasoning skills, knowledge, and tolerance for ambiguity) can increase decision-making difficulties (Shiloh et al., 2001). Moreover, the decision-maker's perception of the complexity of the decision structure and difficulty is purely subjective and may affect the decisions as well. Individuals differ in their abilities to recognize and assess a problem situation, and may approach and tackle decision situations in entirely different ways. In this case what is rational to one manager may well be irrational to another. Differing conceptions of what is rational will often result in the necessity of what Mintzberg et al. (1976) referred to as bargaining, what we generally refer to as discussion, negotiating and sometimes arguing.

Other factors that limit the application of pure rationality are misrepresented, incomplete or unavailable information about possible alternatives, cost and time constraints, failures of communication, organizational precedents and office politics. Under such pressures, a manager, unable to thoroughly examine all the aspects of the decision situation, may decide to address the problem by applying the first and easiest solution that will work, even in part, at a given time. Under such constraints, a manager may just trust intuition, experience or a personal heuristic technique and make a successful decision without even being able to clearly explain how they reached the decision. In many cases, managers make decisions that lead to outcomes that are 'satisfying' and sufficient, rather than optimal (Miller et al., 2002).

In sum, human rationality is bounded due to three major constraints:

1. The decision-maker's limitation in understanding the decision situation, which may be in part a result of personal limitations or biases.
2. The decision-maker's limitation to assess all possible alternatives, inability to compare or calculate criteria, and inability to pick the best alternative.
3. Lack of, or inaccurate, information, and other situational constraints.

Non-Rational Decision-Making

It is these constraints that compel decision-makers to seek 'work-arounds' when addressing difficult decision situations. As we have seen, non-rational approaches such as intuition and heuristics often provide these cognitive work-arounds. In the sense that they often provide the best possible solution, or at least the most sufficient solution, in the face of difficult circumstances, non-rational processes are valuable management tools. Many heuristics, and intuition itself, are based on years of experience that have been consciously, or more often unconsciously, distilled into near-automatic responses to decision situations. Surveys, like the one conducted in New Zealand in 2018 described below (Taskin et al., 2020a; 2020b) found that senior executives tend to trust their own intuition and experiences over data when making important decisions (see Highlight Box 4.5). This should not be surprising, given that they have likely risen to these senior level positions based on the successful decisions they have made over many years.

Highlight Box 4.5

The Extent of Non-Rational Decision-Making in Organizations

A study conducted in New Zealand in 2018 (Taskin et al., 2020a) to find out the extent to which managers use big data and analytics while making strategic decisions (mentioned in Chapter 3) collected data on individual and organizational decision-making. At the organizational level, strategic decision-making processes included judgment (72.1 per cent), past experience (74.1%) and gut feelings when there was not enough information (58 per cent). About 20 per cent of the managers (17.4 per cent for pure judgment, 19 per cent for past experience, and 23.7 per cent for gut feeling) stated they used non-rational decision-making in their organizations at a middling level.

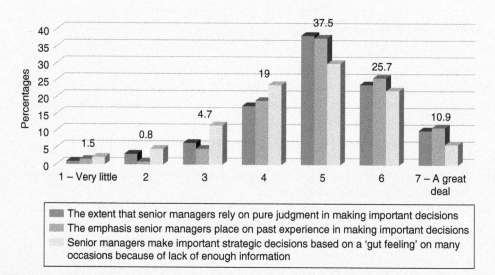

Figure 4.5   Decision-making in organizations – judgment, past experience and gut feeling

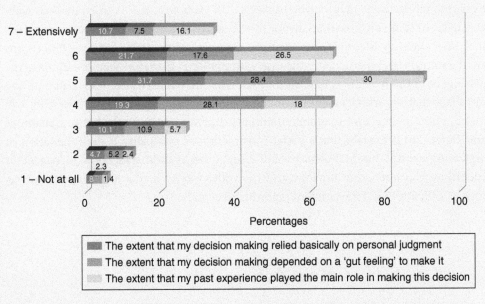

Figure 4.6   Decision-making – judgment, past experience and gut feeling (individual)

Strategic decision-making at organizational and individual level in NZ organizations

At the individual level, for significant strategic decisions, managers also mostly relied on their past experience (72.6 per cent), followed by personal judgment (64.1 per cent), and gut feelings (53.5 per cent). Only a small portion of the managers reported not using either personal judgment (1.8 per cent), gut feelings (2.3 per cent) or past experience (1.4 per cent) while making a strategic decision.

Questions to think about

1.   What kind of decisions do you think can be more appropriately made exclusively by past experience, gut feelings or judgment?
2.   Under what kind of circumstances will past experience, gut feelings and judgment tend to work well?
3.   What are the advantages and disadvantages of relying only on past experience, gut feelings and judgment while making strategic decisions? Expand your answer for different types of decisions.

Of course non-rational decision-making can also be problematic, particularly in some work functions or organizations. Non-rational decision-making is personal, individualized decision-making and hence cannot be replicated or even necessarily explained.

Two managers looking at the same decision situation may make two different decisions. Non-rational decisions may not be backed up by data and may even contradict available data. In some organizations senior level executives may be able to persuade others that their decision is correct, but in many organizations rational data-based decisions are the norm. This is particularly the case with mid-level managers who do not have the experience or the reputation to push through non-rational decisions. It's worth pointing out again that the management discipline is built upon the primacy of rationality and logical philosophical and economic traditions (Intezari and Pauleen, 2019). Cabantous and Gond (2011) explain that a social construction of rationality is the foundation of organizational structure and behavior and is supported by business schools, management education, consultants, technology and the wider society in the form of stakeholders such as Wall Street and government reporting structures.

Consider This Box 4.6

Rationality and Analytics

It is something of a paradox that while huge institutional forces exist that push for and expect rational decision-making, rational decision-making is extremely difficult, if not impossible, to achieve in practice, particularly in the important and often strategic decisions that need to be made in business.

Consider and discuss whether rationality is something of an illusion that persists in the world of business, even as the practitioners of business tend to engage in something else entirely. How can this paradox be managed by individual managers and organizations when it comes to management decision-making?

Consider how and to what extent big data, analytics and other technologies such as artificial intelligence could help to address the factors that are linked to bounded rationality. In what ways could these technologies lead to better provision of data and information and cognitive support that could possibly result in more rational decision-making processes in even complex decision situations?

DUAL PROCESS THEORY: SYSTEM 1 AND SYSTEM 2

A decision is a 'moment, in an ongoing process of evaluating alternatives for meeting an objective, at which expectations about a particular course of action impel the decision-maker to select that course of action most likely to result in attaining the objective' (Harrison, 1995: 5).

According to dual process theory, addressing the moment of decision can be done in one of two ways, through reasoning or intuition: that is, through rational or non-rational means. Dual processing enjoys popularity among researchers of decision-making theory, particularly in the field of psychology. While there are different variations of the dual process theory in cognitive and social psychology, in this book we follow the two-system view popular in the field of managerial decision-making (Wray, 2017).

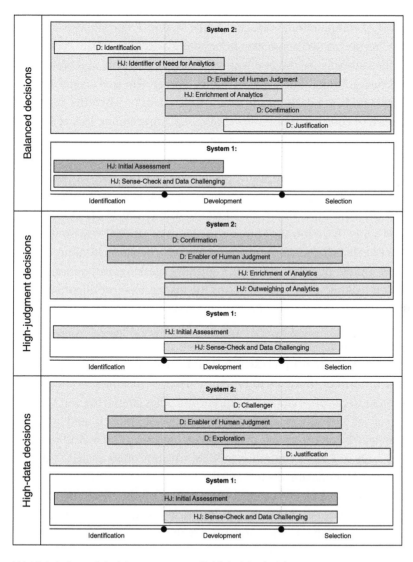

Notes: HJ: High-judgment decision   D: High-data decision

Figure 4.7   Decision-making in S1 and S2 domains (based on three-stage decision-making process)

The two-system view explains that there are two distinct cognitive processes that can result in a decision: intuition and reasoning. These two modes of thought have been labeled under different terms in past research and in this book we call them non-rational and rational cognition. In dual process theory they are usually known as System 1 and System 2 thinking.

Based on research of individual differences in human reasoning by Stanovich and West (2000: 658), the various properties of these two systems can be quite distinctly characterized. System 1 is conceptualized as 'automatic, largely unconscious, and relatively undemanding of computational capacity', while System 2 'encompasses the processes of analytic intelligence'. A decision-maker interpreting a decision situation via System 1 will automatically contextualize the problem, invoking an intuitive, and often biased, judgment (see Figure 4.7 High-judgment decisions). This system is generally applied when a decision-maker finds the decision situation familiar, and/or when the decision-maker is under the kinds of constraints discussed above – e.g. time, money, lack of information, or cognitive ability – and when the decision-maker can confidently rely on their intuition (Bazerman and Moore, 2013).

System 2, on the other hand, can be applied when the decision situation is more regulated or controlled and time and resource constraints are not issues (see Figure 4.7 High-data decisions). These situations allow the decision-maker to decontextualize the problem and apply in a controlled process the kinds of rational steps and principles discussed earlier in this chapter. Such processes lead to a depersonalization of the decision situation and a more objective decision. Generally speaking, in business and organizational decision-making, this system informs the manager's most important decisions, as organizations tend to require and afford greater respect for a logical, conscious and verifiable process of decision-making (Bazerman and Moore, 2013).

While these systems can act separately, they often work together (see Figure 4.7 Balanced decisions). System 1 processes, such as heuristics and intuition, provide support for System 2 in form of shortcuts to prevent a decision-making process from becoming an endless quest to calculate all possible future outcomes (Stanovich and West, 2000). On the other hand, as System 1 processes can lead to biased results if used unconsciously or carelessly, System 2 procedures can oversee these processes. The monitoring of System 1 by System 2 leads to a more controlled process, which is often related to the concept of rationality in decision-making (Evans, 2003).

Both the System 1 and 2 categories suggest that routine decisions are approached through System 2 processes (see Table 4.4). As discussed above these will tend to involve simple or operational type decision situations with clear objectives and limited possible responses. Non-routine and complex decisions, however, are usually approached through System 1 processes. As explained by Simon (1960: 11) 'When we ask how executives in organizations make nonprogrammed decisions, we are generally told that they "exercise judgment," and that this judgment depends, in some undefined way, upon experience, insight, and intuition [...] we may be told that creativity was required'. Even now, in the age of big data, we find executives referring to the 'art of decision-making' and seeking out the 'collective wisdom' when making important decisions (Gressel, 2020).

While System 1 can be compared to non-rational decision-making, and System 2 to rational decision-making, dual process theory recognizes and emphasizes the cooperation and value of both systems working together. In this sense, it fits with the naturalist school of decision-making in that dual process thinking represents the way managers generally make decisions in the real world by combining all their cognitive resources as they deal with numerous situational contingencies. For this reason, we focus on this theory in this book. Explaining how both rational and intuitive sense (can) work together makes an excellent starting point for students of decision-making in the age of big data and analytics by providing a balanced model of decision-making, one that managers can draw from as they work through their own understanding and practice of decision-making. In the next sections, we offer more detail and background on dual process theory and Systems 1 and 2.

Consider This Box 4.7

Would You Make the Same Decision in the Same Way?

Consider your decision to join your current study program. The choice to study at all, the degree you are pursuing, and the university you chose. If you had to make this decision again, look at it from three different angles:

1. Solely using the System 1 approach, relying on your judgment, experience and gut feeling.
2. Solely approaching it from a rational point of view, relying on System 2 processes.
3. Employing a balanced approach, incorporating both systems and their traits. How would this interaction of both systems work?

Compare the different approaches (in hindsight) and the potentially varying outcomes. Consider the benefits and drawbacks of each approach and discuss your decisions with your fellow students.

System 1

From an evolutionary perspective, System 1 is considered the older one of the two systems, as the system's processes are shared between humans and animals (Evans, 2003).

The system is shaped by embodied habits and experiences, making any adjustments to or control of its processes challenging. Other characteristics of this system are identified in the literature and are summarized in Table 4.4. Most commonly System 1 is referred to as fast, automatic and effortless. This enables System 1 processes to generate 'intuitive, immediate responses' (Gilhooly and Murphy, 2005: 282), with the decision-maker only consciously realizing the decision after it has been made and acted on.

In the context of management decision-making, System 1 is often referred to as intuition, which is described as a holistic, time-efficient, emotional, but non-conscious process that relies on learning from experience (Dane and Pratt, 2007). The outcome of this intuitive process is referred to as an intuitive judgment (Kahneman, 2003). A key part of intuition is holistic associations, which describe the process of matching stimuli to known patterns, and fitting 'isolated bits of data and experiences into an integrated picture' (Khatri and Ng, 2000: 60). In this process, the stimuli are matched to either simple cognitive structures, i.e. heuristics, or more complex cognitive structures, which are referred to as expert decision-making perspectives (Dane and Pratt, 2007), the kind experienced senior executives will most likely claim to possess.

Some researchers claim that these expert decision-making perspectives are complementary or even superior to analytical or rational approaches: especially in the case of unstructured or complex problems, where, as we have discussed, rational approaches often do not work. As Dane and Pratt (2007: 49) explain, '[o]ne could argue that the rapid change that characterizes current organizational environments makes intuitive decision-making more necessary today than it has been in the past' (see Highlight Box 4.8). Experts are often found to make competent intuitive judgments without being able to give valid reasons or describe the process leading to their judgment (Simon, 1987). Trying to analyze or understand the decision might even disrupt or affect the quality of the decision.

Highlight Box 4.8

How Experts Arrive at High-Quality System 1 Type Decisions

The rapid arrival at a decision by experts and experienced senior managers can be explained through a rapid fire 'recognition and retrieval process' evoked by a set of premises that leads them to the right conclusion (Simon, 1987: 61), while 'only the final product of such processes is available to consciousness' (Gilhooly and Murphy, 2005: 282). The basis for this retrieval process is a large stock of previously acquired knowledge and experiences, which is anchored in the expert's memory and accessed during the decision-making process (Simon, 1987). This knowledge and experience are skills that managers acquire through decision-making practice, enabling them to make accurate intuitive judgments rapidly and effortlessly (Kahneman, 2003).

Individual differences in managers' experience, cognitive and decision-making capabilities are therefore particularly relevant for the outcome of accurate intuitive judgments (Stanovich and West, 2000).

Questions to think about

1.   In what ways are expert decisions important for organizations?
2.   Discuss the advantages of System 1 decision-making over rational decision-making. When would you prefer System 1 decision-making over rational decision-making? Discuss the role and importance of decision types in such decision-making.
3.   Do you consider yourself as having expert knowledge in a particular area (work, sport, music, hobby, etc.)? How does your decision-making differ when encountering a decision situation in an area where you are expert compared to an area where you are not?

Intuitive judgments of managers are most accurate in situations and environments they are familiar with, as the accuracy of these judgments tends to be very context specific. When confronted with new and complex challenges, the use of personal experience-based judgment can lead to errors or biases. The result of this experiential disconnect may lead to generalizations in situations that should be based on case-by-case decisions (Bhidé, 2010).

In contrast to the complex cognitive processes employed in expert decision-making, simple intuition-based cognitive processes are referred to as heuristics (see Table 4.3). As we have seen, heuristics reduce the decision-maker's processing effort and time as they compensate for a lack of information and reduce complexity. In the dual process view, as a part of System 1, heuristics are considered essential in limiting the number of available alternatives for System 2 processes, which can help the decision-maker maintain a relatively high level of accuracy when making choices and judgments. The finance industry is an example of this, where heuristics are applied in the form of category systems, which help with the evaluation and comparison of firms (Carruthers, 2010). However, when heuristics are applied inappropriately, they can lead to biases that are reflected in the manager's decision (Betsch and Glöckner, 2010).

Many types of heuristics and their related biases have been identified. Here we will focus on three well-known heuristics: the availability, representativeness and confirmation heuristics. The availability heuristic is based on research by Tversky and Kahneman (1973, 1975) and postulates that the ease of information accessibility determines the decision-maker's assessment of an event's probability. While often a useful tool for decision-makers, for example, when assessing the frequency of an event, this heuristic is also fallible as 'An event that evokes emotions and is vivid, easily imagined, and specific will be more available than an event that is unemotional in nature, bland, difficult to imagine, or vague' (Bazerman and Moore, 2013: 7). Vividness of past experiences can promote their availability in the decision-maker's memory, even though they might not be the most relevant ones for the decision.

The representativeness heuristic is applied when the decision-maker has to judge a person, event or process. For this purpose, the decision-maker compares the object in question by its traits or characteristics to established categories or stereotypes. This heuristic is also fallible and if used unconsciously can cause biases in the form of discrimination. The third of the well-known heuristics is considered the confirmation heuristic and can lead to an anchoring bias. The confirmation heuristic is described as the selective use of data when decision-makers test hypotheses, which leads to the neglect of other available information. This can lead to an anchoring bias, meaning that the initial assessment of a situation can affect all further judgment of the situation.

Table 4.4   System 1 and System 2 characteristics

System 1 Characteristics	System 2 Characteristics
Relatively fast processing speed	Relatively slow processing speed
Automatic	Encompasses the processes of analytic intelligence (logical, analytic)
Effortless (heuristic-based)	Rule-based
Acquisition by biology, exposure and personal experience	Hypothetical thinking
Implicit (not available to introspection)	Conscious
Associative	Sequential
Emotional	Controlled
Unconscious	Deliberate
Holistic	Acquisition by cultural and formal tuition
Effortless	Effortful

System 2

Intuitive judgments made by System 1 can lead to a number of biases compromising decision quality, as raised in the previous section. According to dual process theory one of System 2's central tasks is to monitor and correct System 1 judgments if an irrational response is detected (Wray, 2017). The systematic procedures of System 2 allow decision-makers to consciously gather and evaluate information and engage in abstract reasoning and hypothetical thinking. This is an advantage over System 1 in situations that cannot be mastered by relying on previous experience. System 2 processing is captured by rational decision-making models, which, as we have already discussed, consist of deliberate process steps and analysis. Its key characteristics are summarized in Table 4.4.

System 2 is a useful tool for decision-makers, but it also has its restrictions, which can interfere with its key function of monitoring System 1 decisions. System 2 is considered effortful and involves often complex analysis, resulting in a much slower processing speed than System 1's. To engage in System 2 thinking, high levels of fluid intelligence and working memory capacity, as well as experience with statistical thinking, are required. Situational factors around the decision situation such as time pressure and too little (or too much) information can also severely affect a manager's ability to reason out an optimal decision.

When System 2 processes work unencumbered, they consist of a number of analytic steps, as outlined in the section on rational decision-making (Highlight Box 4.2). As we saw, these models contain from three to eight steps with the lengthier models adding sub-steps or including action and evaluation steps.

Highlight Box 4.9

Key Inputs and Outputs in System 2 Decision-Making Processes

In the previously mentioned study conducted in New Zealand and Australia in 2018 (Taskin et al., 2020b) to explore the extent to which managers use big data and analytics while making strategic decisions, we found that a variety of important factors were positively associated with rational System 2 decision-making processes. These factors included: individual characteristics of managers such as their propensity for risk and their domain knowledge; firm-based characteristics, including the firm's orientation to its external environment and to making internal improvements; and the nature of the decision process (i.e. comprehensiveness). Manager uncertainty also had an impact on rational decision-making; however, its effect was negative.

These factors are described blow.

- Comprehensiveness: considering and developing alternative responses, explanations and courses of actions for the decision situation.
- Uncertainty: managers' ability and confidence to estimate the results of a decision; having access to relevant information before making the decision.
- Risk propensity: willingness to act innovatively and maximize the possibility of exploiting potential opportunities.
- Domain knowledge: managers being knowledgeable about core capabilities, goals and objectives of the organization as well as the external environment (i.e. government, competitors, suppliers and customers).

(Continued)

- External orientation: associated with quick response to sector developments and changes; encouraging and training employees to answer or respond better to supplier needs or customer questions; improving the position of the company in the market and having an edge with local competitors.
- Improvement orientation: the degree to which an organization encourages employees to take the initiative to improve their tasks, look for opportunities to improve the organization and self-review their jobs.

The results of the study reveal that rational System 2 decision-making is positively associated with the quality of the decision outcome, efficiency and speed of making decisions, and improved financial and non-financial organizational performance. The decision outcome measures are defined as follows:

- Decision outcome quality: decisions are more accurate, correct, precise, flawless, error-free and reliable.
- Efficiency: arriving at a decision more quickly.
- Financial performance: long-term level of profitability, growth rate of sales or revenues, return on assets, market share and overall financial performance.
- Non-financial performance: greater efficiency of operations, public image and goodwill, quality of service or product, employee satisfaction and social responsibilities.

The survey results can be modeled as shown in Figure 4.8.

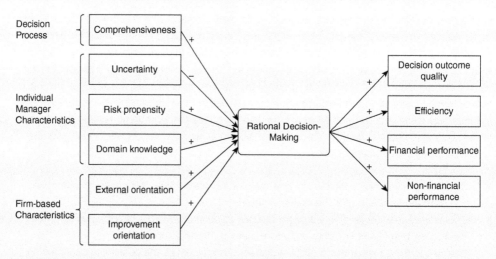

Figure 4.8   Rational decision-making with its antecedents and consequences

Questions to think about

1.   What other factors might affect rational decision-making? Discuss your answer.
2.   Why do you think 'uncertainty' has a negative impact on rational decision-making? Is System 1 decision-making more appropriate for dealing with uncertainty. Explain why or why not?

While all the models differ in certain aspects, three core phases emerge as a common denominator, and can be seen as representative for System 2 processes: firstly, the identification of a problem or decision occasion occurs. This is followed by the development of alternatives, eventually leading to the stage of their evaluation and choice of the best solution to the scenario. Besides these commonalities, each of these models provides an interesting base for the exploration of management decision-making in the age of big data: the assumption being that more data, and more timely data, can enhance the choices made in rational decision-making.

Both System 1 and System 2, have benefits and limitations (Table 4.4). Which processes are most suitable for the decision-maker depends on the nature and context of the decision. It is therefore important to understand the different types of decisions that managers face in today's business world.

DECISION TYPES AND MANAGER RESPONSES

Managers face a variety of decisions (Table 4.5), which can be divided into types based on their characteristics, such as their impact, complexity, or the manager's familiarity with the decision situation (Harrison, 1995). Decision types influence the decision-making process length, thoroughness and need for supporting or relevant data and information. Differentiating between these decision types is important as it informs the manager's approach to decision-making (System 1, System 2 or both), and determines how much time and resources will be allocated to the decision.

Table 4.5 Types of decision situations

	Decision Type	Description	Decision Process
Dimension of Longevity and Impact (Ackoff, 1990)	Operational	Mostly routine, well-defined decisions regarding immediate future	System 2, often data or information based, often automated
	Tactical	Medium-term decisions regarding the organization's efficiency	System 1 and 2
	Strategic	Important, high-level, long-term decisions that influence the organization's goals and objectives	System 1 and 2, will tend to involve a great deal of data and information, but in the end decisions may be made based on experience and judgment of senior executives

(Continued)

Table 4.5   (Continued)

	Decision Type	Description	Decision Process
Dimension of Decision Context (Snowden and Boone, 2007)	Simple/Routine	Decisions or problems are assessed, categorized and responded to with established practices	System 2, often data or information based, often automated
	Complicated	Several potential solutions to a decision require thorough analysis and expertise	System 1 and 2, often data or information based, augmented by human judgment
	Complex	Unpredictable decisions that rely on probing and experiments	System 1 and 2, recursive and iterative, integration of rational and non-rational thinking, along with relevant data, information and experience
	Chaotic	Decisions defined by turbulence and without underlying cause-and-effect relationships	Could be either System 1 or 2, the objective in the first instance is to establish relationships
	Disorder	No other decision type or context is predominant	Could be either System 1 or 2, the objective in the first instance is to establish order

Source: based on Ackoff, 1990; Drucker, 2006; Snowden and Boone, 2007

At one end of the decision-making spectrum are routine decisions. These often concern operational matters and are often immediate and require fewer resources, as the decision-maker is often familiar with the decision situation, which is fairly well contained and often inconsequential (Ackoff, 1990). Routine decisions are sometimes programmable because they are characterized as recurring and predictable, with clear cause-and-effect relationships. Another viable approach for addressing routine decisions is through automated, computational methods, including data and analytics, since the decision criteria are known and include recurring variables.

At the other end of the spectrum are non-routine decisions, which can be described as non-recurring, unique, complex and unprogrammable. These decisions often require intuition, judgment and creativity; heuristics are also applied. Strategic decisions are the most prominent example of non-routine decisions. While they make up a small percentage of the overall number of decisions a manager encounters, non-routine decision situations often require more time and resources than other decisions because of the lack of historical perspective and the fact that these decisions often have effects that extend into the unforeseeable future. Information and knowledge that can inform the decision situation may also be lacking. For example, strategic decisions usually involve significant long-term outcomes and often high levels of complexity.

Ackoff (1990) and Snowden and Boone (2007) offer frameworks that provide more variety and a clearer distinction of the kinds of real-world management decision situations. Ackoff's (1990) framework is used to capture the dimension of longevity and impact, whereas Snowden and Boone's (2007) Cynefin framework is applied to focus on the decision contexts, capturing their complexity and circumstances. Both frameworks' decision types are featured in Table 4.5.

Differentiating decisions according to longevity and impact is commonly used in academic and business contexts. The three decision types are operational, tactical and strategic. Operational decisions are mostly short term and their primary objective is the company's survival. They are considered routine, have clearer descriptions, and can often be approached through quantitative analysis. Tactical decisions are medium term, typically do not exceed the fiscal year, and their primary concern is efficiency. Strategic decisions usually focus on growth and involve a period of time long enough to cover new product development, development of new supply chains, and/or entry into a new business or market. Strategic decisions are complex, infrequent decisions made on a high level, conceptually and hierarchically.

The Cynefin framework focuses on the contextual dimension of decisions (Snowden, 2000). It posits that decision-makers must identify the specific context of the decision at hand and adjust their decision-making approach accordingly (Snowden and Boone, 2007). Five different decision types, or contexts, are differentiated according to the decision situation's inherent cause-and-effect relationships: simple, complicated, complex, chaotic and disorder. Simple and complicated contexts are characterized by clear cause-and-effect relationships, whereas in complex and chaotic contexts this relationship is not immediately apparent. Disorder only finds application if none of the other four contexts is clearly predominant. The decision can then be divided into smaller parts, and each part can be classified as one of the four other contexts.

Simple contexts often involve decision situations with well-structured processes, which mostly result in self-evident solutions that are understood by all affected parties. Complicated contexts differ from simple ones in having several potential solutions requiring more expertise. This context requires an analysis of the available options before deciding on the most appropriate one.

The outcomes of decisions in complex contexts are considered unpredictable because the causes of the decision situation are not always clear. Such contexts are shaped by constant change inherent, for example, in the exploration of new terrains, such as mergers and acquisitions. Only isolated parts of the situation can be understood by the decision-maker, and complete understanding of the context is often only achieved in hindsight (Snowden and Boone, 2007). Complexity is an important indicator for the ensuing decision-making process. This context requires patience from managers, as they have to rely on emerging patterns, probing and experiments to reach a decision.

A chaotic context has constantly shifting cause-and-effect relationships and therefore no determinable patterns. Given this turbulence, the decision-maker must first act to establish order, then sense where stability is present and from where it is absent, and then respond by working to transform the situation from chaos to complexity, where the identification of emerging patterns can both help prevent future crises and discern new opportunities (Snowden and Boone, 2007).

An example of a chaotic decision situation was the Deepwater Horizon spill in the Gulf of Mexico in 2010. This was an emergent situation that had never occurred before with multiple cause-and-effect relationships, many dimensions and levels of interconnectedness and high levels of uncertainty and risk, and huge environmental and financial implications (Intezari and Pauleen, 2019). It took many attempts to try and stem the immediate chaos of the explosion and leaking oil and years to try and stabilize the widespread impact of the event.

Decision types influence the decision-making process and as we can see, managers face a variety of decisions, which can be divided into types based on their characteristics, such as their impact, complexity or the manager's familiarity with the decision situation. Differentiating these decision types is important and is the first step when encountering a decision situation. Understanding the decision type informs the manager's approach to decision-making and determines the time and resources that should be allocated to it. While strategic decisions only make up a small percentage of the overall number of decisions a manager encounters, this decision type requires more time and resources than other decisions because of their significant long-term outcomes and often high levels of complexity. On the other hand, routine operational decisions tend to be easier to make because they tend to be fairly structured and require less resources and the decision-maker is often familiar with the decision situation. Between simple and complex decisions lies a full range of decision types, many of which are unique and each of which will require a conscious and often considered approach to address them.

CHAPTER SUMMARY

This chapter has provided an in-depth introduction to management decision-making providing background into the history and importance of management decision-making and especially into the decision-making processes as exemplified by rational, non-rational and naturalist decision-making. We have given special attention to the dual process theory of decision-making because we believe it is an excellent starting point for management students who wish to become effective decision-makers. Dual process theory also allows us to adopt a more naturalist perspective on decision-making, which we believe provides a solid basis for managers to incorporate and balance both human and data-driven methods to optimize the decision-making process.

We stated earlier that it is the manager's job to anticipate decision situations and actively search for problems to solve. Traditionally this was done by observation and the measuring of current performance against standards. The abilities to observe and measure are part of a fundamental set of management KSAs. In Chapter 1 we discussed what mindsets and KSAs are necessary for managers to succeed in management decision-making and in Chapter 7 we will discuss how organizations can improve data-driven decision-making. Table 4.6 highlights some ways that managers and organizations can improve decision-making performance with a focus on dual process decision-making. Improving System 2 approaches are fairly non-controversial; however, many of the KSAs related to System 1 thinking will come off as 'new age'. Nevertheless, these approaches underpin System 1 processes and are all now part of management discourse.

Table 4.6 Improving Systems 1 and 2 decision-making performance

Decision-Making	Improvement	Suggested Methods	Sources
System 1	Improve Non-rational Cognition	• Accessing imagination • Developing insight • Reflecting on experience • Embodying wisdom • Engaging in mindful management practice	Patvardhan, 2017 Intezari and Pauleen, 2019 Küpers and Pauleen, 2015 Kudesia, 2019
System 2	Improve Rational Cognition	• Training in orderly and probabilistic thinking • Training in statistics • Directed and standardized organizational operating procedures	Simon, 1960 Kahneman, 2003

In many decision situations a manager's capability to anticipate and react and identify solution alternatives is significantly limited in depth and scope by cognitive abilities and a host of situational factors such as lack of time and access to quality and up-to-date data and information. Now, managers can utilize advanced business intelligence systems, big data and analytics, allowing them to quickly collect data and information from numerous sources inside and outside their organizations, and apply sophisticated statistical analyses to support System 2 type decision processes. Even System 1 expert judgments and heuristic-based decisions can now be supported or confirmed with timely data.

As we have discussed in previous chapters and will again in Chapter 5, big data and analytics are potential game changers in management decision-making. They represent a significant enabler of rational decision-making in organizations. The increasingly growing volume of data (big data), as well as advances in technology in acquiring and analyzing massive volumes of data in a very limited time, may significantly improve many management decisions. For example, real-time analytics and deep contextual analysis of data can help managers identify trends, anticipate changes in the market, mitigate risks, provide customized services, and improve customer experience. While presenting opportunities, the novelty of big data and advanced analytics can also be expected to pose additional risks for managers. Lacking the knowledge of how big data can help decision-making or the ability to use and understand statistical analysis can hinder System 2 decision-making, while the often abstract nature of data and knowledge can cause distrust among System 1 decision-makers, who may develop a psychological distance from this form of knowledge (Bryant and Tversky, 1999).

From a dual process theory standpoint, though, big data and analytics do not and cannot replace human judgment and other System 1 cognitive skills such as intuition, insight and imagination. Moreover, people still play the fundamental role of determining how available technologies are to be used in the decision-making process. As both naturalist decision-making and dual process theory demonstrate, individual managers take different approaches to decision-making and will individually decide the roles of data, information, knowledge and personal judgment when making decisions. Different decision situations will engage different decision-making processes, which then engage a variety of approaches. The approaches are interrelated in a recursive process of problem finding and problem solving. These are points worth keeping in mind in a business and technological environment that is moving full-steam ahead with what has been called hyper-rational thinking and technological solutionism (Dalal and Pauleen, 2018).

KEY LESSONS

In this chapter we have introduced management decision-making and decision-making theories. The most important takeaways can be summarized as:

1. Management decision-making is as much an art as a science: data, analytics, rational thinking, judgment, intuition and imagination all play a role.
2. The key is that the decision-maker needs to be acutely aware of the decision situation, contingencies involving the decision situation and their own decision-making style with all its strengths and weaknesses.
3. Experience in decision-making will increase managers' awareness of the decision context and key variables but might also lead to preconceived ideas and biases. Reflection and evaluation of decisions are therefore a key part of decision-making that should be practiced by all decision-makers, independent of their seniority.

5

ANALYTICS IN MANAGEMENT DECISION-MAKING

Contents

Highlight Box 5.1

Asking the Right Questions

Analytics and big data have become powerful trends in business and government, popping up everywhere in the practitioner, academic and popular press. They seem a bit mysterious to most, act as game-changers for those in the know and are considered a business opportunity for the vendors marketing them. In our view, they are just a management tool. They may be a powerful tool when used intelligently, but they also have the potential to be misunderstood and misused. Asking the right question and defining the requirements is critical to the effective use of analytics. These questions refer to the cause or reason for the analytics effort, the metrics that need to be defined for the effective use of the data and analytics, and the benefits that are being sought. Asking the right question is the required starting point of the analytics process, and it is also seen as a critical skill for decision-making.

As the Head of Data of a large financial organization advises: 'Start with the question, not with the data. Where do you believe value could be in your business? And then, what's the fastest, cheapest way for you to demonstrate a test of where that value could be? Do you need to develop an analytical model or can you simply create a set of simple hypotheses to test? If you don't even know where to start, you probably want to do some analysis, and some interpretation of insights.'

A business analyst confirmed this approach by saying: 'First I define the problem, or what I need to do, what do I need to look at, what kind of information do I think I need for answering those questions, or doing the analyses.'

A senior manager at the same financial organization also expresses that the need to ask the right questions is critically important to intelligently use analytics: 'I pride myself because I know what questions to ask.' Having a thorough understanding of and experience with data analytics benefits this starting point of the analysis. 'I have a sixth sense in being able to understand if the data is accurate from my questions and from what I hypothesize in my head and I know how to format or present data so that it helps to tell a story.'

Questions to think about

1. What do you think managers need to know in order to ask the 'right' questions about using big data analytics?
2. Why do you think it is important to have a question before beginning data collection and analysis?
3. What do you think about analytics being a management tool? What do you think the role of information technologists should be?

CHAPTER 5 KEY LESSONS

1. Effective management decision-making involves both human judgment and data/analytics.
2. Different decision situations require different combinations and applications of judgment and data.
3. Appropriate management KSAs and organizational support are essential in achieving effective balanced, high-judgment and data-driven decisions.

INTRODUCTION

In Chapter 3 we covered the history of analytics and related technologies, the types of analytics in current use, and the relationships between big data and analytics. We noted three key points: 1) while analytics have been around for a while, advanced analytics powered by sophisticated technologies and big data are products of the twenty-first century; 2) advanced analytics offer significant new opportunities for organizations to assess environmental conditions and to support data-driven decision-making; and 3) the use of analytics should be moderated with human input and judgment. In Chapter 4 we introduced management decision-making and the kinds of decision-making processes presented in theory and used in practice, with special focus on dual process theory, a theory that tries to account for the way people really make decisions, using combinations of rational and non-rational cognitive processes. We noted that data analytics sits firmly in System 2 processes as an important support tool for rational decision-making.

In this chapter we focus on *how* managers use analytics in decision-making. Specifically, how the *roles* of human judgment and data analytics work separately and together through the decision-making process. We also investigate the contextual factors that affect these roles, and how data analytics can be used more effectively in management decision-making. Much of this chapter is based on the results of five years of qualitative and quantitative research in the use of big data and analytics in management decision-making (Taskin et al., 2019, 2020; Gressel, 2020).

THE ROLE OF ANALYTICS IN DECISION-MAKING

While advanced analytics and big data currently pose challenges for organizations, traditional analytics capabilities and IS tools supporting decision-making have been used for decades. Decision support systems (DSS) and knowledge management systems (KMS) have provided managers with valuable insights and played a prominent role facilitating decision-making. DSS are designed to follow System 2 processes and assist the decision-maker by introducing an optimized structure, particularly into unstructured and semi-structured decision types (Courtney, 2001). As unfamiliarity with big data and analytics may contribute to the complexity of decision-making, especially for those without the knowledge, skills and abilities to effectively handle them, managers employing big data could significantly benefit from DSS capabilities when faced with challenging decision situations. While providing technological support and structure, DSS still leave room for managerial judgment and act in a supporting role (Bohanec, 2009). A KMS can be another important tool for the exploitation of big data, as it assists in the acquisition, creation and storage of knowledge, which is often derived from data.

The general influence of these and other information systems is addressed in Huber's (1990) theory of the effects of advanced information technologies on organizational design, intelligence and decision-making. Huber proposes that using communication and decision support technologies leads to several significant changes, such as fewer time-consuming meetings, and an increased variety of people acting as information sources for decision-making (Figure 5.1). At the same time, Huber stated, the number of employees involved in the decision-making process is expected to decrease, as these technologies can function as a source of expertise and therefore substitute for the respective expert. However, recent research has found this may not be the case as the use of advanced data and analytics by managers often requires information technologists and may still require domain experts when decision situations are complex (Gressel, 2020).

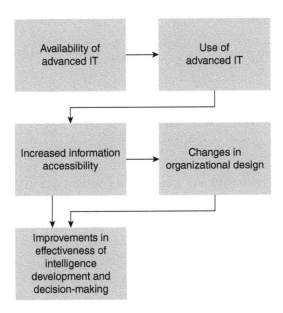

Figure 5.1   Simplified version of Huber's 1990 theory of the effects of advanced information technologies on organizational design, intelligence and decision-making

Overall, the use of advanced information technology is proposed to have a positive effect on the identification of opportunities and problems, and to facilitate less time-consuming and higher quality decisions (Huber, 1990). While Huber's theory was published in 1990, the pursuit of more accurate and timely decision-making continues. More modern methods of data analysis and information technology offer additional benefits and insights to managerial decision-making. These insights are gained when information is extracted from big data, using fundamental principles of data science (Provost and Fawcett, 2013). This extraction, which is related to data mining, processes raw data into meaningful information and knowledge.

As discussed in Chapter 2, when data is used as the basis for decision-making, its value lies in the quality of the data. Good data is critical to creating useful insights. Only with rigorous data selection can descriptive, diagnostic, predictive, prescriptive and autonomous analytics offer valuable opportunities to the decision-maker. Figure 5.2 incorporates the role of analytics into Huber's decision-making theory. The specific roles of analytics in the decision-making process – enable, confirm, challenge, identify, explore and justify judgment – are explained in detail in this chapter.

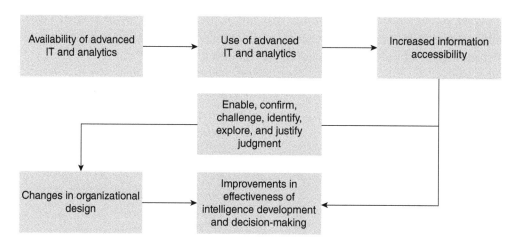

Figure 5.2   Analytics' role in DM and organizational design

Source: adapted from Huber, 1990

The quality of the data sources and whether the data matches the organization's needs not only affects the quality of the results or insights, but also the decision process itself. When the decision-maker is overwhelmed by too much data or lacks trust in it, this can result in a 'paralysis by analysis' and a prolonged decision-making process. Analysis paralysis is an often occurring problem, as 'individuals tend to want too much rather than too little information and may take too long to arrive at decisions' (Harrison, 1995: 12). Decision-makers have to weigh the necessity of gathering additional information against the cost and time of acquiring it. The objective is to reach a close proximity to the optimum amount.

Deciding how much data or information is enough requires human judgment and is a critical part of any decision-making process. Furthermore, the decision-maker has to know what data or information is required. These contextual and computational types of managerial knowledge are discussed in Chapter 1. Essentially, managers must know enough about data and analytics to be able to ask the right questions (Highlight Box 5.1) and to use their own judgment and expertise. These human factors can be considered assets in the decision-making process.

This is essentially the position taken in this book. As we have argued in earlier chapters, managers require a balanced set of KSAs that span technical and managerial areas. Effective management decision-making requires knowledge of decision-making processes, supporting technologies, and an awareness of one's own decision-making preferences (Chapter 6) as well as the ability to make conscious adjustments to the process, as environmental constraints require.

SPECIFIC ROLES OF ANALYTICS IN MANAGEMENT DECISION-MAKING

As we saw in Chapter 4, in dual process theory, rational and non-rational cognitive processes play distinct but often complementary roles in the decision-making process. Data analytics, as a conscious effort, is solely found in System 2, whereas human judgment is associated with System 1 as well as System 2. The academic literature focuses on the importance and extent of intuition, judgment and data in decision-making, but not to the level of differentiating between distinct roles in any given decision situation. In this chapter we identify specific roles and their place in the decision-making process. These roles are based on original research (Gressel, 2020) and assessed in the context of the dual process theory.

Traditional decision-making relies heavily on judgment, whereas data-driven decision-making in recent years has put more emphasis on the role of data analysis. However, data is not necessarily seen as a substitute for judgment, but as a complement. While data can enrich management decision-making, it also has its limitations. Managers need to find a balance to incorporate both judgment and analytics in their decisions, as they have different influences on the decision-making process and function differently in the various stages of the process. In this book we categorize data and human judgment into roles. These roles reflect data analytics' and human judgment's influence and their specific use in the decision-making process. Based on our research, we have categorized five distinct roles of human judgment (See Highlight Box 5.2) and seven distinct roles of data analytics (Table 5.2) (Gressel, 2020).

Highlight Box 5.2

Human Judgment in Decision-Making

While data-driven decision-making focuses on the role of data and analytics, traditional decision-making relies heavily on judgment. In our research (Gressel, 2020) we found human judgment is used primarily in five roles: 1) in the initial assessment of the problem, 2) to enrich the use of

(Continued)

analytics, 3) as a sense-check and data challenging tool, 4) to identify the need for analytics, and 5) to overrule analytics. These roles are discussed below, and summarized in Table 5.1 and their relationship to the analytics roles are illustrated in Figure 5.3.

Table 5.1 Human judgment roles

Human Judgment Role	Description	Illustrative Quote
Initial Assessment	Human judgment is used by managers to create an initial impression of the situation	'I think at the beginning I use my intuition to say, "You know, it's probably here."'
		'Given my history and experience, that was a logical place to start.'
Enrichment of Analytics	Human judgment adds valuable insights and additional aspects to the data analytics results	'Managers are looking at what comes back from the data and then overlaying that with intuitive knowledge or saying, "Why would that be?"'
Sense-Check and Data Challenging	The analysis results are challenged and run through a sense-check	'Data is great, but you have got to have a little bit of intuition behind it and reconfirm and check the data's integrity, quality and make sure the way it's been presented is impartial.'
Identifier of Need for Analytics	Decision-makers recognize the need for additional, more sophisticated decision-making support	'So first of all, I start thinking about how would I tackle this problem or question. And then based on that I am thinking, what kind of information would I need to tackle this problem?'
Overruling of Analytics	Factors such as relationships, intuition and cultural aspects can outweigh fact-based analytics results	'Data might say one thing, but there might be other influences that are actually more important. You might not see that in the data, so intuitively you have to weigh that up and say, "Hang on, there are these other key influences here that need to be accounted for."'

Initial Assessment

Managers will often use human judgment to form an initial assessment of the decision situation they are facing. In these cases, managers rely on their previous experience, knowledge, intuition and business understanding. These initial assessments can assist managers in determining a starting point in the decision-making process. However, initial assessments should not be the only influence in the decision-making process as they may introduce biases into decisions and lead to misplaced assumptions that can carry through the decision-making process. Managers are often aware of these biases and recognize the limitations of initial assessments and so they may combine this role with analytics in the roles of confirmation or challenger (Table 5.2).

Enrichment of Analytics

Human judgment can also function to enrich the use of data analytics. As analytics has limitations, the managers' experience and business understanding can often add nuance and context not captured by data. The development of scorecards, which facilitate lending decisions, is one example that heavily relies on data analytics, but also requires the input of human judgment. Human judgment is used to enrich the outcome of data analytics with managerial insights. Decisions that involve a degree of creativity and include artistic elements incorporate a significant amount of human judgment. While data and information can provide objective insights into a situation, human judgment enables managers to make more holistic assessments. In particular, wisdom is valued for its inclination to combine experience from several (human) sources, i.e. collective wisdom.

Sense-Check and Challenging

While data analytics is seen as a more objective resource for decision-making than human judgment, it also has limitations, and should be questioned. Blindly trusting data can be one of the pitfalls of data-driven decision-making. The sense-check and data challenging role is used when confronted with 'something that doesn't make sense'. To be able to challenge and question data used in decision-making, managers need to understand the data's origin and how it is used. Familiarity with data and recurring metrics enables managers to be more sensitized to spotting errors and inconsistencies in the data. Data challenging not only involves the detection of incorrect data analytics, but can also point out human error in the interpretation of the data and its analysis or the omission of relevant data. To sense-check data analytics results, a manager may follow a set process: for example, by beginning with challenging the calculations, and particularly, outlying data points and then more widely considering a broader range of factors that might negatively affect the data analysis, such as the data sources or the selected analytic process. Data challenging requires leadership support and needs to be rooted in the organizational culture (Chapter 7).

Identifier of Need for Analytics

Human judgment is seen as critical not only in challenging data, but also in recognizing the need for (more) data analytics. To ask for supporting data or begin an analytics initiative, an initial assessment of the situation is required. Managers must carefully assess the decision situation and determine its requirements. Human judgment can therefore be used as part of the initial assessment role to identify further information needs. A list of questions may help get this process started: 'What information do I need? And how can I get it? Who can I talk to? What do I need to make sure that I have an informed base on which to make a decision?' However, the role of identifier of need for analytics can also extend beyond the initial stage of the decision-making process and recur at a later stage, when data results are not clear, or the results need to be challenged.

(Continued)

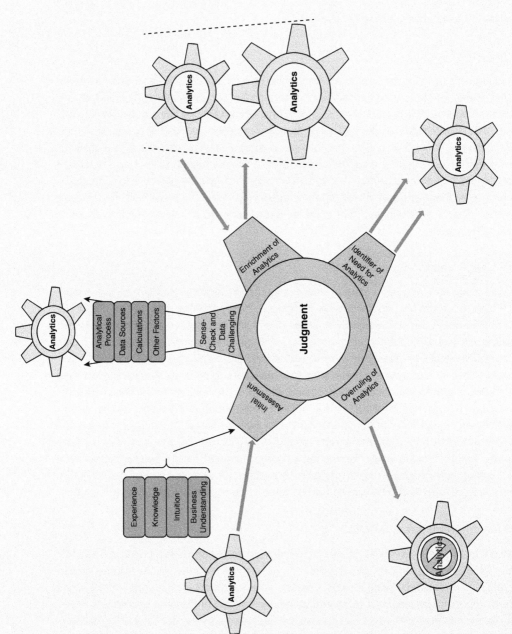

Figure 5.3 Roles of human judgment

Overruling of Analytics

Human judgment can also take on the role of overruling analytics results by factoring in different aspects into a decision that cannot be captured by data. The overruling of analytics results often occurs in the later stages of the decision-making process. In these stages, human judgment is often seen as the last chance to get the decision right. Data analytics may be a factor in getting to that point in the decision process, but it may be overruled by intuition and overwhelming gut feelings. As one manager described it: 'At the end of the day, you [have] just got to make the call.'

The role of overruling analytics becomes critical when analytics cannot consider all relevant factors. Such factors are, for example, learning opportunities or the improvement of relationships that can be an intangible outcome of decisions. Upholding business relationships may not always be cost-effective, but may have benefits that data cannot capture. Relationships play a major role in the field of human resources and people management, as data analytics is limited in capturing relevant factors: 'Intuition plays a big part when it comes to people, because that's the most difficult bit to get right with data and analytics', related one manager. Recruiting decisions fall into this category, as the assessment of organizational fit is often characterized as an 'intuitive feel'. Altruistic motives may also be reasons to overrule data analytics, especially in the not-for-profit sector, where data-based decisions may be overruled by organizational values.

The seven distinct roles for the use of data analytics in the decision-making process are: 1) as an enabler of judgment, 2) for confirmation, 3) as a challenger of judgment, 4) identification, 5) exploration, 6) justification and 7) as a 'no-brainer'. These roles are summarized in Table 5.2 and discussed below.

Table 5.2   Data analytics roles

Data (Analytics) Role	Description	Illustrative Quote
Enabler of Judgment	Data is applied to choices that are too complex to determine without analytics	'Previously we were kind of flying a little bit blind, when we didn't know what sort of results we were getting. So it is quite refreshing now to [have the data to better] understand the situation.'
Confirmation	Data is used to confirm initial assessments	'So you have a theory, check the data. What does it tell you? Does it confirm or deny your theory? Check before you jump.'

(Continued)

Table 5.2 (Continued)

Data (Analytics) Role	Description	Illustrative Quote
Challenger of Judgment	Initial assessments and cognitive biases are challenged with the assistance of data analytics	'I think it gave them a few surprises [...] There is always a bit of push back. But once you could show and compare [...] it was starting to make sense, and the data allowed for it to be a much more facts-based discussion rather than emotive.'
Identification	Analytics (e.g. reporting) identifies a previously unknown problem or opportunity that requires a decision	'When we look at data, things like customer satisfaction over time, and it becomes clear that we were failing in that. So then we needed to find a different model to deal with all those customers.'
Exploration	Data sources are explored for trends explaining a phenomenon, or for potential solutions to problems	'Analytics generally would be the use of statistical modeling or sophisticated tools to try to unearth patterns in the data that might not be evident to intuition.'
Justification	During the selection stage, data analytics results are used as objective validation to justify decisions	'We had lots of [departments] that were disappointed [...] So then we walked them through the process and said: well, here's the numbers [...] So it was the data that saved our decision-making, because we could go back to it: well here is the fact. You're in or you're out.'
No-Brainer	Data analytics results are so certain that they are the sole basis of a decision	'Sometimes intuition takes over data, and sometimes data is so black and white, that it's a no-brainer.'

The figures (Figures 5.4 through 5.10) that follow represent the respective role of analytics and how it interacts with judgment in decision-making. In these figures, both analytics and judgment are drawn in the form of cogwheels. Their interaction with each other and the way they turn demonstrates how they work together in a decision-making process. Judgment is located in the top right corner representing its primary role in complex and high-impact decisions. Analytics is located closer to the bottom and to the left as it represents primarily lower-impact and more automated types of decisions, such as operational decisions.

Enabler of Judgment

Decisions that incorporate a number of variables are often too complex for managers to judge confidently. For example, when a marketing manager of a large retail chain looks at launching a new campaign, various questions may arise: what other campaigns are currently running, how are they performing, what timing might be preferable to get the most out of the new campaign, or are other external factors such as the season or something else relevant? Data and analytics, accounting for a plethora of factors, can assist managers in these cases to make a prudent decision. Managers value the input of data in this role, as it provides them with greater confidence in their decisions (Figure 5.4). As they describe it, without data and analytics, they might be 'flying blind'. Data as an enabler of judgment can therefore assist managers in making decisions that their human judgment cannot evaluate completely.

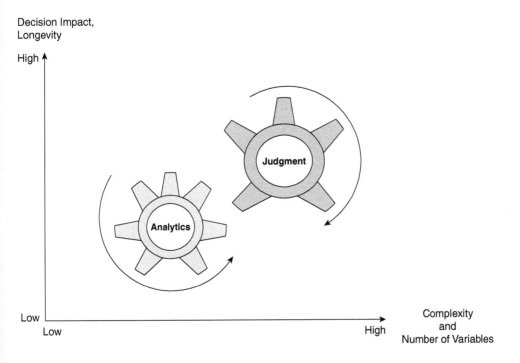

Figure 5.4 Role of analytics: enabler of judgment

One of the key benefits of this role, especially for early-career professionals, is that it offers managers the opportunity to balance a lack of personal experience and business understanding with solid information derived from data relevant to the decision situation. The potential and extent of this role depends on the available data and the analytics capabilities of the organization. If organizational prerequisites are met, the role of enabler of judgment can become quite extensive and prescriptive. In one company we are familiar with, they employ a tool that assesses current workloads, assigns priorities, and enables them to plan more efficiently.

Confirmation

While traditional decision-making is based on making judgment calls informed by intuition and experience, managers can use the additional support of data to confirm their initial assessments and increase confidence in their decisions (Figure 5.5). This can be described as 'trying to support your own thinking and testing your hypothesis'. In addressing the balance of human judgment and data analytics, this role of data does not diminish the value of human judgment, but simply adds to it. As one manager described it: 'I think you probably use intuition just as much, but you've got the data now to better prove or disprove your intuition.' Interestingly, once managers are accustomed to relying on data to confirm their assessments, the unavailability of data in certain situations becomes apparent. In these situations, managers might not have the expected data at hand, which can lead to insecurity about their decisions.

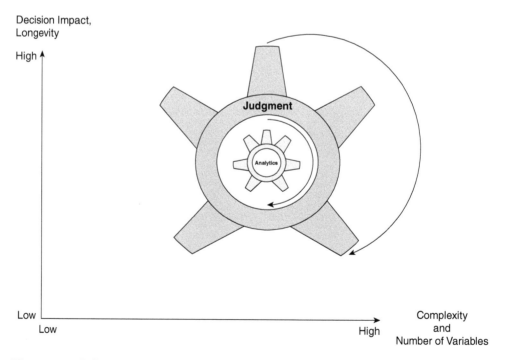

Figure 5.5 Role of analytics: confirmation

While the role of confirmation is particularly relevant in strategic and high-impact decisions to confirm initial assessments or theories, its role is less pronounced in operational decisions. In these day-to-day decisions, confirmation can still be a valuable contributor, but the data analysis is likely to be less time consuming. These decisions are mostly likely to be informed by personal experience and knowledge, with the data functioning as confirmation. When it comes to collecting data for the role of confirmation, the amount collected depends on the manager, and how confident they feel about the decision at hand. As one manager advised: 'Get as much data as you can to ensure that you are satisfied that the decision you've got to make is the right one.'

Identification

In this role, data analytics is used to identify decision situations. These decision situations may be problems or represent opportunities. Data that fulfills this role usually presents in the form of recurring reports. Managers do not always take immediate action when report data points out problems, as sometimes this data can be monitored over a period of time to observe developments, as in the case of monitoring customer traffic on a company web page. Outlying data in reports or ad hoc analyses can also highlight errors or negative circumstances that require immediate attention. This identification often originates from the analytics or business intelligence department, for example in the form of unexpected 'bubbles' that are detected in recurring reports. These bubbles can be understood as sudden spikes or drops that need to be investigated further. When reports or ad hoc analyses reveal outlying data, this data is usually forwarded to the respective business unit for clarification.

Other sources of identification may originate in business units that are doing their own research, market observations, or engaging in their own internal analytics efforts. Data can also be provided by external sources such as supply chain partners, financial analysts and banks. Such external market data can sometimes trigger internal strategic decision-making. Issues can also be identified during an analysis for a different purpose, and potentially highlight further tactical or even strategic issues. In sum, the role of identification can be very valuable as it provides managers with insights and points out issues that they need to be aware of (Figure 5.6).

While the identification of decision situations is accomplished through data analytics, human judgment is required for later stages in the decision-making process. Conveying data results to other business units or top management is an example of this, as the uncovered insights might be sensitive or highlight shortcomings of other departments and current policies. Human judgment is also required for sense-checking and data challenging (see Highlight Box 5.2), as outlying data could also be the result of an analytics error.

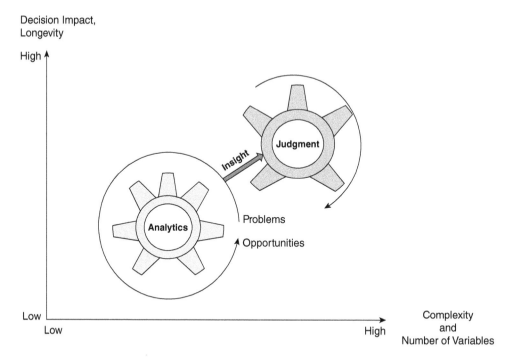

Figure 5.6   Role of analytics: identification

Exploration

Whereas data as identification concerns new problems or opportunities, data as an exploratory tool provides managers facing existing decision situations with the opportunity to assess a wide range of complex factors and their potential influence on the decision situation. Often, the number of variables involved in a decision becomes too large to accurately assess with human judgment alone (Figure 5.7). In many cases, managers might not know all the contributing or confounding factors in a decision situation. These situations benefit from insights provided by data: for example, with the use of statistical modeling or sophisticated tools to try to unearth patterns in the data that might not be evident to managers. In this role, data analytics can be used to explore correlations and dependencies to assess business performance and determine significant influences.

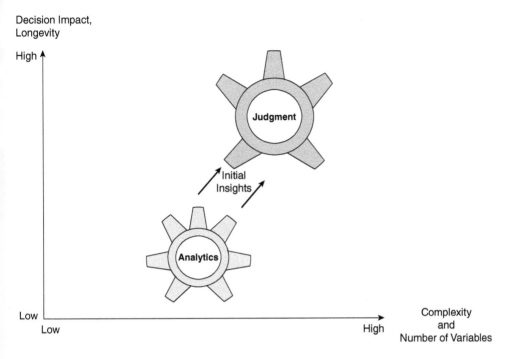

Figure 5.7   Role of analytics: exploration

Business analysts may use data to explore a wide range of relations to identify enablers, disruptors, risks and opportunities. Particularly in the field of marketing, data analytics for exploration can be valuable to assess consumer behavior by evaluating marketing channels, the effectiveness of campaigns, and to look for trends. These decisions can inform future investments and marketing plans. Exploration may also play a significant role in operations where it can be used to determine the cause of operational issues as well as ways to address these issues. Data analytics in this capacity contributes to the daily business and provides managers with an understanding of current events. Analytics can be used to probe deeper, to assess the root cause of an operational problem and plan further steps to mitigate the situation.

Justification

The role of justification is considered critical to managers in data-driven organizations, as well as in companies that require formal decision processes, which involve stakeholders or funders. Whereas decisions solely based on judgment might be accepted in some more traditional organizations, a data-driven environment demands the support of these judgments with data and facts (Figure 5.8) (see Chapter 7 for more on the role of organizational culture in data-driven decision-making).

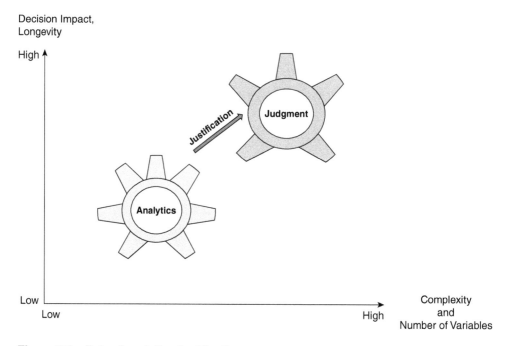

Figure 5.8 Role of analytics: justification

Data allows for a more objective form of reasoning, and – since data analytics results and related efforts can be easily documented – functions as a basis for discussion and justification of the decision. In particular, controversial decisions benefit from the support of data analytics, as they enable decision-makers to provide an objective form of justification that is not solely based on subjective judgments. While this form of justification is the norm for data-driven companies, organizations in earlier stages of their data journey, as well as not-for-profits with an often more traditional organizational culture, can also benefit from using data analytics for justification. Not-for-profit organizations particularly require data to obtain and manage funding. Data analytics in the role of justification is often included in business cases, when presenting decisions and key information to stakeholders or higher authorities for approval. Managers use data for this role to realize projects that do not have widespread support from the outset. While senior management might support the general notion of a new project or decision, the backing of analytics is often needed to advance to the next stage.

Challenger of Judgment

In contrast to the data as enabler of judgment role, this data analytics role is a challenger of human judgment. Due to its perceived highly rational and objective nature, data is often seen as a neutral source of information that can challenge cognitive biases and initial heuristic-based assessments (Figure 5.9).

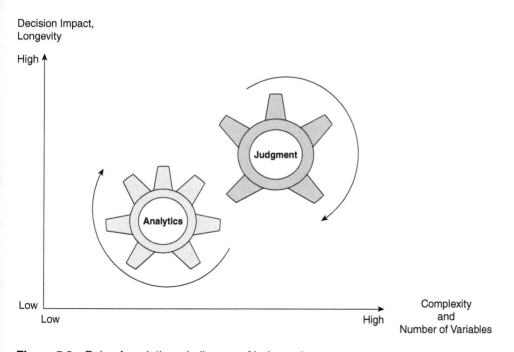

Figure 5.9   Role of analytics: challenger of judgment

This role contrasts with and complements the roles of human judgment in sense-checking and challenging data (Highlight Box 5.2). In our research, managers find that 20–30 per cent of their initial intuitive judgments were not backed up by the data and that having the data helped prevent negative outcomes (Gressel, 2020). The more data that is available and the more trustworthy the data, the more effective this role of data analytics is in preventing mistakes.

Managers may not only use data to challenge their own perceptions regarding their own decisions but may also use it to change or challenge colleagues' initial assessments and biases, especially in decision situations involving organizational change. In one instance, an executive introduced a data-informed profitability analysis that allowed the company to re-evaluate their customer base and therefore increase their profits (Gressel, 2020). The results of this analysis had contradicted other executives' prior assumptions on the customers' value and was a valuable piece of evidence supporting the first executive's case. The challenging of human judgment is often necessary, especially when the judgment is based on outdated experience or old knowledge that is applied to new or emerging circumstances. As a result, managers particularly value the role of data analytics as a challenger in strategic and high-impact decisions. As one general manager explained: 'I believe that you should look at the data any time you're looking at changing policy or moving a customer demographic from your sweet spot.'

No-Brainer

Data is seen as self-evident and the sole basis of a decision in its role as 'no-brainer'. In such cases data takes precedence over human judgment and is the main or

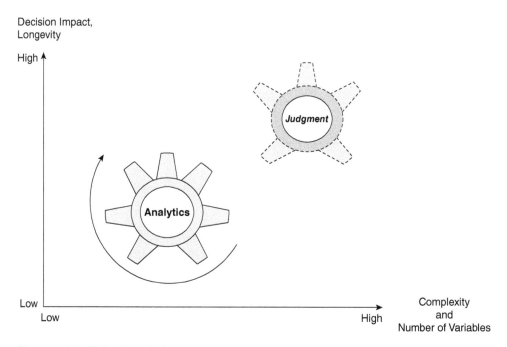

Figure 5.10   Role of analytics: no-brainer

sole factor considered in selecting the best alternative in the decision-making process (Figure 5.10). These decision situations often involve simple operational decisions that have limited consequences and follow a structured, predefined approach. Often, they can be automated and run by data-driven processes. Particularly in the non-profit industry or for companies that have strict requirements for decision justification, data is often used as the sole criterion for decision-making, and therefore takes on the role of no-brainer.

Roles in Action

In relating the human judgment and analytics roles to dual process theory, we can see that the human judgment roles can primarily be understood as System 1 processes and the data analytics roles as a part of System 2 processes. A careful reading of the human judgment and data analytics roles (Highlight Box 5.2 and in this section above) demonstrates, as dual process theory explains, that the roles of human judgment and data analytics are in practice deeply linked when it comes to managers dealing with real decision situations. For example, while a negative gut feeling may lead managers to further investigate or ignore certain data sources, a data set presented by a colleague might induce a manager to modify or abandon their initial assessment of a decision situation. Consider This Box 5.3 highlights some of the ways that these roles interact.

Consider This Box 5.3

How Human Judgment and Analytics Roles Work Together

As dual process theory posits, the roles of human judgment and data analytics can work together. Data analytics and human judgment roles can interact in a variety of ways, balancing the inherent limitations of each role and strengthening the decision-making process. Exactly how they work together depends on the given decision situation. Here are some examples:

1. The roles of initial assessment as well as sense-check and data challenging match System 1's role in providing the analytical parts of the System 2 decision-making process with shortcuts and rapid feedback. In the age of big data, this is useful for managers to narrow the focus of the decision, minimize required data analytics efforts and evaluate analytics results.

(Continued)

2. However, as discussed in Chapter 4, System 1 shortcuts or heuristics can lead to cognitive biases. Relying on outdated knowledge or insufficient experiences can result in misinformed judgments. Preventing negative outcomes from these biases is part of System 2's monitoring task. Biases, however, cannot be avoided completely. Rational analysis is also biased, as quantitative approaches are based on assumptions and perceptions as well. Intuition and judgment are therefore also inherent in System 2. Three of the identified human judgment roles can be attributed to System 2: identifier of need for analytics, enrichment of analytics and overruling of analytics. These roles are conscious processes that demand the manager's attention and full analytical capabilities.

3. Data analytics also takes on a number of roles in System 2 processes. As analytics always requires conscious thought and action, all data analytics roles are attributed to System 2. When making decisions, data can identify situations that require decisions and enable a manager's judgment when the alternatives are too complicated to judge using only previous experience and intuition. Data can also fulfill the roles of exploring decision factors and can function as a no-brainer in clear situations that do not demand any further human judgment.

Questions to think about

1. Can you think of other decision situations where the roles of human judgment and data analytics can work together to improve decision-making processes and outcomes?
2. Assume that you are a manager, making a strategic decision. What would you do if the analytics contradict your judgment (i.e. intuition, gut feeling)? How would you make a decision in such a situation? Can you think of examples of such cases?
3. How do you think judgment and analytics work in a group decision-making environment?

Perhaps the most important takeaway from this section is that knowledge of and competence with both human judgment and data analytics roles should be considered required management skills in order to use data and analytics successfully in decision-making. Equally important is that managers need to be aware of their personal strengths and weaknesses with these roles and be conscious of how they are applying them in any given decision situation (see Chapter 6). As Wirth and Wirth (2017: 36) state, 'A proper understanding of the challenges to be addressed, plus critical thinking when it comes to turning data into insights, are probably more crucial success factors than the using of the latest Big Data analytics tools.'

However, self-awareness and recognition of the different human judgment and analytics roles alone are not sufficient. Managers also need to develop an understanding of these factors in interaction with their environment (further discussed in Chapters 7 and 8). The interactions between roles, decision types, the ways they are applied by managers and their effects on the decision-making processes depend heavily on the decision types as well as on the decision context. This is discussed in detail in the next section.

CONTEXTUAL INFLUENCES ON DATA-DRIVEN DECISIONS

In this section we explore the contexts under which data-driven decisions are most likely to take place and in what ways data analytics is likely to be used. The context of a decision concerns all the factors that pertain to the decision situation, which we defined in Chapter 1 as a decision-demanding situation. Decision situations may be concerned with solving problems or taking advantage of opportunities. As noted in earlier chapters, decision situations may be obvious, or they may be hidden. The four main contextual factors in decision situations are:

1. decision triggers
2. decision types
3. manager KSAs
4. organizational culture and capabilities.

In this section we look at all four and explore how they drive or inhibit the use of analytics in decision-making.

As discussed in this chapter, analytics can play a role in identifying hidden problems or opportunities. Managers, however, remain central in identifying and addressing decision situations. If they are knowledgeable about analytics and can understand the data and ask the right questions, they will be able to spot problems and opportunities missed by other managers with less knowledge and fewer skills. If organizations support a data and analytics culture and are reasonably advanced in their use, then it is more likely that decision triggers leading to opportunities will present themselves to these organizations than to those who do not have supportive cultures.

Another contextual factor that plays a role in the use of analytics in decision situations is the decision type that needs to be addressed. As seen in Chapter 4, decision types may range from simple to complex, and from operational to strategic, and data and analytics will play different roles in each case. The last two contextual factors are manager KSAs and organizational culture and capabilities. These are briefly introduced in this chapter and discussed in more detail in Chapters 6 and 7.

DECISION TRIGGERS

Both human judgment and analytics can identify a decision situation, which may be either a problem or an opportunity. These roles also work in tandem to strengthen or challenge initial decisions regarding the situation. Table 5.3 illustrates these actions and interactions. In all situations where decision identification is triggered, analytics play a role. In particular, analytics operates in the role of enabler of human judgment and it is often used to confirm decisions.

Table 5.3   Decision identification – triggers

Trigger	Description	Role of Human Judgment	Role of Data Analytics
Evaluation	An internally triggered, intentional review of current practices, or an evaluation of future opportunities	Judgment is used for an initial assessment of the situation or for the enrichment of analytics results	Data analytics allows exploration, confirms anomalies or opportunities, and can enable judgment
Routine Check	An ad hoc problem identified during a routine check or review	Judgment is used for an initial assessment of the situation, or overruling analytics	Data analytics identifies issues and challenges or enables judgment
External Trigger	An external impulse, i.e. opportunity or problem, prompting a decision	Judgment is used for an initial assessment of the situation, or overruling analytics	Data analytics confirms decision or enables judgment
Anecdotal	Concerns, often longstanding, based on employees' perceptions that require a decision	Judgment is primarily used for an initial assessment of the situation	Data analytics can enable, confirm or challenge judgment

The roles of human judgment and data analytics cannot be classified as negative or positive influences per se. In practice a certain role can be either a contributor or a disrupter of successful decision-making. While a certain influence may be considered negative by one manager, another might consider it a positive influence. For example, most managers consider human judgment to be a positive factor when making an initial assessment, but if the assessment is biased and leads to complications during the decision-making process, it is considered a clearly negative factor.

DECISION TYPES, DECISION PROCESSES AND THE ROLES OF HUMAN JUDGMENT AND ANALYTICS

In Chapter 4 we introduced decision types and classified them in one of two ways: 1) simple, complicated and complex (plus chaotic and disordered), and 2) operational, tactical and strategic. For this section, we will combine the classifications into:

- simple/operational
- complicated/tactical
- and strategic/complex.

to simplify our analysis and cross-reference them with decision styles as we relate them to the roles of human judgment and analytics (Figure 5.11).

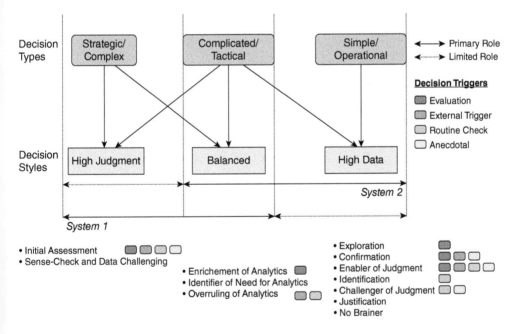

Figure 5.11   Mapping decision types, decision styles and decision triggers

Decision styles (introduced in Chapter 4), based on System 1 and 2 processes, are classified as either:

- balanced decisions (balanced mix of rational and non-rational cognitive processes)
- high-judgment (primarily based on human judgment) or
- high-data decisions (primarily based on data analytics).

These three decision styles can be associated with specific decision types: e.g. strategic decisions tend to be balanced decisions (as shown in the Figure 5.11). In our models, we use Mintzberg et al.'s (1976) three-stage decision-making process of identification, development and selection to frame the decision styles. The preferred or personal styles of the decision-maker may also have an impact on the selection of the decision style (see Chapter 6).

Balanced Decisions

Most decisions that a manager must deal with in today's business environment are likely to be balanced decisions. These decisions display high levels of data analytics and human judgment use. Most strategic decisions can be categorized as balanced, requiring an interplay of non-rational (e.g. intuition) and rational decision-making elements (Calabretta et al., 2017). With these decisions managers try to gather input from several data sources, which can often be difficult to access or acquire. This data is then balanced with the experience and judgment of (senior) management.

Case Study 5.1

Balanced Decision-Making

What does a balanced decision look like and how does it come about? This example comes from our research (Gressel, 2020) and demonstrates how judgment and analytics can work together throughout a strategic decision-making process.

A company in the transport industry wanted to explore a new business segment. They hired a former Head of Operations who had experience in this business segment. The CEO wanted this new Business Development Manager to determine whether there was a strategic opportunity for the company to break into this new market. He went to work and basically relied on his experience and judgment during the identification stage and the initial stages of development including his preliminary assessment of opportunities and risks. The second part of the development phase led to a pilot project and the start of a formal business case process.

Internal company data was gathered during this pilot and was used to develop the case. What was also critical during this pilot stage was that the Business Development Manager heavily consulted with his former business, gathering information based on their experience and knowledge. Through this pilot period the team, led by the manager, would go back and forth between the data they collected, the original assumptions about the opportunities and risks of the new venture, and the judgment of the former colleagues. They decided the business case was solid and based on it began a full nationwide launch of the new business segment, eventually becoming a big player in the new business segment.

In this case, the pilot began with both domain-specific knowledge and experience and data from their existing business. In this balanced approach, data was used to support judgments and to mitigate risk. As the pilot developed and after the launch was initiated, the company accessed market data collected by external agencies. The data reinforced what they were learning from their customers and the customers were corroborating what the data was indicating. The result of this balanced decision-making was strategic decision-making success.

Questions to think about

1. Identify and discuss the roles of judgment and analytics as they were used in this case.
2. What other roles of analytics and judgment could have been used to achieve a similar success with such a strategic decision?
3. Discuss whether/how this decision process and outcome could be improved.

Decisions with considerable impact, such as strategic decisions, demand managerial experience, but also call for further validation and a business case to support or justify the decision to senior management and stakeholders. Collecting data and information has been found to be a key success factor for decision-making performance and leads to more effective strategic decisions (Kaufmann et al., 2017). Strategic decisions consume a considerable amount of time and resources due to their complexity and long-term effects.

Complexity is a standout characteristic in the balanced cluster. Complex decisions are seen as unpredictable and rely on probing and experiments (Snowden and Boone, 2007). Complex decisions benefit from an initial assessment that is based on experience and intuition, followed by data-driven piloting and experiments during the development and selection stages. This approach also serves complicated strategic and tactical decisions, as they often have a number of potential solutions and therefore require thorough analysis and expertise (Snowden and Boone, 2007). Data is usually easier to acquire for complicated decisions, as they tend to have more measurable components.

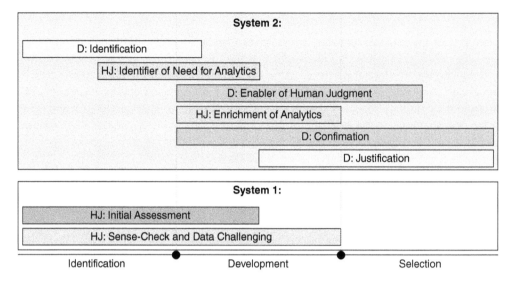

Figure 5.12   Balanced decision-making process

Source: Gressel, 2020

The balanced decision-making process is illustrated in Figure 5.12, which displays the interaction of Systems 1 and 2, as well as the most common data analytics and human judgment roles used by managers. The thoughtful and considered approach behind balanced decisions is seen in the stage of identification. Most decisions are triggered by the conscious effort of evaluation and routine checks, which matches Mintzberg et al.'s (1976) depiction of managerial decision identification. Simon (1960) states that executives spend a considerable amount of time identifying changes in their environment that require a decision action.

Following identification, the development stage can often involve a significant amount of data in the form of reports, ad hoc analytics, experiments and pilots. This high use of data requires analytics-savvy employees to be involved in the decision-making process. These may be managers with the necessary KSAs or specialist business analysts. Current insecurities around the emergence of big data and advanced analytics means managers and organizations may require the services of data analytic specialists to be involved in their decisions. Furthermore, including relatively new data sources and unfamiliar data types may lead to loops in the development stage, as data often has to be sense-checked. A risk of this is analysis paralysis. The increasing availability of data analytics is, however, providing managers with additional options to develop and assess alternatives during the development stage.

The selection stage is mostly based on data. In the majority of strategic decisions in the balanced cluster, managers use data in this stage to confirm their previous assessments or to justify their choices to other stakeholders. As data analytics is an important part of this final decision-making stage, managers may encounter related obstacles such as a lack of trust in the data, misunderstandings of the results, or remaining biases that need to be overcome.

High-Judgment Decisions

Decisions in the high-judgment cluster involve high levels of judgment, and only low to moderate levels of data use. In these decisions, business understanding and domain experience are more relevant than the input of data. Complex, tactical decisions dominate in this cluster, but there can also be a mix of complex and complicated decisions. The main differentiating factor between the high-judgment cluster and the balanced cluster is the decision type. While managers usually make extensive efforts to get access to data for strategic decisions (for example, by running experiments, pilots and so forth), tactical decisions, on the other hand, are considered to have less significant consequences, and the time and cost to gather relevant data is usually not deemed proportionate to the decision impact. Instead, managers rely on human judgment.

Case Study 5.2

High-Judgment Decision-making

Marketing used to be the home of high-judgment decisions. Think Mad Men! These days big data and analytics are integral to marketing. Think social media and the Internet. But high-judgment decisions still figure prominently in marketing, especially for those experienced executives who have built successful careers based on their judgment, experience and knowledge. Here's an illustrative case of a high-judgment marketing decision based mostly on the gut feeling of the leadership team.

The case centers around the decision of a large construction supply company to go with a 'new' marketing channel. In the past, the company had tried the channel, but it was a major flop. They had invested a lot of money and got nothing back for it. Since then the channel had been off the table. However, during the past few years, the idea of using the channel was brought up periodically in executive meetings. Then the decision situation was triggered again when the company's advertising agency produced data that supported the adoption of this channel. Although the company had no internal data to compare with the external data provided by the marketing agency, the executives said: 'OK, let's give this another shot.'

(Continued)

They contacted two different agencies that could support the creation of required materials for the new marketing channel. They came back with offers on what they could produce and costings. Based on this information, but no specific supporting internal data, the executive team made a decision based primarily on gut feeling. They asked themselves, 'Was the market ready for it? Was it creative enough to stand out from the competitors?' And they decided yes it was. The decision went to the board and was approved.

Their brand awareness was very weak at that time but they started to see business picking up. The development of the new marketing channel represented a large investment for the company. The result was a lift in customer spending. Although the advertising agency produced monthly reports on the performance of the various channels, including the new and old channels, it couldn't differentiate the data enough to prevent data overlap, so it was not possible to draw definitive conclusions about the effectiveness of the new channel. For the future, the company is considering using better tracking mechanisms, such as QR codes, specific hotlines, etc. to specifically track their customers' response to the diverse channels.

Because it was difficult for the company to track this new channel, it was not possible to say whether it was this channel that was producing the renewed interest in the company or if it was a general unrelated uptick in business. While the company did not have definitive data proving the new channel's effectiveness, they nevertheless believed they could 'feel' the difference. The marketing manager assessed the outcome as positive, stating, 'I think it was a good decision in the end.'

Questions to think about

1. In this case, external data led to the reconsideration of an old decision situation, and judgment substituted for a lack of internal data. What kinds of internal data could have supported this decision?
2. Identify the decision type explained in the case. Explain your answer.
3. Discuss how this decision-making process could have been improved.

The importance of business understanding and experience is also underlined by the high number of complex decisions found in this cluster. The novelty and open-endedness of complex decisions often leads to unclear decision requirements, solutions and difficulties in evaluating outcomes (Mintzberg et al., 1976). These decision situations are sometimes referred to by managers as being 'all over the place'. As neither their process nor their outcomes can be predicted or clarified by data, judgment is often the only way to proceed.

Such intuitive approaches are also suitable for decisions that are characterized by incomplete information and knowledge, which is often the case in dynamic business environments (Khatri and Ng, 2000). The factors and variables of these decisions are not always quantifiable, and a manager's experience is more valuable as a decision-making input.

The Theory of Unconscious Thought supports this process, explaining that more complex decisions benefit from the use of unconscious thought and lead to higher quality outcomes than conscious decisions (Dijksterhuis and Nordgren, 2006). However, while this theory explains successful judgment-driven complex decisions in this cluster, the flip side is that negative outcomes are also more likely in complex decision situations if the judgment-driven decisions are being made by managers who lack previous experience and relevant understanding of the decision background.

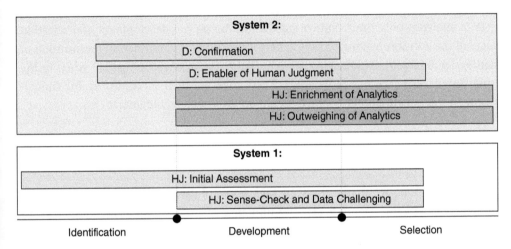

Figure 5.13   High-judgment decision-making process

Compared to the balanced decision cluster, System 1 is more prominent in high-judgment decisions and spans across all three decision-making stages (see Figure 5.13). Human judgment roles also tend to outweigh and overrule the analytics roles applied by managers during the process. An early indication of this judgment-driven approach can be found during the identification stage: most decisions are likely to be triggered externally. External triggers often lead to the problem of a lack of internal reference points, which impedes the manager's capabilities to assess the external data for organizational fit. This corresponds to the veracity criterion referred to in the definition of big data, which posits that big data needs to be checked for credibility but also for target audience suitability (Jagadish et al., 2014). Due to a manager's inexperience with data or a lack of suitable data, decisions often have to be made based on incomplete information, which leads to the high emphasis on human judgment in this cluster.

The high reliance on human judgment is particularly noticed during the development and evaluation of alternatives. In these stages data analytics is usually used to confirm judgments or to take on minor roles in enabling judgment for more complicated scenarios. The majority of these development and selection stages rely on a manager's experience, business understanding and intuition. These judgments, however, can be error-prone, particularly as the use of System 1 processes can lead to cognitive biases (Stanovich and West, 2000; Bazerman and Moore, 2013). Also, more analytical System 2 processes that rely to a large extent on human judgment may lead to incomplete assessments, as the managers' lack of experience can negatively affect the decision outcome. Experience is a critical contributor to decision-making, particularly for human judgments (Dreyfus and Dreyfus, 1980). As managers require experience in the matter under consideration as well as the ability to assess internal and sometimes external data sources, any lack in these KSAs is likely to lead to negative outcomes.

Data analytics only finds limited application during the development and selection stages of the decision-making process, where it functions as confirmation for intuition or managerial judgment. If sufficient data is available, it can enable judgment when facing more complicated factors and contexts. These roles are then succeeded by the human judgment roles of enrichment of analytics or are overruled by judgment.

High-Data Decisions

High-data decisions are characterized by high levels of data analytics, and low levels of human judgment use (Figure 5.14). The influence of human judgment is usually limited throughout all the decision-making process stages in this cluster. Data analytics is considered much more significant by managers and finds application particularly in the development and selection stages. High-data decisions tend to involve more complicated decisions compared to complex or simple decision types. This is because complicated

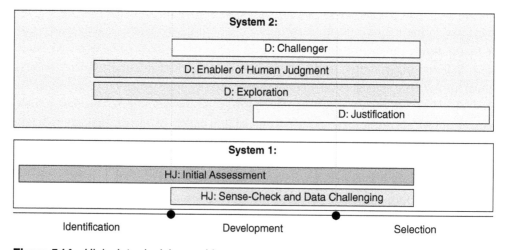

Figure 5.14   High-data decision-making process

decisions require a high level of analysis and expertise to determine the best solution among a large number of possibilities (Snowden and Boone, 2007). The expertise and judgment that managers require for these complicated decisions plays a supporting role to the data. For this cluster, managers must have high levels of analytical KSAs. Most of these kinds of data-driven decisions are, therefore, likely to be found in organizations that have very high levels of analytics maturity, in which managers are mostly able to follow established processes.

In contrast to balanced and high-judgment decisions, high-data decisions' System 2 processes comprise primarily data analytics roles. Human judgment roles are limited to System 1 processes. While this means a significant reduction in the application of human judgment, System 1 processes are still used to some extent during all three stages.

Case Study 5.3

High-Data Decision-Making

The growing interest in big data and analytics should lead to more and better data-driven decisions. Why else expend so much effort and expense collecting and analyzing data? High-quality, high-data decisions are most likely to be found in organizations that have high levels of data maturity. This case demonstrates how data-driven decision-making works when it works well.

The scorecard is at the core of this financial services company's business. Credit is their bread and butter. It is the company's core strategic competence to understand their credit risk appetite at any point in time. They have a statistically based credit scorecard that they use to provide a credit profile for customers. That profile is used to make decisions about how much they will lend to a customer and what price they will charge for the services that they provide. To produce a score for a customer, the company brings together the data from the customer's application and evaluates it against the scorecard, which comprises large amounts of internal and external third-party data. Based on the analysis of this data, the customer is given a score, and then moves into a segmented customer profile, that enables the company to make a decision about the customer. It is the richness of the data set as well as the applied analytics that allows the company to make much better credit decisions than those in the past that were based on human judgment alone.

Because data is so critical to this process, the company periodically, and in an established and highly structured process, reassesses the performance of their scorecard. This regular evaluation of the scorecard begins with the question: 'What kind of data are we using and how effective is it?' To answer this question, they employ data analytics to assess the impact of previously determined and recurring variables used in the scorecard. In this assessment, the company looks at the rate of defaulted loans, for example, as well as other factors that indicate whether their lending guidelines achieve the desired results. Data analytics plays the most significant role in this assessment: human judgment is used in a supporting capacity.

(Continued)

In this case, the importance of data and analytics in the decision-making process is evident. Both in the decision about whether to lend money to a customer and the decisions concerning how to improve the scorecard, data analytics takes the top spot, with human judgment a clear second.

The manager driving the regular reviews of the scorecard reflected on his 25 years of experience and considered himself to be a reasonably capable judge of customer creditworthiness, but admits he cannot come close to achieving the same level of performance as the current system. As a result of this decision-making process the company has achieved an exceptional portfolio performance, which gives them a competitive advantage in their industry. How did they achieve this level of performance? In the early years of the company, the decisions now informed by the scorecard relied on human decision-making. Then, the scorecard was developed with external partners who had expertise in automating the decision-making process. The regular iterative review of the scorecard informed by the company's internal data and comparison data of competitors, moderated by executive judgment, has led to a state-of-the-art system.

Question to think about

1. Discuss the roles of analytics and judgment in the decision in this case.
2. What type of decision is described in the case? What are the advantages of using analytics for such decision types? Discuss whether it would improve the success of the decision outcome to combine judgment with analytics for such decision types.
3. Can you think of any limitations to these kinds of data-driven systems? What are the dangers, if any, of automating decision-making processes and limiting the role of human judgment?
4. The financial crisis of 2007–8 (see Chapter 3 Box 3.4) was precipitated by loans approved by the kind of system described in this case. The variables used to predict creditworthiness were either intentionally or carelessly programmed into the algorithms running the analytics. Human judgment as 'overruler' of analytics was missing. A near-global recession for many years was the result. Could it happen again? Explain your answer.

In the identification stage, in contrast to the high-judgment cluster, high-data cluster decisions rely primarily on the analysis of various internal and external data sources. The triggers identified in this cluster, similar to balanced decisions, match Simon's (1960) description of this stage, characterizing it as time-consuming scanning of the environment.

In high-data decisions, data drives the development and selection stages, since the decisions often involve numerous variables and data sources that make the use of judgment difficult, if not impossible. Human judgment is restricted to initial assessment and consideration of the analysis results' validity during development and selection. Its active impact on the creation of alternatives is limited.

Data has a significant and diverse impact on the decision-making process, particularly the role of exploration, which is used extensively. Data is employed in the role of exploration, as judgment is usually not sufficient to identify all, or the best, alternatives when making a decision. Data in these cases is used to identify all the relevant possibilities and to discover more in-depth insights. This approach is only likely to be used in organizations with very high analytics maturity. Particularly in Dot-Com organizations, analytics is preferred to intuition in decision-making, regardless of the decision type (LaValle et al., 2011). In their study, LaValle et al. (2011) found a clear correlation between performance and analytics-driven management. The analytics maturity of an organization is an important factor in this style of decision-making and is further discussed in Chapter 7.

This section facilitates a deeper understanding of actual managerial decision-making, highlighting the impact and diverse influences of data analytics as well as human judgment on the different decision clusters. These representations are informed by actual decisions, and represent a realistic picture of decision-making in the age of big data. Two important factors in the decision-making context have been alluded to in the above sections – manager KSAs and organizational culture and level of analytics maturity. These are discussed in more detail in the sections below.

MANAGEMENT KNOWLEDGE, SKILLS AND ABILITIES

We have discussed the importance of management KSAs in Chapter 1 and various other places in the book. Indeed the objective of this book is to help students and practitioners develop the KSAs necessary to thrive as professionals in a data-driven organizational environment: both managers and the information technologists working on the data side of the organization. By delving deeply into the decision-making process and investigating the effects of both human judgment and data analytics roles on it, both sides gain a deeper appreciation of the factors that affect decision-making. By studying the three decision styles and the ways that judgment and data are used in the decision stages, students can grasp the nuances of decision-making and consciously work at improving their own decision-making. Understanding the way data and analytics can support you in your decision-making will be immensely helpful once you become a manager. If you are on the data analytics side of things, then understanding the decision-making process and the way human judgment and analytics can work together will help you to understand what the business side of the organization needs and how and when to provide it. Management decision-making types, self-assessment exercises and ways to improve both judgment and analytics KSAs are discussed in depth in Chapter 6.

ORGANIZATIONAL CULTURE AND CAPABILITIES

We have also seen in this chapter and throughout the book some discussion of how organizational culture and data analytics maturity of the organization can have an impact on the use of data in the decision-making process: for example, companies like Google and Amazon, that were founded in the Dot-Com age, have developed sophisticated data-driven cultures. In our research and the literature, we see clear evidence that data-driven decision-making requires a readiness on the part of organizations for big data and analytics-driven decisions (Jagadish et al., 2014; Gupta and George, 2016; Shah et al., 2017). Managers reporting high-data decisions work in a data-ready environment and because of this tend to experience successful decision outcomes. Although strategic decisions usually require high levels of human judgment, an organization's level of maturity will enable managers to benefit from sophisticated and tested data analytics methods, which already incorporate individual and organizational expertise. In such environments, data and analytical approaches prove more reliable and often lead to better outcomes than decisions based on judgment (Khatri and Ng, 2000; Dijksterhuis and Nordgren, 2006). In Chapter 7 we will cover in detail the organizational prerequisites for data-driven decision-making including the role of organizational culture, environmental factors and the maturity of analytics capabilities.

As discussed above, the characteristics of the decision clusters can be attributed to the decision type and other contextual factors around the decision situation. In the next section we take what we have learned above and apply it to summarize a number of 'lessons learned' and how these can help managers and organizations to more effectively use analytics in decision-making.

USING ANALYTICS EFFECTIVELY

Based on our research with managers we have developed several 'lessons learned' on how to use analytics effectively to assure successful data-driven decision-making. In this section, we focus on describing 'ideal' decision-making processes. By accumulating managers' perceptions on requirements to improve decision-making, as well as lessons learned from their previous decisions and overcoming obstacles, we identified four key requirements for managers and organizations (Figure 5.15):

1. finding a balance between judgment and data in decision-making
2. building trust in data analytics
3. transforming reactive into proactive decisions
4. creating processes and guidelines around decision-making.

Finding Balance in Decisions

Finding a balance between data and human judgment is a key concern of managers and often seen as a shortcoming in current decision-making. Data input and judgment are often both necessary for decision success. Even if data shows a certain result, past experiences will always be mixed into the decision-making process as well. Maintaining this balance is important, as both human judgment and analytics have limitations. For example, analytics reaches its limits when the decision parameters are unclear or impossible to model. The roles of human judgment and individual knowledge are also limited and, as we have discussed in Chapter 4, are prone to biases. A manager's knowledge formed by their own experiences might differ from another manager's and from the organization's collective knowledge or procedures. To balance knowledge- and experience-based decisions, analytics can be used to mitigate biases which can promote more uniform organizational decision-making and work outputs. A balanced approach can, however, produce contradictory results. If, for example, an initial judgment-based assessment is not supported by the data, managers may become conflicted about the selection of an alternative. The solution to this 'clash' of intuition and data may be in developing sufficient understanding of analytics, which can build trust in data results.

Building Trust in Data Analytics

Trust in data analytics is a significant factor for successful data-driven decision-making. Reasonable data quality and access to information are essential prerequisites. However, to build organization-wide trust in data demands further steps, as it requires a cultural shift in the organization (see Chapter 7). If this trust is not built, managers face difficulties when using the data analytics results to justify their decisions, particularly when results contradict the intuition or judgment of other stakeholders involved in the decision. Analytics may provide valuable insights, but not all involved decision-makers may be willing to accept the results. When the organizational culture is 'stuck' at this level, it is necessary to implement strategies that can facilitate understanding of the significance of analytics and to create trust in its results. One strategy is to share positive experiences with data-driven decisions. Showing and comparing data results with co-workers and stakeholders helps to make sense of data. These kinds of 'show and tell' can lead to more fact-based discussions rather than emotive ones.

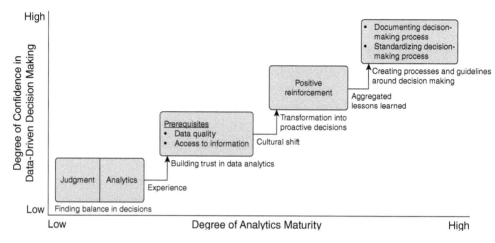

Figure 5.15   Model of mature data-driven decision-making

Transforming Reactive Decisions into Proactive Decisions

Usually, once managers have their first successful experiences with data analytics, the lessons they learned are incorporated into further decision-making. This kind of positive reinforcement can result in managers incorporating analytics into decision-making at the beginning of the decision-making process, rather than using them in another role such as verifying or justifying a decision that has already been made. This data-driven approach leads to a more proactive decision-making process, one that may prevent errors and avoid negative outcomes. Positive data-assisted decisions may lead to the establishment of regular data-driven reporting that can enable organizations to make more proactive decisions and to identify negative developments early on.

Creating Processes and Guidelines Around Decision-making

To convert the lessons learned in early stages of data-driven decision-making into actionable insights for others, managers often need to define decision-making processes or guidelines. Clearly structured decision-making and business cases are particularly valued in data-driven organizational cultures and are mostly used for strategic and complex decisions. There are obvious limitations though: for example, the availability of suitable data and experiences are restricted when dealing with decision situations concerning the future. As one manager described the future, 'You don't have a lot of knowledge about how it's likely to work.' In general, managers see structured decision-making guidelines as a benefit and, based on past positive outcome decisions, often want the policies to be documented. Documenting and standardizing decision-making processes, however, needs to be done with consideration as the processes may not be applicable across different business areas.

CHAPTER SUMMARY

In this chapter, to gain a deeper understanding of the management decision-making process in the age of big data, we have provided an extensive analysis of the roles of human judgment and data and analytics in the decision-making process and aligned them with dual process theory. We have also accounted for the effects of key contextual factors in the decision-making process. In this chapter we focused primarily on the effects of decision triggers and decision types, while briefly introducing how manager KSAs and organizational culture and capabilities can have an impact on decision-making. These will be covered in greater depth in the following two chapters. Finally, we presented a model of mature data-driven decision-making that identifies and explains the four key requirements necessary for managers and organizations to systematically improve the use of data and analytics in decision-making.

KEY LESSONS

In this chapter we have introduced the roles analytics and judgment play in decision-making. The most important takeaways can be summarized as:

1. Effective management decision-making involves both human judgment and data/analytics.
2. Different decision situations require different combinations and applications of judgment and data.
3. Appropriate management KSAs and organizational support are essential in achieving effective balanced, high-judgment and data-driven decisions.

6
TYPES OF MANAGERIAL DECISION-MAKERS

Contents

Highlight Box 6.1

Getting to Know Different Types of Managers

Managers are individuals. They bring different experiences, knowledge, skills, abilities and personalities to their jobs. As such we can expect them to have different decision-making preferences and approaches. Here we introduce four different managers to you. They are all facing decisions on a regular basis and they are all choosing different approaches to finding the best solutions. The following sums up their approaches:

Manager A takes a mostly data-driven approach: 'I definitely take that information-gathering step, find out as much information as I can. Before doing this, I first think, "What am I trying to find out? What data could help me?"'

Manager B tries to use data and judgment equally. She values data, as according to her, 'it beats the gut', but she also knows that intuition is required to 'reconfirm and check the data's integrity, quality and to make sure the way it's being presented [is] impartially'.

Manager C is not sure if data can be trusted. He does not have a lot of experience with it and believes in his judgment until he's proven wrong: 'I think by now I would have found out if my guesses and intuition are wrong. If that were the case, I might have to question myself more. At the moment, though, I have no reason to. I'm going to believe I'm right.'

Manager D is quite traditional and even though she might have experience with data, she sticks to using her judgment: 'Basically all of my decisions are based on experience. I can pull reports and I use those to an extent, but I essentially use gut feel over the top of them. I sort of overwrite the analytics with common sense.'

Questions to think about

1. Which of the decision-makers do you relate to most? Why?
2. What could cause you to change your decision-making style?

CHAPTER 6 KEY LESSONS

1. Managers have individual styles of decision-making.
2. Data and analytics are increasingly seen as having a critical role in decision-making.
3. Organizations and individual decision-makers need to take into account these decision-making types to optimize decision support policies and systems.

INTRODUCTION

In Chapter 5, we extensively covered the roles analytics and judgment play in decision-making as well as related factors including decision types, decision styles and other contextual elements involving the decision situation. We touched upon the knowledge, skills and abilities needed by managers to find the balance necessary to make the best use of analytics and judgments. But where does a manager begin in assessing their relative position and their use of human judgment and data analytics as a decision-maker?

In this chapter, we offer some help in answering this question by introducing a taxonomy of management decision-makers based on original research (Gressel, 2020). Four different types of managers are explored and illustrated with vignettes to demonstrate their various data and analytics needs, as well as their decision-making behaviors. These types describe a manager's experience, aptitude for and interest in analytics, their preferences for analytics or judgment, and other factors. Students and individual managers can use this taxonomy to better understand their own capabilities and preferences, while organizations can benefit as the taxonomy can help them to accommodate the different needs of managers and offers diverse tools to address potential weaknesses. An assessment tool is also introduced, which can help students to identify their preferred decision style, along with exercises to help them expand their decision-making repertoire.

TYPES OF MANAGERIAL DECISION-MAKERS

In Chapter 5, we saw in some detail how managers perceive and balance the use of analytics and human judgment in the decision-making process. Looking at managerial decision-making more deeply, we can also see that managers can be grouped according to their use of analytics and judgment into four distinct types of managerial decision-makers. These types are based on shared views, certain personality characteristics and comparable decision-making behaviors. Classifying and understanding these distinctive decision-maker types is important for at least two reasons.

First, it is an important prerequisite for organizations to understand how to best support individual managers' needs. In order to build a data-driven workforce, all managers need to be comfortable with the use of data and therefore share an informed understanding of data analytics. The taxonomy of managerial decision-makers enables organizations to cater for their employees' needs with customized approaches that match both employee and organizational characteristics and preferences.

Second, understanding these decision types can also assist students, and managers, in developing skills that will help them to become better decision-makers and make more effective use of data analytics in their decision-making. Students and managers can use the assessment tools introduced in this chapter and find out what type of managers they are or will probably be. By understanding the different types of decision-makers, they can then identify further characteristics and requirements of their decision-maker type. This information can then be used as a basis for building up the KSAs needed to become a more effective decision-maker.

Table 6.1 gives an overview of the four different managerial decision-maker types arranged according to their use of intuition and data analytics in decision-making. Their characteristics and requirements are summarized in the respective quadrants. The four types are summarized as follows:

- Type A consists of managers that have an 'analytics bent' and are therefore quite adept at and experienced in using data and analytics. They often hold business analyst or related positions and tend to have more faith in data than in human judgment, which leads to mainly high-data decisions.

- Type B managers are 'all-rounders', who usually hold senior management roles. They are comfortable with the use of analytics and have accumulated a significant amount of contextual and domain experience, which enables them to make balanced decisions.
- Type C managers can be characterized as 'uninformed or uncertain' about data-driven decision-making. They are mostly lacking analytics training and experience, which leads to skepticism and avoidance. Their decisions tend to be spread across all decision styles, depending on the extent of collaboration with others. If analysts or Type A managers are involved, even high-data decisions are possible for this type.
- Type D managers can be considered as 'old-fashioned' decision-makers. Old-fashioned does not necessarily mean they are old or in senior management positions. They could be any age and in any level of management. It just reflects their decision-making style, which is to mostly trust in their own experience and judgment, and they are most likely to hold positions in companies that are not very data-driven. They have either not been exposed to data or are data-averse.

Table 6.1 Types of managerial decision-makers

Type A 'Analytics-Bent'	Type B 'All-Rounder'
Characteristics:	Characteristics:
• lower or middle management • data-driven • analytics experience • trust in data • critical of judgment	• senior management • business understanding and domain experience • trust in data • good communication skills
Requirements:	Requirements:
• access to high-quality data • co-workers open to analytics • skills to relay data to others	• access to quality data and personnel • data-driven environment • visualization tools
Type C 'Uncertain'	Type D 'Old-Fashioned'
Characteristics:	Characteristics:
• all levels of management • judgment-based decision-making • skeptical towards data • no analytics training • no exposure to analytics successes	• all levels of management • non-data-driven industries • data-averse or lack of exposure • rich domain experience • requirement for high-judgment decisions
Requirements: • leadership encouragement • sharing of analytics successes • analytics training	Requirements: • leadership guidance • analytics training and peer support • communication of culture change

Data-driven

Judgment-driven

Consider This Box 6.2

One Decision – Four Perspectives

Let's assume four different managers – each of them displaying clear characteristics of one manager type – are facing the same decision. The decision at hand? Approving a loan application, which you can see in Figure 6.1. So, how do our different manager types approach this decision? What do they take into consideration?

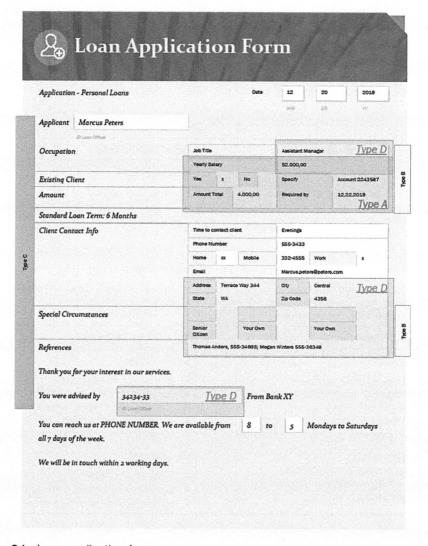

Figure 6.1   Loan application form

Type A is very data-driven, so mainly focuses on the key numbers provided in this application: salary, loan amount and a potential loan history of the applicant. Type B on the other hand is an all-rounder. While B also focuses on these essential numbers, their focus expands further: they consider the occupation of the applicant, as well as the references provided by the applicant, and special circumstances. Type B wants to get the full picture before making a decision and therefore considers all angles, including human aspects. Type C is uncertain, might be inexperienced, and takes in the whole form. It is unclear what Type C might focus on, and whether it is the most relevant information to make this decision. Type D bases the decision on gut feel and experience. Type D therefore looks at the occupation and might follow a bias that certain professions always, or never, pay back their loans. Other biases might figure into the decision as well: where the applicant lives, their name, etc. They also pay a lot of attention to human aspects and therefore will not only check the references provided by the applicant but might also have a conversation with the loan officer that consulted the applicant in the beginning – to get additional insight.

The following sections introduce the different manager types and highlight their shared characteristics, such as experience, skills and preferences, in more detail. We also explore how these characteristics affect their decision-making behavior. Vignettes of real-life examples are included to illustrate the qualities and characteristics of each type.

Type A: Analytics-Bent

Type A managerial decision-makers are those who have the 'analytics bent', a description offered by the managers we interviewed. It describes the mindset of data-driven decision-makers: managers with an analytics bent are characterized by their extensive experience with analytics and their trust in data. They may be of any age and at any level in the organization, but they tend to be younger and in lower or middle management positions, reflecting the recent emergence of the use of big data and analytics in both business and education. Type A managers mostly follow high-data decision-making processes and value data as decision input more than judgment. Using data analytics for decision-making enables them to better understand situations in contrast to those who solely trust their intuition and 'jump to confusions', as one Type A manager wryly put it.

Type A managers see analytics as enriching judgment-based decisions, a source of accumulated experiences from others represented in the form of data, and a chance for objective validation. These managers view intuition and gut feelings as being burdened by assumptions, biases and limited applicability. As discussed in Chapter 1 these managers possess a computational mindset. Because of their reliance on data for decision-making, these managers require access to high-quality data sources and colleagues and senior managers who are open to data analytics results. Therefore, these managers also need the necessary KSAs to be able to easily and effectively communicate data and analytics results to others.

Jan, the analyst of a financial services organization, shared the following decision with us. It involved an anecdotal trigger, suspected fraud, which was followed by data analysis, and eventually a final talk/consultation with the sales department. This led to a recommendation, and an eventual decision by the CEO. The process has since been established as a periodic approach to fraud detection. This is Jan's account.

> The trigger for the event was in our organization, in our collections department, which follows up on customers who haven't paid back their loans. The collections department found that quite a few customers from one of our retailer groups were not re-paying loans. They suspected fraud. The details about applicants in our system didn't match up, particularly the personal references they provided. So we wanted to investigate what was happening.

> So that was the trigger that led to the analysis and eventually to the decision. From that I looked at the retail chain to determine: what would constitute good behavior from that retailer; what constitutes bad behavior; what percentage of their customers were good versus bad, and how much business do they do in general with us? I gathered that data and then as a comparison point, I looked at a few of our other chains and did the same analyses on them, and compared the results. I found important differences; for example, that customer scores, based on information we collected, were substantially higher in the stores where the customer loans were going bad and the number of customers that were not paying up. The customer scores assess the risk of the customers. Higher scores should mean a lower risk of default, but here the opposite was happening – higher scores were correlated with higher risks. Then I looked deeper and did some spot checking on individual applications from customers that were rated highly and repaid loans on time and those that were rated highly but defaulted on their loans. We immediately saw problems.

This financial services company has two main systems collecting customer data. One collects data from loan applications and the other, the Accounts system, collects loan repayment data from customers. The data in the applications system cannot be changed, and it is this data that determines if the customer gets a loan. Once a loan is approved an account is set up. The data in the account system can be updated by customers. A careful analysis of the data in the two systems showed that in the cases of the defaulting customers, the data in the two systems were different: i.e. same customer, different data. Jan continued with her story.

So those two different systems are the main systems that I gather my information from. The quality in those two systems is very high. I compared both of [them] to see what's the truth in one system versus what's the truth in the other system.

What Jan and her team eventually found, along with the management of the retail chain was that the sales people in the retail chain were gaming the system and using 'cheat sheets' to enter false customer data into the applications system that they knew would meet the parameters of a successful loan application. When the loans came through, the customers, who were unaware of the deception, would change incorrect details in the accounts system. After discovering this, Jan's company instituted new policies and more rigorous checks into the two systems. Jan's discovery of the fraud was heavily based on good data analysis of the company's internal data. Jan summarizes the case:

I was heavily involved in this decision to change processes. My part was really the analytical side of things. The sales manager investigated the different stores and the retail channel. And then both of us made a recommendation as to how to proceed and then ultimately the CEO was the one who made the final decision and said, 'Okay, we're going to cut them.'

While the analytics-bent Type A managers can provide their teams and organizations with valuable insights from data, these managers have certain requisites to make successful high-data decisions, namely access to high-quality data, colleagues who are open to data results, and the KSAs to communicate analytics results to others.

Access to quality data is a key requirement for Type A managers to make successful decisions. If an organization's IT infrastructure does not support Type A's preferred way of making decisions and required data is not available, managers have to rely solely on their judgment, which may lead to negative decision outcomes. Limits to data access can be due to budget and time restraints. Particularly in large organizations, the ownership of different data sources can be spread across several departments or units, which can complicate access to data or analysis and make data acquisition and analysis a much more time-consuming job.

The other two requirements for Type A decision-makers are closely related: managers with the analytics bent require co-workers that are open to data-driven decision-making, and need to have the necessary KSAs to communicate data analytics results to their colleagues. This often means having good knowledge of the decision situation, the ability to clearly explain what the data means, and often the persuasion skills to convince colleagues who are skeptical about using data for decision-making. It's equally important, however, to keep a certain balance when using data not only in the decision-making approach, but also when relaying data analytics results to others. Depending on the audience, e.g. levels of seniority or the organizational culture, the amount and details of presented data may need to be adjusted, so as to not overwhelm others with too much information. Information or data overload can be a real issue for some managers. As Jan explained, 'What these managers want is an opinion or a decision, not necessarily the proof of how you got there.'

Type A managers can be summed up as very data-driven and data-savvy decision-makers, whose experience is centered around analytics and not contextual or domain knowledge. They require a fitting organizational environment for successful decision-making.

Type B: All-Rounder

Type B managerial decision-makers are considered all-rounders, as they not only have an excellent grasp of data analytics but also extensive domain experience. This combination of computational and contextual knowledge allows them to make balanced decisions. Their comprehensive set of KSAs also enables them to make both high-data and high-judgment decisions successfully, although their preferred decision-making process is balanced. Type B decision-makers tend to hold senior management positions, which is the reason for their extensive business understanding and domain experience. Similar to Type A managers, they have a good grasp of analytics and trust in data, albeit not to the same extent. What also characterizes Type B managers is their excellent communication skills, which enable them to communicate decisions based on their subjective judgments as well as objective analytics.

All-rounders mostly see equal value in data and judgment as decision-making inputs. Analytics is considered as enrichment, a chance for objective validation, and they generally trust data. Therefore, they require an organizational culture and environment that is supportive of data-driven decision-making. This extends to the need to access quality data and analytics personnel that can support managers with more sophisticated data needs. As they are aware of the need to communicate analytics results to others, they also value visualization tools, which bring data into a more accessible format and facilitate the communication of analytics results.

Shane, the general manager in charge of operations in a large New Zealand company, often has to make strategic decisions concerning the business's cash management processes. Decisions around this cash business are complex. These decision situations rely on equally high amounts of data and human judgment. He relates:

> Our strategic decisions are particularly challenging, because there are so many dependencies around the organization. We're always challenging ourselves on our cash management processes, asking, 'What can we do to make sure we're the most efficient that we can be?' Not just in terms of our company, but in global terms around cash management, for example. What could we do differently or better? Are there any other examples from other countries that are doing things differently or better? How do their economies compare to ours in terms of cash use, and cash per capita – and that's where we simply start by using Google for our research.

Because the company has little internal data and because there is no relevant data in New Zealand, Shane says it's necessary to look internationally for data and it's like trying to find a needle in a haystack. So Shane and his team start by Googling for answers to questions like branch distribution, access to cash, distribution costs, geography of the countries, etc. to try and build up a coherent analysis. He explains:

> So through this process I start to understand which countries in the world are doing related things. And I've got some contacts I'll just tap into and ask them: are you aware of anyone else who's doing stuff like this, and can you point me in that direction? And maybe they have got a very good relationship with other relevant people and so I learn more this way.

There is risk in this process because Shane cannot know if he is getting the best information or not. But the process does help to test his own views on things. Eventually he needs to make a decision:

> Obviously, I have to justify it as strongly as possible; for all the right reasons financially, let alone logically and also taking people and a lot of other factors into account. And I sort of debate it back and forth. Is the financial case strong? Could we do it better in some way? And then I make my recommendation and go for it.

This recommendation is mostly based on financial reasons and in the end it comes down to: how compelling is the financial outcome at an operational cost level? And then, if it's a low cost, Shane says, 'Let's do it', but if it's a high cost, he asks:

> Hmm, what is the risk are we taking by implementing it? We always ask these questions and we relate the risks we are taking by going down this path at a customer level, at a staff

(Continued)

level, at a company reputational level, all of those components get incorporated into the decision. And then we write a business case.

In this case, although the business is short of formal data and analytics, they do make a systematic effort to collect whatever information and data they can. In the end, they work through a balanced process of using data and human judgment in a rational process of challenging and supporting possible decisions, before making the final decision.

Type B decision-makers also recognize the limitations of data analytics. While they see data as a valuable decision input, they still believe in human judgment or intuition to reconfirm and check the data's integrity and quality and to make sure that it is presented impartially. They challenge data and use their judgment according to decision contexts and data availability. They believe that human judgment helps to ensure that analytics enriches the decision-making process but does not overwhelm it. On the other hand, while they recognize the value of intuition and experience, they also see their limitations, such as the risk of cognitive biases, assumptions and potentially limited applicability.

As Type B all-rounder decision-makers still rely on data analytics, their requirements are similar to managers that have an analytics bent. Type B decision-makers require an environment that supports and is open to data-driven decision-making. Type B managers often make their careers in data-driven environments, which influence their way of decision-making. All-rounders also require access to quality data, but also to the right personnel that have sufficient analytics skills to support the managers with their more complex data needs. Type B managers have a good understanding of data, but mostly still require specialists for the data analysis. They may know what questions to ask concerning data, but they may not know how to get and analyze the needed data.

As Type B managers might not have the same extensive computational skills of Type A decision-makers, they may benefit from tools that facilitate easier access to data analytics results. Part of their role is to relay their decisions and the supporting data analytics results to other stakeholders. Visualization tools are particularly useful in such situations as they have the potential to reach a broad audience with varying analytics skills und understanding. Visualization in the form of 'dashboards', for example, can bring insights, trends and other key data-based information in easy-to-grasp pictorial representations, which makes communication and persuasion much easier.

Type B managers benefit from visualization, as might Type C managers. Type A analytics-bent decision-makers, on the other hand, may prefer to interact with hard data, which has not been previously interpreted or manipulated. This signifies the varying needs among the different decision-maker types, but also highlights how both strengths and insecurities can manifest in different ways in the decision-making process. This is further explored in the next section on uncertain managerial decision-makers.

Consider This Box 6.3

When Different Types of Decision-Makers Have to Work Together

A potentially large issue for organizations in general and individual managers in particular is that different levels of computational competence with data and analytics among different employees can cause difficulties and inhibit individual and organizational performance. As noted, Type A decision-makers require an openness to data-driven decision-making and from their perspective Type C and D colleagues, with their insecurities around data and analytics, can be a hindrance. Types C and D, however, are often successful senior executives with experience and knowledge gained over long careers and they might be put off by analytics-bent Type As spouting numbers. Given the right mix of individual knowledge, skills and abilities, as well as organizational support and encouragement, all types of decision-makers should be able to work together to achieve the best decision outcomes. However, in reality, there are bound to be clashes in style that affect decision-making processes and outcomes as these mini scenarios from our research attest (Gressel, 2020).

To encourage Uncertain Type C managers, Type A managers can relay both their analytics results and also basic explanations of analytics to these managers, which may encourage the use of data analytics. Type C managers, on the other hand, need to become more familiar with the benefits of data and analytics and be able to understand the lingo. As one Type C manager we interviewed somewhat regretfully recalls:

> I've just lost a guy who had a real bent, and passion for analytics. And actually until he came along I didn't appreciate what we could be getting if we get it right. So it was really unfortunate to lose him.

Helping managerial decision-makers to understand the basics of data analytics was seen as a necessary approach to address Type C's insecurities, as it reduces the impression of complexity and inaccessibility. This was emphasized by one executive:

> Use cases showing the ways analytics can help are one way of helping to persuade people that this is a good approach. But once you start putting it in a black box and no one understands what the black box is, no one's going to believe it.

Understanding of data analytics by all decision-makers is a prerequisite for successful organizational data-driven decision-making. A general understanding allows all types of managers to sense-check and challenge analytics results, either as individuals or in a group. This Type B

(Continued)

manager emphasized the importance of understanding analytics so that he can use his intuition effectively in data-driven decision-making:

> If I don't understand the data myself, I'm probably not going to question it. I should be able to understand what's going on in the data. The situation should never be that I just solely rely on the data and nothing else.

As we proposed back in Chapter 1, the answer is developing a set of KSAs that allow the computational experts and the contextual experts to build shared mindsets to effectively share information and work together.

Questions to think about

1. Describe decision situations and environments for one successful and one unsuccessful decision where different types of decision-makers work together. You can reflect on your own experiences if you have some relevant to the case in question.
2. Discuss some approaches that can help overcome obstacles for decision-making by different types of decision-makers.

Type C: Uncertain

Type C decision-makers are used to a judgment-based decision-making environment and are often uncertain around the topic of big data and analytics. Often, they are part of organizations that have a traditional decision-making culture and have only recently embarked on the journey to a more data-driven approach. Type C managers are skeptical towards data, as they have usually not received any formal analytics training and have not had sufficient exposure to analytics successes. They lack an understanding of analytics' potential and are not confident or proactive about gaining the skills necessary to work with data. In terms of decision-making approaches, Type C cannot be assigned to a specific decision style. These decision-makers might avoid using data altogether, or they may experiment with it to some degree. This uncertain use of data and analytics can make their specific decision process unpredictable.

Uncertain decision-makers might generally be open to the use of analytics but lack several prerequisites, effectively preventing them from engaging in data-driven decision-making. They lack trust in data, analytics skills and access to quality data, and they may not be able to deal with the time commitment data analytics requires. As they mostly rely on their own experience and intuition, leadership encouragement and analytics training are required to engage Type C managers in data-driven approaches. Sharing positive results and use cases related to data-driven decision-making can also be a helpful tool in creating more trust in data and demonstrating its value.

This is a complex tactical decision made by Sue, a head of department of Transport Company A, which was triggered externally by an opportunity provided to them by Transport Company B. The decision turned out poorly, and can be blamed on a lack of KSAs with data analytics. Sue explains:

> This decision cost us a lot of money. We took on Company B's work, and we put up estimates of how long we thought it would take to do that work, but we really didn't have experience with this kind of job. So we calculated how long the work would take and how much to charge them. We believed that there would be a profit and possibly a relational benefit to working with this company. Our calculations were off. The work was a lot more significant than we thought it was going to be.

The job involved the task of taking data, storing it and analyzing it, and then advising Company B what to do next. Sue thought that this was pretty much the same management task that they did in their own company and based cost calculations on the cost of hiring another person to do this work. But as Company A found out, the job entailed far more than they bargained for. Company B's data was formatted differently and it had to be loaded into Company A's system, which proved to be very difficult and time consuming. Sue had this to say: 'the one thing I have learned from this is: anything that involves taking data from one place to the other is hugely costly'. And Sue went on explaining:

> So we went around and looked at different companies and the management software they used to manage their assets, to decide when maintenance is due, what work is [needed to] do, etc. So it requires a massive database and software capable of making forecasts about what is going to happen next. So the actual software is $80,000 a year, but to move all your data could cost you millions; because taking the data from one system and putting it into another is much more than copying it over. Moving data is an expensive business. I've learned a lot since, and I guess now I know about moving data and paperwork, and how many errors and problems there can be with it.

In this case, Sue started out as a Type C manager and her lack of KSAs about data resulted in a costly business transaction. Now, however, after this incident, she has educated herself and will probably be able to engage in more balanced decision-making in the future.

While some Type C managers might be willing to adopt data-supported decision-making, many will be unwilling or unable to face up to the challenges of adopting data-supported decision-making. This insecurity can lead to negative decision outcomes, based on bad judgments related to a lack of familiarity with analytics. On an individual level, Type C managers can usually benefit from data and analytics training.

Another contributing factor to this uncertainty is the lack of direction or support from senior managers or the analytics maturity of the organization. If the systems in place are not easy to use and training is not provided, even managers interested in data-driven decision-making face difficulties. This means that the organizational environment can contribute to managers being categorized as Type C, even though they might be very capable of becoming Type B decision-makers. When organizations shift to data-driven decision-making, Type C managers can come to see the potential for data analytics in augmenting otherwise high-judgment decision-making, but they require support and encouragement from leadership and, at minimum, basic analytics training. They also benefit from the sharing of positive data analytics results or cases. As the organizational culture shifts to data-based decision-making, these employees will need to be brought along.

Leadership support can be a significant factor for successful data-driven decision-making. In some organizations leadership support may be provided by introducing the element of gamification and competition. For example, using leader boards and traffic-light color coding to track error-free data entries and related activities may lead to healthy and playful competition among team members and more engagement with data analytics and peer support as this manager explains: 'What we were able to do was to create almost like a competitive environment among the different stages, where it became almost like a game, with monthly ranking of who was performing well.'

Sharing of positive results is another way of encouraging uncertain decision-makers to use the information systems in place. Fostering more widespread understanding of data analytics, and demonstrating its value, for example, by showing and explaining the relationship of analytics to enhanced performance during team and company meetings, can build trust and commitment to data-based approaches. As one manager related, 'There is that opportunity for some quick wins that we should be able to demonstrate.'

While Type C managers often avoid data-driven decision-making because of their uncertainty around the topics of big data and analytics, another management type, Type D, reject data outright in favor of their own experience and judgment. This type of manager is discussed next.

Type D: Old-Fashioned

Type D decision-makers can be characterized as 'old-fashioned'. Managers classified as Type D share certain characteristics. They tend to work for companies in non-data-driven industries that required high-judgment decision-making and therefore rich contextual experience. Old-fashioned managers tend to have negative perceptions of data analytics or a lack of exposure to it. They definitely prefer high-judgment decisions. Old-fashioned decision-makers that lack exposure to data analytics are usually found in organizations that are in the very early stages of their data journey. Type D's currently high-judgment decision-making might evolve with the progression of the organization towards a more data-driven environment. However, there are also Type D managers that consciously avoid using data in their decision-making process. This may be because these managers are in working environments that require judgment-driven decisions demanding creativity and have very little use for data analytics.

Another reason for avoiding high-data decisions is negative experiences with analytics. Managers that fall into this category have experienced the limitations and often difficult to attain requisites of data-driven decision-making. These limitations include personal, organizational and environmental factors including a lack of analytics skills, low quality or no data, and the time and resources consumed by data analysis. Therefore, to move old-fashioned decision-makers from these views requires significant organizational support to engage in high-data or balanced decision-making. This support includes leadership guidance and the communication of the cultural change to a more data-driven environment, but also access to reliable data and data analysts. Type D managers can also benefit from analytics training and peer support.

An example of a decision by a Type D old-fashioned decision-maker was provided by Bob, the CEO of a start-up advertising agency. The decision was made based on Bob's judgment with only minimal data input. In fact, using his rich experience, which he implicitly trusted, Bob over-ruled contrary data. The decision involved hiring a new person for the company. Based on the salary required for this hire and the fact that revenues would not support it, the decision should have been not to go forward with the hire. Bob explains:

> I had to make a decision on the first person we hired. I knew how much revenue was coming into the business and I knew how much the salary was, and based on this analysis I knew that it didn't work. So I ran the numbers in a number of ways and they told me that we couldn't afford to hire that person. Although I didn't think the new hire would bring in more work, I did believe he would be able to effectively share the work we had, which would free me up to scout out more business. So I hired him, and the business grew and we've gone on to hire more.

Although the analytics based on internal sales data and billings and expenditures told Bob that it wasn't possible to hire another employee, he nevertheless believed that the hire would result in the growth of the company. And therefore, he took a gamble and overruled the numbers. But according to Bob, it was an educated gamble based on forecasting, thinking and intuition. As he explained:

> So that person isn't in the numbers. And while the numbers tell me that that's not a good idea, my understanding of the business and my gut feel and my slightly gambling nature goes: 'Let's do it anyway!' And it will be fine. And a lot of that confidence comes from previous positive experiences in similar situations.

Old-fashioned decision-makers tend to be particularly adept at making successful high-judgment decisions, as they rely on their vast contextual experience and domain knowledge. Even though the role of analytics in these decisions is usually minimal, Type D managers still incorporate facts in their decision-making process. This factual information is usually not extensive or diverse data, but it still provides objective validation for the managers' assessments.

Type D managers are often data-averse due to a general resistance to change or more often a specific lack of computational KSAs. To encourage these managers to engage in data-driven decision-making will require leadership guidance, clear communication of the change to a more data-driven decision-making culture, and at least basic analytics training and peer support.

A key prerequisite for old-fashioned managers to adopt a more data-driven decision-making style is leadership guidance. These Type D managers want to continue doing things the way they always have and often display a general resistance to change. They therefore present a challenge to those who want to move with the changing times. As one Type A manager/analyst put it: 'So you have people sitting and murmuring that "this idea sucks and I like doing it the original way, because I've been doing it for 35 years"'. Leadership support in these cases is critical, as the reluctance from superiors who are not behind data-driven decision-making may spread to their employees. In extreme cases different departments in the same company may follow different decision-making processes in accordance with their office managers.

Clear, consistent communication of changes in the organization's decision-making culture is essential for reliable decision-making success. The sharing of positive results is a valuable technique to not only communicate the change itself but also its benefits. This communication and sharing of positive results can be instrumental to changing the organizational culture as part of an organization's data evolution.

Another factor contributing to the resistance of old-fashioned managers can be a lack of computational KSAs. In these cases, peer support can be particularly effective, as these Type D managers may be less hesitant in approaching peers for help than asking superiors. If managers are not familiar with data analytics and lack essential training, their avoidance of it can be due to fear. This form of insecurity is a common trait of Type C and Type D managers. While Type D managers make a more conscious choice to rely on judgment-driven decision-making, both types benefit from basic data analytics training. A lack of basic training might be the root cause of numerous processing errors while analyzing the data, which can in turn lead to faulty insights and misinformed decisions. Additionally, insufficient training and a lack of policies around data use can lead to managers using their own processes (e.g. avoiding analytics), which lack consistency. Training, as well as access to data, can be adjusted to the level of the respective manager and their data needs. Not every manager requires the same level of data access and analytics skills, as their needs depend on their positions and the types of decisions they make.

In this section, we have explored in detail the different types of management decision-makers. Individuals can make use of this information by determining the type of decision-maker they tend to be and then working on developing the KSAs that can help them to become a more well-rounded decision-maker capable of effectively using both judgment and data. Organizations can benefit from determining the types of management decision-makers working in the organization in order to provide the training, as well as the data and support systems to meet and improve their varying skills and preferences. Differing requirements have to be met for the specific types to optimize decision-making outcomes organization-wide.

ASSESSMENT: WHICH MANAGER DECISION-MAKING TYPE ARE YOU?

This short assessment tool provides you with an opportunity to reflect upon your own decision-making style and determine what type of manager you are – or could be.

Please answer all questions in the following four sections according to how you most commonly make decisions as part of your role in your current organization or with an organization you worked for in the past. If you wish you may also consider a personal decision-making situation, for example, selecting which university to attend or academic program to enroll in. Think back, about how you approached these situations and what factors were important to you.

Type A – Analytics-Bent

I have concerns about using only judgment for decision-making

Strongly disagree	Disagree	Neither agree nor disagree	Agree	Strongly agree
☐	☐	☐	☐	☐

I have a better understanding in situations using data analytics for decision-making

Strongly disagree	Disagree	Neither agree nor disagree	Agree	Strongly agree
☐	☐	☐	☐	☐

I value data as a decision input more than judgment

Strongly disagree	Disagree	Neither agree nor disagree	Agree	Strongly agree
☐	☐	☐	☐	☐

(Continued)

I generally use analytics for most situations when making decisions related to business

Strongly disagree	Disagree	Neither agree nor disagree	Agree	Strongly agree
☐	☐	☐	☐	☐

I believe analytics is the best way to add more objectivity to experienced-based decisions

Strongly disagree	Disagree	Neither agree nor disagree	Agree	Strongly agree
☐	☐	☐	☐	☐

I perceive the use of analytics as the best way to minimize issues around assumptions and biases

Strongly disagree	Disagree	Neither agree nor disagree	Agree	Strongly agree
☐	☐	☐	☐	☐

We have the required technical infrastructure and co-workers that are open to data-driven decision-making in my organization

Strongly disagree	Disagree	Neither agree nor disagree	Agree	Strongly agree
☐	☐	☐	☐	☐

I hold a junior or middle management position in my organization

Strongly disagree	Disagree	Neither agree nor disagree	Agree	Strongly agree
☐	☐	☐	☐	☐

I have a very good understanding about analytics and analytical tools

Strongly disagree	Disagree	Neither agree nor disagree	Agree	Strongly agree
☐	☐	☐	☐	☐

I have extensive experience using analytics

Strongly disagree	Disagree	Neither agree nor disagree	Agree	Strongly agree
☐	☐	☐	☐	☐

I have high confidence in system-generated data used for decision-making

Strongly disagree	Disagree	Neither agree nor disagree	Agree	Strongly agree
☐	☐	☐	☐	☐

Type B – All-Rounder

I actively communicate my decisions with other colleagues

Strongly disagree	Disagree	Neither agree nor disagree	Agree	Strongly agree
☐	☐	☐	☐	☐

I can use visualization tools to communicate how data and analytics are used in supporting a decision

Strongly disagree	Disagree	Neither agree nor disagree	Agree	Strongly agree
☐	☐	☐	☐	☐

I value having analytics support that can help me with more sophisticated data needs

Strongly disagree	Disagree	Neither agree nor disagree	Agree	Strongly agree
☐	☐	☐	☐	☐

Typical decisions I make require both data/analytics and experience/knowledge-based judgment

Strongly disagree	Disagree	Neither agree nor disagree	Agree	Strongly agree
☐	☐	☐	☐	☐

I see both the use of analytics and my judgment as equally reliable validation for the decisions I make

Strongly disagree	Disagree	Neither agree nor disagree	Agree	Strongly agree
☐	☐	☐	☐	☐

I use analytics as a way to minimize the risk of cognitive biases and assumptions

Strongly disagree	Disagree	Neither agree nor disagree	Agree	Strongly agree
☐	☐	☐	☐	☐

I believe that human judgment provides a necessary check on the use of analytics in the decision-making process

Strongly disagree	Disagree	Neither agree nor disagree	Agree	Strongly agree
☐	☐	☐	☐	☐

Management and culture in my organization support and are open to data-driven decision-making

Strongly disagree	Disagree	Neither agree nor disagree	Agree	Strongly agree
☐	☐	☐	☐	☐

(Continued)

I hold a senior management position in my organization

Strongly disagree	Disagree	Neither agree nor disagree	Agree	Strongly agree
☐	☐	☐	☐	☐

I have a good understanding about analytics and analytical tools

Strongly disagree	Disagree	Neither agree nor disagree	Agree	Strongly agree
☐	☐	☐	☐	☐

I have extensive knowledge and domain experience in my business area

Strongly disagree	Disagree	Neither agree nor disagree	Agree	Strongly agree
☐	☐	☐	☐	☐

I can determine when data is trustworthy and useful when making decisions

Strongly disagree	Disagree	Neither agree nor disagree	Agree	Strongly agree
☐	☐	☐	☐	☐

Type C – Uncertain

I do not feel confident about working with data when making decisions

Strongly disagree	Disagree	Neither agree nor disagree	Agree	Strongly agree
☐	☐	☐	☐	☐

I do not have the time that data analytics requires me to commit for decision-making

Strongly disagree	Disagree	Neither agree nor disagree	Agree	Strongly agree
☐	☐	☐	☐	☐

Although I do not use data for decision-making, I sometimes experiment with it

Strongly disagree	Disagree	Neither agree nor disagree	Agree	Strongly agree
☐	☐	☐	☐	☐

I tend to rely more on my judgment rather than use of analytics when making decisions

Strongly disagree	Disagree	Neither agree nor disagree	Agree	Strongly agree
☐	☐	☐	☐	☐

I mostly rely on my own experience and intuition when making decisions

Strongly disagree	Disagree	Neither agree nor disagree	Agree	Strongly agree
☐	☐	☐	☐	☐

I can make decisions using analytics depending on the extent of collaboration with others

Strongly disagree	Disagree	Neither agree nor disagree	Agree	Strongly agree
☐	☐	☐	☐	☐

Data-driven decision-making is not common or is very new in my organization

Strongly disagree	Disagree	Neither agree nor disagree	Agree	Strongly agree
☐	☐	☐	☐	☐

I hold a management position in my organization

Strongly disagree	Disagree	Neither agree nor disagree	Agree	Strongly agree
☐	☐	☐	☐	☐

I have limited exposure to analytics or analytical tools

Strongly disagree	Disagree	Neither agree nor disagree	Agree	Strongly agree
☐	☐	☐	☐	☐

I have limited training or experience using analytics

Strongly disagree	Disagree	Neither agree nor disagree	Agree	Strongly agree
☐	☐	☐	☐	☐

I am skeptical about data generated by information systems when making decisions

Strongly disagree	Disagree	Neither agree nor disagree	Agree	Strongly agree
☐	☐	☐	☐	☐

Type D – Old-Fashioned

Although I do not use analytics, I incorporate facts in my decision-making process

Strongly disagree	Disagree	Neither agree nor disagree	Agree	Strongly agree
☐	☐	☐	☐	☐

(Continued)

I make judgment-based decisions and avoid using data in my decision-making

Strongly disagree	Disagree	Neither agree nor disagree	Agree	Strongly agree
☐	☐	☐	☐	☐

I consider myself data-averse when making decisions

Strongly disagree	Disagree	Neither agree nor disagree	Agree	Strongly agree
☐	☐	☐	☐	☐

I prefer relying on my judgment and experience rather than data for decision-making

Strongly disagree	Disagree	Neither agree nor disagree	Agree	Strongly agree
☐	☐	☐	☐	☐

Decision-making in the organization I work in requires use of judgment rather than data or analytics

Strongly disagree	Disagree	Neither agree nor disagree	Agree	Strongly agree
☐	☐	☐	☐	☐

I hold a management position in my organization

Strongly disagree	Disagree	Neither agree nor disagree	Agree	Strongly agree
☐	☐	☐	☐	☐

I have no training or exposure to analytics or analytical tools

Strongly disagree	Disagree	Neither agree nor disagree	Agree	Strongly agree
☐	☐	☐	☐	☐

I have vast contextual experience and domain knowledge in my business area

Strongly disagree	Disagree	Neither agree nor disagree	Agree	Strongly agree
☐	☐	☐	☐	☐

I do not rely on data generated by the system when making decisions

Strongly disagree	Disagree	Neither agree nor disagree	Agree	Strongly agree
☐	☐	☐	☐	☐

Calculation

In order to assess what type of decision-maker you are, first, you need to answer all the questions from the self-assessment tool as best as you can. When you finish answering the questions by ticking one of the options between 'strongly disagree' and 'strongly agree', you will need to assign a score for each question. Give a score for each option between '1' and '5' (Strongly disagree = 1; Disagree = 2; Neither agree nor disagree = 3; Agree = 4; and Strongly agree = 5). Get the average of the scores for all questions under Types A, B, C and D separately. Write your average scores for each type in an Excel file as shown in the table part of Figure 6.2 below. Select the last four columns with different decision-maker types and the two rows (with heading row and the average values row). Select the radar-with markers option from the insert-charts ribbon in Excel. After choosing the radar-with marker option, you should see a chart similar to Figure 6.2.

	Type A – Analytics-Bent	Type B – All-Rounder	Type C – Uncertain	Type D – Old-Fashioned
Average from the assessment tool	4.5	2.2	1.8	2.3

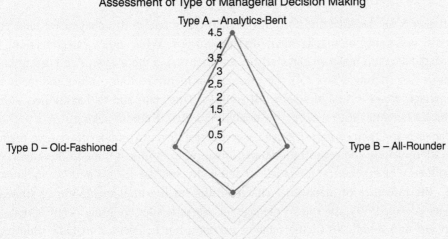

Figure 6.2   Example spider graph of management type

(Continued)

Interpretation

The type for which you score highest indicates your dominant type. For example, in Figure 6.2, the decision-maker is primarily a Type A decision-maker with an analytics bent. Tendencies to other decision-maker types are low. The decision-making type you are may be in part determined by the kind of decision type you are facing. It is worth retaking the assessment with another decision type in mind to see if your manager type remains the same or changes. If it remains the same, it indicates strong tendencies to this type of decision-making. While this figure can be useful to identify your dominant type, specific strengths and potential improvement areas, as described in the text, can be identified. If you plan to transform or are transforming into another type, you can use this tool for monitoring purposes to see your strengths and potential areas of improvement as described in the sections above.

By understanding the kind of decision-maker you are, you can then identify further characteristics and requirements of your decision-maker type. This information can be used as a basis for building up the KSAs needed to become a more effective or well-rounded decision-maker.

CHAPTER SUMMARY

In Chapter 5 we classified decisions into certain types, and in this chapter we have presented a taxonomy of management decision-makers. While other categorizations of managerial decision-making characteristics are discussed in the academic and practitioner literature (see Highlight Box 6.4), our research has identified four distinct and memorable manager types – Analytics-Bent, All-Rounder, Uncertain and Old-Fashioned – that emphasize how they use (or don't use) analytics in their decision-making.

Managers and their characteristics have been researched in a number of contexts related to decision-making and organizational performance. Examples of these studies report on the influence of experience, tolerance for ambiguity and risk (Gupta and Govindarajan, 1984), the influence of managerial characteristics on the implementation of strategic change (Boeker, 1997), the role of managerial characteristics on group decision-making (Shepherd and Rudd, 2014), the reliance on intuition in decision-making (Hensman and Sadler-Smith, 2011), as well as studies that differentiate decision-makers by their characteristics (Shah et al., 2012). Furthermore, there are psychological assessments for practitioners, such as the Myers-Briggs Type Indicator, which help managers to recognize the impact their personality preferences have on their decision-making style (Cristofaro and Cristofaro, 2017; Hirsh and Hirsh, 2010). In this chapter, we have included a simplified self-assessment exercise that can help students gain some understanding of their decision-making type.

Highlight Box 6.4

Manager Decision-Making Styles: What the Literature Says

Studies relevant to decision-making have reported on the influence of managerial characteristics on decision-making in individual and group contexts and cover a wide range of factors. In team contexts, characteristics such as demographic information (tenure, education, diversity, age) as well as diversity in cognitive style and personality have been shown to influence the use of rationality, intuition, financial reporting and several other components of the decision-making process (Shepherd and Rudd, 2014). In a study exploring intuitive decision-making in the banking and finance industry, Hensman and Sadler-Smith (2011) showed that experienced executives' reliance on intuition depended on the task at hand, individual factors (such as the executives' experience and confidence), and also the organizational context.

In an expansive research project evaluating 5,000 employees by Shah et al. (2012), the researchers differentiated between three different groups of decision-makers, the first of which are 'unquestioning empiricists', who trust analysis over judgment and value consensus. This group can be broadly compared to Type A managers, although Type A decision-makers were mostly focused on data results without needing too much input from other parties. The second group, 'visceral decision-makers', distrust analysis and prefer to make decisions unilaterally. Also, this group shows similarities to Type D managers. However, these traditional managers mostly value collaboration and the exchange of opinions with other parties. The closest match can be found with the third group, the 'informed skeptics', and Type B managers. These informed skeptics are characterized as balancing judgment and analysis, with solid analytics skills and willingness to consider differing opinions.

While Shah et al.'s (2012) results offer confirmation for the key decision-maker types presented in this chapter, the typography outlined here delivers more in-depth insights that account for different decision types and contexts as well as the organizational environment. Furthermore, this study identified a fourth category of managerial decision-makers, Type C, to account for uncertain managers that are in a transition phase – a significant group representing a large proportion of managers today.

The insights presented in this chapter offer important clarity to practitioner and academic understanding of how managers apply analytics in decision-making. This knowledge highlights the different types of managers and how they work with analytics and has practical applications for students, managers and organizations. Students can take in this information, assess their relative strengths and weaknesses, and address them in their current studies. Managers who aim to improve their decision-making can benefit from the categorizations by identifying which decision-maker type they belong to and taking action to further develop their KSAs to become more balanced decision-makers.

Organizations that are interested in becoming more data-driven can tailor their change management approach to the respective managers in their current workforce as well as developing criteria for hiring, a subject covered in more detail in the following chapter.

KEY LESSONS

In this chapter we have introduced types of managerial decision-makers. The most important takeaways can be summarized as:

1. Managers have individual styles of decision-making.
2. Data and analytics are increasingly seen as having a critical role in decision making.
3. Organizations and individual decision-makers need to take into account these decision-making types to optimize decision support policies and systems.

7

ORGANIZATIONAL READINESS FOR DATA-DRIVEN DECISION-MAKING

Contents

Highlight Box 7.1

Managers' Knowledge of Their External Environment

In our research on managerial decision-making (Taskin et al., 2020b), we collected data from New Zealand and Australia. With a total of 654 participants, 83.3 per cent held senior management roles including executive management and directorship/board membership roles, 11.5 per cent held middle management roles and the remaining 5.2 per cent held first-level, supervisory or other roles in their organizations in public, private or not-for-profit sectors. The size of the organizations participating in the study varied from small to large enterprises: 16.8% of the organizations had 50 or less employees, 52.2 per cent of organizations had 50 to 500 employees and 30.9 per cent of them had more than 500 employees. One particular set of questions in

(Continued)

this research asked managers' opinions about the level of knowledge managers in their organization possessed about the external environment the organization operates in, organizational goals and capabilities, as well as key factors required for the organization's success.

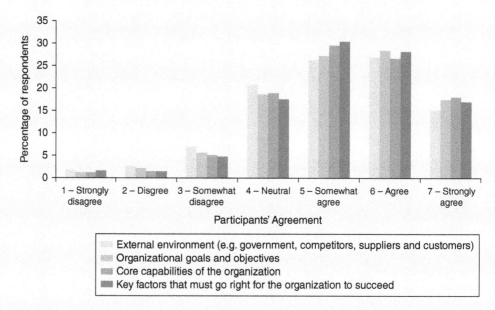

Figure 7.1   Organizational knowledge areas

As Figure 7.1 shows, more than two-thirds of the participants (68.2 per cent) agree that managers in their organization had a high level of knowledge about the external environment that the organizations operate in. This included knowledge about government and other parties including competitors, suppliers and customers. However, 11.2 per cent of the participants disagreed about the organization having a high level of knowledge of the external environment, while 20.6 per cent of the participants did not or could not state whether they agreed or disagreed about the level of knowledge that existed in the organization. Similar trends appeared concerning the knowledge the organization possessed about organizational goals and objectives, core capabilities of the organization, and key factors leading to success of the organization.

Questions to think about

1. Do you think managers generally have the information they need about internal and external factors to make good decisions? Discuss your answer with some examples.
2. Identify a potential decision situation. This can be strategic, tactical or operational. Discuss what kind of information managers need beforehand to make this decision successful.

CHAPTER 7 KEY LESSONS

1. The environment within which organizations operate can have a significant impact on attitudes towards the use of data and analytics.
2. Organizational culture is the key to driving organizational data analytics use and maturity.
3. Analytics maturity is an important concept that measures an organization's readiness and actual use of analytics on a daily basis.

INTRODUCTION

As we have alluded to throughout the previous chapters, data-driven decision-making does not operate in a vacuum. In order for big data and analytics to be used most effectively in decision-making, organizations must be prepared for their use. This is of course the case with Internet-era organizations, but what about more traditional organizations? In this chapter we take a close look at the factors that influence organizational readiness to embrace data-driven decision-making. These factors may be internal or external to the organization. We use an ecological framework to position the factors that influence organizational readiness and to discuss the interrelationship between these factors. We also introduce an analytics maturity model, which charts the different stages organizations usually take in their data journey and maps out the changes in organizational culture necessary to become an analytics-mature organization. This model provides students, managers and organizations with an explicit understanding of how an organization's analytics maturity connects to decision-making processes and affects how individual managers engage in decision-making and their ultimate success.

AN ECOLOGICAL FRAMEWORK OF MANAGEMENT DECISION-MAKING

We begin this chapter by providing a high-level overview of an ecological framework outlining significant factors that influence management decision-making. This framework builds the foundation for the rest of the chapter. The framework models the hierarchical levels of the diverse influences on organizations and managers as well as their relationships to each other and their effects on decision-making. Bronfenbrenner (1977, 1979) originally created the ecological framework suggesting that an individual's development is influenced by their environment, which consists of hierarchical levels. The model has since been used in different contexts, including in research on bullying, immigration assimilation and decision-making (Harrison, 1995).

The hierarchical levels of the framework are the macrosystem, exosystem, mesosystem and microsystem, with the individual at its center (Bronfenbrenner, 1977). Here we use the ecological framework to illustrate the key contextual factors that have been discussed in detail elsewhere in the book (Figure 7.2).

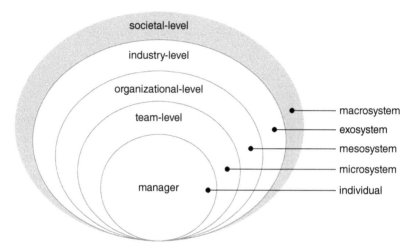

Figure 7.2   Ecological framework of managerial decision-making

Source: Gressel, 2020

The individual at the center of the framework is the manager, the individual decision-maker. The microsystem includes department-level influences, such as colleagues and direct report managers. The mesosystem consists of interactions among microsystem factors, such as different departments within an organization. The exosystem extends these influences and encompasses further environmental aspects. These influences can be understood as industry-level influences, such as best practice in the financial services industries and may also relate to university research and collaboration with industry. The macrosystem, containing factors such as economic, legal, social, technological and political systems, comprises the larger factors at play in society (Harrison, 1995). These are covered in some depth in Chapters 9 and 10.

Figure 7.3 illustrates the kinds of factors that are to some degree likely to influence an individual manager's decision-making. These factors are based on the academic and practitioner literature and our own research. There is considerable overlap in the factors affecting decision-making between levels. This is especially true at the individual, team and organizational levels and again at the industry and societal levels.

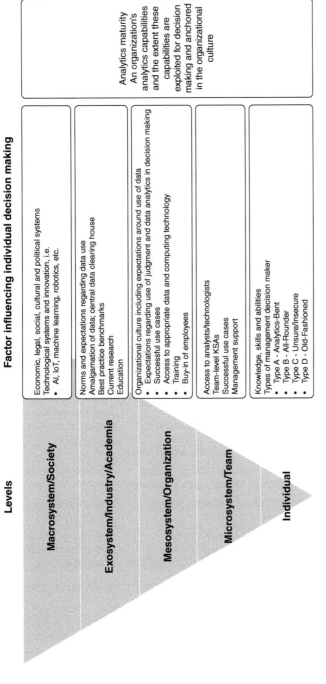

Levels | **Factor influencing individual decision making**

Macrosystem/Society
Economic, legal, social, cultural and political systems
Technological systems and innovation, i.e.
• AI, IoT, machine learning, robotics, etc.

Exosystem/Industry/Academia
Norms and expectations regarding data use
Amalgamation of data; central data clearing house
Best practice benchmarks
Current research
Education

Mesosystem/Organization
Organizational culture including expectations around use of data
• Expectations regarding use of judgment and data analytics in decision making
• Successful use cases
• Access to appropriate data and computing technology
• Training
• Buy-in of employees

Microsystem/Team
Access to analysts/technologists
Team-level KSAs
Successful use cases
Management support

Individual
Knowledge, skills and abilities
Types of management decision maker
• Type A - Analytics-Bent
• Type B - All-Rounder
• Type C - Unsure/Insecure
• Type D - Old-Fashioned

Analytics maturity
An organization's analytics capabilities and the extent these capabilities are exploited for decision making and anchored in the organizational culture

Figure 7.3   Effects of the different levels on management decision-making

Source: based in part on Bandura, 1978; Harrison, 1995; Bumblauskas et al, 2017; Wirth and Wirth, 2017; Gressel, 2020

We covered the individual level in Chapter 6, discussing the four types of management decision-makers and their relative mix of KSAs. In the following four sections the other levels – from micro/team to macro/society – are discussed in detail. Later in this chapter, we introduce a Data Journey to Analytics Maturity Model (DJAMM), which we suggest is related to and affected by all levels in the ecological framework.

Team-Level Influences: Analyst Support

The decision-making environment at the team level represents the manager's most immediate influence on their decision-making process, as it entails direct work relationships with colleagues and co-workers. Team members with KSAs related to analytics and their use in decision-making, easy access to information technologists, successful use cases and management support are all important decision-making influences at the team level (Table 7.1).

Table 7.1   Team-level influences on use of analytics in management decision-making

Team-level Influences	Contribution to DM Process	Effects on Decision-making
Co-workers	Provide support and motivation	Increased use of data-driven DM
Information technologists	Assist in understanding and using data in decision-making	Develop managers' confidence in the use of data and data-driven decisions
	Can challenge managers' assumptions of various factors in decision situation	More balanced decision-making
	Provide information and knowledge of what is happening in the organization	Enable proactive instead of merely reactive decisions
Access to well-maintained data	Provides reliable and fitting data for managers' use cases	Ensures reliable data-driven results
Successful use cases	Provide guidance in use of data analytics	Institutionalize organizational use of data analytics
Established roles and processes	Provide guidelines to managers and analysts regarding their responsibilities and accountabilities	Ensure efficient and effective data-driven decision-making processes

For example, according to Wirth and Wirth (2017), one of the key challenges of organizations is the definition of use cases when it comes to analytics use. They outline the importance of first clarifying the requirements and how the data will be used before wasting time and financial resources on unnecessary data collection and analysis.

Bumblauskas and colleagues (2017: 16) confirm this and identify a manager's 'lack of vision' to ask questions that can be answered with data as a key problem of big data analytics.

However, when it comes to data-based management decision-making what may be more important than the general influence of co-workers is the manager's access, or lack of access, to business or data analysts. At the team level, individual analysts can contribute to data-based decision-making in two important ways. First, in their capacity to 'challenge', which may include challenging a manager's judgments and heuristics as well as the manager's motivation and reasoning behind using data and analytics in the decision-making process. Second, individual analysts also provide managers with a learning opportunity that allows them to improve their own data and analytics skills, giving managers a better understanding for the decision inputs and, as a result, confidence in their decisions.

An analyst as a team member can provide significant inputs and advantages to a manager's decision-making processes. A manager's ability to interpret the outcomes of analytics, and their understanding of the relationships of problem variables significantly improves decision quality. Moreover, according to self-efficacy theory (Bandura, 1978), managers can develop confidence in their data analytics abilities and become comfortable in the realm of data-driven decision-making through their interactions and exposure to analysts.

These aspects are discussed in more depth below and include short illustrative vignettes. It is worth noting here that at the organizational level, centralized business intelligence (BI) units or analytics departments grant all departments in an organization access to well-maintained, high-quality data sources as well as skilled analysts that can support organizational, team and individual decision-making processes. Analysts working in these centralized departments have similar influences as team-level analysts on managers' decision-making and these similarities are mentioned in this section as well.

As explained in Chapter 5, one of the roles of data analytics is as a challenger of judgment, and analysts can contribute to a manager's decision-making simply by challenging them. Analysts may challenge the manager's judgment with its inherent biases and assumptions or they may challenge the manager's motivation and reasoning behind using data and analytics in the decision-making process. In the latter case, this 'challenging' can lead managers to more clearly define the purpose of the data collection as well as the expected results, before the analyst engages in actual data collection and analysis. This contribution on the part of an analyst particularly supports the identification steps of the decision-making process, and enables managers to avoid oversights and redundancies in the development and selection steps.

Skilled and experienced business analysts often take on the 'challenging' role when they are approached by business managers for data input. In response, analysts ask the managers why they require certain information. With this, analysts want to ensure that managers have thoroughly defined the problem and requirements. Managers value the challenge, as this head of department points out:

> The team challenges me. I've got a data analyst now, this fantastic guy who challenges me. I say, 'This is what I want to know', and he'll ask me, 'Why, why, why?'. A challenge at this point, before potentially irrelevant data is collected and processed, prevents the misspent use of human and financial resources.

While the relationships between managers and analysts need to be established in the context of an organization's data analytics level of maturity, companies that are mature in terms of their analytics capabilities can take advantage of this dynamic. For example, in a mature organization, requests for data input may be made through a requirements document, which outlines the purpose of the data collection. In such organizations, the analyst might in turn provide the manager with raw data and summary data and then allow the manager to draw their own conclusions. In organizations where business intelligence or analytics are more centralized the analysts themselves may become a font of information about the organization and the business environment as they respond to requests for data and analysis from all parts of the organization. In this sense, they function as the corporate librarian of old, providing managers with the advantage of 'shared information and shared knowledge of the business'. As one executive explains:

> If these analysts are actively engaged in the business, of course they will see things and hear things themselves. And we engage with them when we are asking for data and putting criteria around it. And when they're presenting data back, they may point out to us other relevant queries and data sets they are aware of. This I think is that next step and where the real power is.

This shows the potential benefits that close access and a working relationship with analysts can have on management decision-making and demonstrates that analytics maturity is in a reciprocal relationship with team- and organizational-level influences on individual decision-making.

Besides challenging managers in their decision-making, analysts can also 'educate managers' in using analytics tools for themselves, which has several obvious benefits.

For one, as managers learn to work with data and analytics, it saves them time in their decision-making, as they are not as reliant on co-workers for their data analysis. It also improves the managers' understanding of the data that is incorporated in their decisions as well as their ability to explain to others what the data means. Finally, this kind of on-the-job training helps to raise the organization's level of analytics maturity. These effects all work to increase understanding that improves decision-making quality.

In one example from our research, a manager describes how he and two analysts regularly collaborate to create business cases and work insights from data into presentations. For in-depth reporting, both the manager and analysts approach the company's central business intelligence unit for detailed data. As a team, they then work on analyzing that data together, with the manager being heavily involved. He explains: 'They kind of give us the raw SQL data query "thingy". And then we would "Pivot table" it or whatever'. While his statement clearly indicates a lack of familiarity with the specific analysis techniques, he is still involved in the process. This enables him to have a basic understanding of which data is used in his decision-making, and ultimately leads to more confidence in the decision itself.

While working closely with team-level analysts can enrich an individual manager's decision-making, management decision-making across the organization can especially benefit from centralized BI and analytics departments. These departments have access to consolidated high-quality data that gives managers access to well-maintained databases and specialized individuals such as data analysts, data scientists and other information technologists with the skills to gather, clean, analyze and extract insights from data. While managers require a basic understanding of analytics to ensure high decision quality, dedicated analysts have superior skills and experience in analyzing data that benefit managers in their decision-making process. The centralized nature of these teams enables all departments of an organization to access required data and human resources instead of having skilled individuals scattered across departments and teams. In contrast, if analysts and data are spread across the organization, it may be a hurdle for data-driven decision-making. While managers may still be able to find the needed information, the search can be effortful and time-consuming.

One manager explained that internal and political issues are often to blame for problems with accessing data sources. As data analytics departments take on an internal supporting role in organizations, they are generally not revenue-generating, which often leads to underfunding and resulting shortages of resources:

> The reality is that data makes no profit for the company – it's the decisions from data that make profit. So, these teams are potentially underfunded, and under-resourced, and you go through this horrible circle of wanting more data, but no one is being able to get it. So, then you try and avoid having to deal with it.

Access to analysts is a critical requirement for organization-wide data-driven decision-making. However, a general acceptance of data-driven decision-making, leadership support and funding, as well as a shortage of skilled talent, are key problems that organizations face when setting up analytics departments or even hiring individual team-level experts. Once managers have been exposed to a data-driven environment and access to analytics departments, they tend to become big supporters of this type of environment and advocate for data-driven decision-making when they move to other departments or companies.

Coming from a very data-driven environment in his previous role, one head of department recognized the benefits of analytics for decision-making and supported co-workers in his new position to employ a more data-driven decision approach themselves. Taking on this advocating role had a transformative effect on his environment. He explained:

> When I moved into my current position, I was fascinated that we did not correlate the data and information we had. I use the term 'pixels' here as an analogy ... I've had the challenge of turning pixels into pictures, because with information people make decisions; with data they get annoyed. This is an industry-wide problem. People tend to separate their systems. But if you put them all together and look at their relationship, you can then understand where your problems are emerging. So we've spent the last four or five years pulling together that data that enables us to draw that picture. So it's about categorizing data, so that you can draw relationships.

Managers and their co-workers not only have an immediate impact on each other, but can also change the decision-making culture on an organizational level. The organizational culture and its role in the managers' decision-making environment is further explored in the following section.

Organizational-Level Influences: Data-Driven or Traditional Culture

The organizational level is the second tier of the hierarchy of environmental influences on managerial decision-making (Table 7.2). Having a consistent decision-making culture across the whole organization is a key component for successful decisions, whether they be data-driven decisions, data-supported decisions or judgment-based decisions. For high-data or balanced decision-making, the most significant influencing factor is the organization's acceptance of and support for the use of analytics. Organizational culture is critical for achieving company-wide acceptance and use of data-driven decision-making at the individual level: it may be even more critical for a manager than overcoming technological challenges or mastering analytics techniques.

Table 7.2 Organizational-level influences on use of analytics in management decision-making

Organizational-level Influences	Contribution	Effects on Decision-Making
Organizational culture	Leadership support	Recognition of data-driven decisions
	Data analytics champions	
	Explicit preferred decision-making styles	Consistent and reliable decision-making process
	Availability of use cases in data-driven decision-making	
Investment in data and analytics	Centralized data analytics centers	
	Data access and analytics support at departmental levels	
	Business intelligence software on managers' desktops	High-quality data and reliable, well-informed, data-driven decisions
	IT governance and risk management (security)	
	Use of social media and Internet in organizational operations	See Chapter 9
HR initiatives	Providing training in data and analytics	Increases involvement of key decision stakeholders
	Targeted recruitment of analytics capable employees and managers	Increases an organization's analytics capability

In most organizations today, organizational culture affecting managers and their decisions can be understood as either traditional or data-driven. While traditional and data-driven cultures can be considered diametric opposites, most organizations are likely to be in an in-between stage – somewhere on a spectrum ranging from traditional to data-driven.

Highlight Box 7.2

Traditional Decision-Making

Traditional decision-making culture is defined by the acceptance and practice of human judgment, intuition and experience for decision-making. Before the age of easy data access, most organizations engaged in traditional decision-making. These days, organizations that cannot afford or do not understand the advantages of data analytics continue to engage in traditional decision-making. These are often small and medium size organizations. However, even in some large organizations, senior leadership might prefer to rely on traditional decision-making based on their experience, knowledge and judgment, with their preferences strongly influencing employee decision-making. In a traditional decision-making culture employees generally reject the use of data in their day-to-day tasks, and tend to rely on their judgment and experience. One head of department describes her company's culture as follows:

> It's quite old-fashioned if you like. That's the culture that we work in: very conservative. They base it on years and years of knowing, 'this thing will lead to this thing'. We're still back, like in the 70s, we behave like that. And we are in an industry like that.

Besides describing the effects of the organizational culture on individual decision-making, this manager also illustrates the perceived effects of the industrial environment on organizational culture. However, she also added that there were other departments in the organization that were further along in changing their culture, particularly accelerated by several younger new hires. This highlights the fragmentation of organizational culture due to team-level and individual factors, and the close relationship between the different environmental factors.

Highlight Box 7.3

NZ Managers Value Intuition as well as Analytics

A 2018 study conducted in New Zealand examined the use of intuition and analytics in decision-making (Taskin et al., 2020a). Data was collected from 116 supervisory-level managers to upper executives from organizations of various sizes: 3.4 per cent of participants were from small organizations (1 to 20 employees), 12.1 per cent were from medium-sized organizations (21 to 50 employees), and the remaining 84.5 per cent were from larger organizations (51 or more employees working in NZ). Across the range of companies the findings were similar. Roughly 50 per cent of all managers tended to value the use of intuition and analytics in decision-making equally (50 per cent in small companies; 50 per cent in medium companies, and 45.9 per cent in large companies). Managers either favoring using intuition in decision-making or analytics in decision-making were also relatively close: favoring intuition (small companies – 25 per cent, medium companies – 28.6 per cent, and large companies – 25 per cent); favoring analytics (small companies – 25 per cent, medium companies – 21.4 per cent, and large companies – 29.6 per cent).

The results reveal that, overall, all three types of organizations – small, medium and large – show similar trends in terms of trusting analytics when making strategic decisions. The number of small and medium-sized organizations was limited in the study, mirroring the smaller number of companies using analytics for strategic decision-making. Results from large organizations show that managers trust analytics over intuition and experience. An established organizational culture, expectations and procedures in such organizations about decision-making, availability of more data and technology for analysis, as well as more resources to hire qualified analysts can be some of the reasons for valuing analytics more.

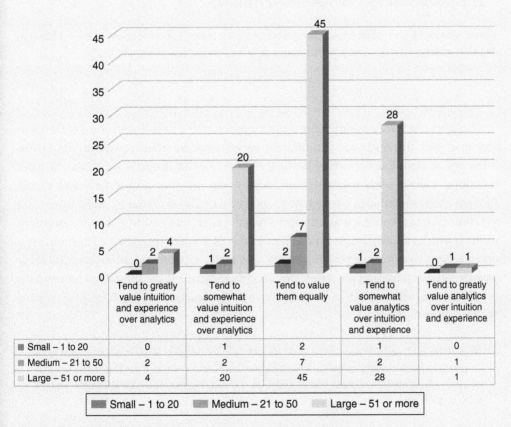

	Tend to greatly value intuition and experience over analytics	Tend to somewhat value intuition and experience over analytics	Tend to value them equally	Tend to somewhat value analytics over intuition and experience	Tend to greatly value analytics over intuition and experience
Small – 1 to 20	0	1	2	1	0
Medium – 21 to 50	2	2	7	2	1
Large – 51 or more	4	20	45	28	1

Small – 1 to 20   Medium – 21 to 50   Large – 51 or more

Figure 7.4 Managers' use of intuition/experience and analytics

Data-driven culture, on the other hand, describes an organization that values data and often requires analytics as a form of objective validation when justifying decisions. Judgment-based decisions alone are usually not accepted without some form of data backing them up. In organizations that are transitioning from a traditional to a data-driven culture, this can lead to changing expectations that can catch managers off guard. For example, while the organizational culture might not necessarily change the way individuals make their decisions, it can affect how these decisions are relayed to superiors.

When asked if the shift in organizational culture influenced his decision-making, a head of department replied: 'Good question. I don't know if it influences my decision-making, but it might change the way I would try and sell a decision.' Another manager had this to say:

> Organizational culture can be a challenge when presenting your decisions. It can lead you to be broader based or it can make you very defensive.

These reflections show that organizational culture is an important component in the managerial decision-making environment and managers definitely recognize its significance.

Managers can have a variety of reasons for promoting a data-driven culture. Data can give managers and organizations different perspectives on strategy and can help them break out of traditional thinking about problems. As one manager explained, 'a more traditional culture leads to average decisions based on what people have historically thought about something'. Given how so much data today is driven by social media and web traffic, data allows for a greater focus on customers and customer-focused decision-making, which can help organizations better meet customer expectations. However, even organizations with mature analytics capabilities and a data-driven culture may still favor balanced decision-making processes. One analyst summarized the prevalent culture of his organization as using both human judgment and data analytics to reach the best possible decision outcome:

> What does your gut tell you about what it's going to be, what is analytics telling you what it's going to be and really question the validity of both, and then go from there. So, our culture is really to involve at least some analytics and also experience – 'best of both worlds' kind of approach.

Changing an organizational culture to a more data-driven approach requires the buy-in of employees and this requires time and commitment. Organizations need to ensure that users understand the value of data-backed decisions. Building belief in the system by demonstrating results to the management team may take one to two years of concerted effort. During this process of slow cultural change, leadership support and governance are critical. While changing the organizational culture facilitates long-term benefits, obstacles may be encountered on the journey. An inherent challenge is selecting the right approach to change management that will facilitate a smooth transition to a more data-driven culture and gain organization-wide acceptance.

Particular challenges arise in organizations that are driven by the intrinsic motivation of their employees, as is often the case in not-for-profit organizations. These organizations often still rely on experience-based decision-making and the best judgment of their employees, as their decisions are often affected by emotions and intangible factors. Changing this culture to a more rational, objective data-based approach can be especially challenging.

Organizations with centralized analytics units can benefit managers by providing them with organization-wide data, state-of-the-art analytics capabilities and sufficient and capable human resources to support their data needs. LaValle and colleagues (2011) state that centralized analytics units include several benefits. As a center of excellence, these units can provide advanced insights, manage the available resources efficiently and provide governance around data analytics use. They add that these centralized units should be an addition to existing local resources and should not detract from the often valuable close relations that local analysts might have with their departments. One of the key obstacles to establishing centralized analytics units and even staffing local units is the lack of qualified information technologists (Alharthi et al., 2017; Chen et al., 2017). As discussed in Chapter 1, organizations face a shortage of skilled individuals with sufficient experience with data analytics and an understanding of its business applications. Overcoming these obstacles is part of the data journey that organizations begin on their way to transforming their traditional culture into data-driven decision-making.

Just as individual managers operate within teams and are influenced by their organizational cultures and environments, so organizations operate within industries and the larger society. In the next section we look at how industries influence organizations in general and management decision-making in particular.

Industry-Level Influences

In the ecological framework (Figure 7.2), the industry level sits at a critical position between organizations and society. The industry level is often in the form of trade organizations, such as the Australian Electrical & Electronics Manufacturers Association, the European Banking Federation, the Hospitality Association of New Zealand, and the National Association of Manufacturers in the United States, who act as buffers, filters and guides between government and society and the organizations they represent. Other significant participants at this level include universities, think tanks, and academic, industry and government-supported research centers. The activities of these participants including education, research into best practices, and the setting of policies and agendas can significantly influence organizations and in the case of education, individual management decision-makers (Table 7.3).

Table 7.3   Industry-level influences on use of analytics in management decision-making

Industry-Level Influences	Contribution	Effects on Decision-Making
Industry and Trade Bodies	Set data and other technological standards	Provide an ethical framework and guidelines for data-driven decision-making
	Availability of industry-wide data	
	Industry data reporting requirements	
	Lobby government for laws, regulations and policies on data	
	Set ethical standards	
Universities and Research Centers	Educating future organizational managers and information technologists	Preparation of future key decision stakeholders
	Research into best practice in decision-making	Enabling sophisticated data modeling
	Research into technological development and use of data and analytics	

Organizations are experiencing these industrial influences in the form of restrictions on their business processes imposed by industry standards or regulations. Industry-wide safety regulations or financial reporting practices may affect organizations' freedom to make decisions by limiting options. This was highlighted by a head of department in a financial services company, who reported, 'We can work out how we're going to do it within our own business – but to a large extent we're managed pretty strictly by outside influences.'

There are many industries that are already highly reliant on data or quickly moving into data-based spaces. Obviously, the tech-based industry, represented by companies like Facebook and Amazon, began and remain data-reliant (Keenan, 2015). Insurance and financial services have long been data- and information-based, but in the age of computer and network technologies, the influence of data is growing rapidly (Hensman and Sadler-Smith, 2011; Goepfert and Shirer, 2018). Many other industries, like retailing, power generation and pharmaceuticals, have adopted technologies that allow them to make increasing use of data and analytics. Individual companies within these industries must get on board or risk being left far behind.

The participants in our research perceived the influence of the industry on their decision-making to varying extents depending in particular on the level of restrictions that the industry regulations entailed. For example, reporting requirements set by the financial industry and safety requirements in the transportation industry can affect managers' decision-making processes and decision choices. The relevance and extent of these industry standards and restrictions to individual decision-making will vary depending on the decision situation and decision type. Operational decisions that involve safety will clearly be affected by industry regulations. Strategic decisions about new financial products will also likely need to take into account industry standards.

One industry-related factor that is affecting organizations and individual managers is industries' involvement in the gathering, analysis and provision of data. Industries are demanding that organizations supply data and this entails the formal reporting of data by managers. On the organizational and individual decision-making side, the availability of external industry-wide data is changing the way companies strategize and the way managers approach decision situations. For organizations and businesses operating within data-intensive industries, such as technology, insurance and finance, the increasing availability of data simply extends the range of their data and analytics capabilities and may lead to decision situations involving new products and strategies.

Organizations with data-rich histories include the financial and technology industries. Due to strict guidelines and regulations, companies in the financial services industry are used to data-driven decision-making. Customers and competitors expect data-derived insights in the age of big data and this further increases the relevance of data in this industry. As one manager observes, 'Nowadays, I think there's an expectation from the customer as much as competition from our peers around using data for even more powerful conversations.'

For other, more traditional industries that have had less access to data in the past, the increasing availability of data means that they will need to begin to address the collection and use of data. Such systemic changes in these industries' use of data are bound to affect the organizations and managers, likely leading to major rethinking of their decision-making culture and resulting in a reconsideration of the need for data-driven decisions.

Not all organizations are used to relying on data to inform their decision-making, as certain industries tend to have less access to data, and therefore adopt a more traditional approach. This low access to relevant data tends to result in high-judgment decisions. This is particularly the case in creative organizations and some more traditional non-profit organizations. In these industries, managers tend to heavily factor in the importance of relationships and values in their decision-making and often give them precedence over objective data. This is changing as data becomes more available and these industries become increasingly more networked. Non-profit organizations' dependence on funding, in particular, requires a change in decision-making cultures, as funders are increasingly data-oriented. Funding decisions now depend on numbers and data.

Funding for non-profits is limited and highly competitive. Grants that may have once been disbursed based on personal relationships and well-written proposals are now increasingly data-driven. As one executive working in the non-profit sector emphasized:

> Funding, finding new sponsors and partners is data-driven. We have to prove the benefits of our organization and the service to the community. So full quantitative data is required.

One executive described this as a new development that can be attributed to the evolution of big data analytics. Funders are more aware of the relevance and the insights provided by data, and therefore require objective data results in support of non-profit decisions. She said:

> I think what's happening is that traditional NGOs (non-government organizations) like ourselves have to be a lot more responsive to what funders expect of us, and properly measuring and evaluating what we do. But it's a very recent, very new thing. And it's not something we're afraid of. Because eventually, in my view, it helps build our case for saying we should be allowed to do more instead of funding other organizations who aren't as effective as us.

This change in non-profit organizations reflects the evolution in data-driven decision-making that is happening in all organizations. In this respect, non-profit organizations resemble for-profit businesses that need to justify their actions to stakeholders.

This growing importance of data access and analytics reliance among traditional organizations exemplifies a gradual shift and evolution. The tendencies towards more data-driven cultures can be perceived across almost all industries, with organizations struggling to achieve the necessary cultural change. This organizational journey to more data-driven decision-making is further discussed later in this chapter, where we outline the different stages and obstacles of this journey.

Societal-Level Influences

As understood in the ecological framework, the societal level includes economic, legal, social, cultural, political and even technological systems within which industries, organizations and individual managers operate. These systems shape industries and organizations in fundamental ways, most of which are beyond the scope of this book to discuss. What we are interested in here is the way societal factors affect how industries and organizations and even individual managers make decisions (Table 7.4).

Table 7.4   Societal-level influences on use of analytics in management decision-making

Societal-level Influences	Contribution	Effects on Decision-Making
Government(s)	Laws and regulations	See Chapter 9
Society	Cultural influences (e.g. expectations of privacy)	See Chapter 9
	Crime (e.g. hacking)	
	Ethical mores (e.g. standards of behavior)	
Technological Development	Emergence of new technologies	See Chapter 10
	Security standards	

The societal factors critical to individual decision-making, especially as it relates to the use of big data and analytics, primarily involve the influences of legal, political, social and technological factors. We have seen throughout this book how technological innovation around big data and analytics including the systems that support these technologies have influenced decision-making. We have traced the evolution of decision support technologies (Chapter 2), introduced the information systems, such as social media, that are resulting in the production and use of big data (Chapter 2), and discussed the increasing sophistication of data analytic tools (Chapter 3). All of these technological factors have a direct influence on management decision-making by making data-driven decision processes available to most organizations and individual decision-makers. The way data affects decision-making is discussed in detail in Chapter 5. In Chapter 10, we will investigate how emergent technologies, such as artificial intelligence, machine learning and the Internet of Things, may affect decision-making.

The legal, political and social factors around the use of big data, analytics and related technologies have, in a sense, been the elephant in the room that until recently only a very few people or organizations have been discussing (see for example, Electronic Frontier Foundation www.eff.org). But in the last couple of years, legal and ethical issues around data privacy and ownership have become increasingly raised in business, consumer and political contexts. Until recently, political and legal issues around data have been mostly ignored, but given widespread and well-publicized incidents of mass hacking of individual, organizational and government data, as well as potentially intrusive data collection methods by government and businesses, these issues are now firmly on everyone's radar. How these issues are resolved will have potentially large effects on industries, organizations and ultimately individual decision-makers. Because these issues are so important, we have included a separate chapter (Chapter 9) to survey current issues around data security, privacy and ethics, as well as current government laws and organizational practices and the possible effects of these on management decision-making.

ORGANIZATIONAL MATURITY OF ANALYTICS CAPABILITIES

Based on the ecological framework of management decision-making (Figure 7.2) and the discussion of the mutual/interlinking influences of its various levels on organizational data analytics culture, we know that different organizations are in different places in their data analytics journey. From the framework and the research we have done, we can see the reasons why different organizations may be in different stages and also why and how organizations may (have to) evolve and progress in their data analytics abilities.

From our research (Taskin et al., 2019; 2020b; Gressel, 2020) it is clear that most individual managers' engagement with analytics and big data does not include a full understanding of their use or potential. Furthermore, our findings suggest that big data and even basic analytics are not as ubiquitously used by organizations as current literature and vendors suggest. While vendors market big data as an effective solution for many organizational challenges, many managers at middle and senior levels still struggle with basic analytics tools and are not ready to adopt big data. Nevertheless, most organizations are aware of the growing availability and relevance of data and are aiming to become more data-driven. From our research data, it is clear that most organizations seem to be going through similar stages and experiences with big data and analytics.

Consider This Box 7.4

A Window into the World of Data Analytics

China and New Zealand are two of the countries we collected data from for our multinational research project exploring the effects of big data, analytics and related technologies on management decision-making (Taskin et al., 2020a). Among the 139 managers from China who participated in the study, 44.9 per cent were in senior management roles, 37.7 per cent in middle management role, and 12.3 per cent of the participants were at first-level management or similar roles. While 7.2 per cent of these managers indicated that they were not familiar with analytics tools, 41 per cent of the managers claimed they were somewhat familiar with the analytical tools. The remaining 50 per cent were almost equally distributed between being slightly and moderately familiar with analytical tools.

New Zealand data presented a somewhat different story. Of 116 total participants, almost twice (84.5 per cent) as many senior-level managers participated in the study compared to China, while middle managers were about 6 per cent of the total participants and 6.9 per cent were first-level managers or similar roles. Out of these participants, 3.4 per cent stated they had no familiarity with analytical tools, 16.4 per cent were slightly familiar, 26.7 per cent were somewhat familiar, and 47.4 per cent were moderately familiar with analytical tools. About 6 per cent of the participants claimed they were very familiar with analytical tools.

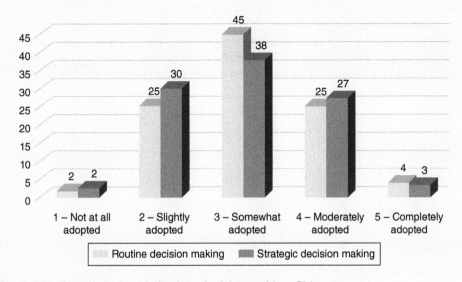

Figure 7.5   Adoption of analytics into decision-making: China

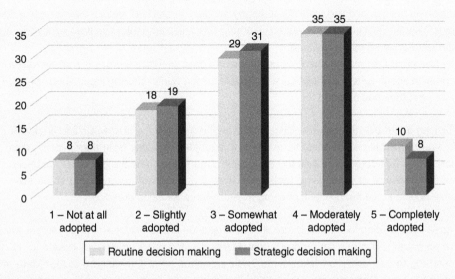

Figure 7.6   Adoption of analytics into decision-making: New Zealand

(Continued)

As seen in Figures 7.5 and 7.6, the adoption of analytics into routine and strategic decision-making differs somewhat for New Zealand and China. New Zealand tends to be further along in moderately or completely adopting analytics into decision-making, while China seems to be in earlier stages of adopting analytics for decision-making. These figures can be viewed in light of the DJAMM (Figure 7.7) introduced in this chapter.

Questions to think about

1. What do you think explains the differences in adoption rates of analytics between China and New Zealand?
2. What effect do you think the different management levels of participants have on their perception of analytics in their organizations?
3. What changes in the rates of adoption might you expect to see in the next five years?

Case Study 7.1

The Data Journey to Analytics Maturity

In this section, we look at how organizations can work their way up to data analytics maturity, especially as it relates to management decision-making. Here we highlight the advice of one very perceptive department head, Dan, of a highly data-driven organization that has been championing the use of data within his company but also across his industry. Giving regular conference talks, Dan's experience is valued by other companies embarking on the journey towards greater data-driven decision-making.

The first point Dan makes about an organization's data analytics journey is that there is a lot of confusion about data and analytics, with people having wildly differing ideas about what they are and what they can be used for:

> Thinking about the difference between reporting and insights, and analysis and analytics. To a lot of people data means the number of gigabytes they buy from their Internet provider; others, of course, understand the power of data and know the distinction between the management of data, using tools to analyze it and extract insights, and some even know how to solve the problem of using these insights for value creation.

The answer, according to Dan, is education. The challenge is that the level of engagement within any given organization can vary a great deal. Managers and other employees have a lot to do, and learning to use analytics takes time. The perception among managers is that 'data and analytics are hard'. Dan says:

Data should be a tool that managers can use to support them, but in a lot of cases data is seen as a convenient excuse for not being able to do something. And until we get them help in using and learning about data and analytics, there is no point really thinking about where these technologies fit into the business.

According to Dan, it's important to have someone in the organization to show the business that working with data and analytics is not really that difficult. Dan has this role in his organization and understands the difference it makes. He points out that there are myriad tools and data sources as well as vendors who can help with getting data, preparing it for analysis, analyzing it and producing answers. The real challenge, Dan says:

> is knowing the right questions, and that those questions should be driven from understanding what you believe can create value in your business, value that can be driven by data. So in a lot of cases I meet business people who say, 'I've got a need or an issue, and I believe that data can help.'

Dan is one of the 'go-to' data experts in his organization. When co-workers come up to him with a data-related problem, he shows them how easy it is to get that answer. But more than that, he challenges them by asking:

> Now that you have your answer, what are you going to do with it? How will you use it to create value?

At this point, what Dan has discovered is that answering this question is the hard bit for the managers, and this is because fundamentally it has to do with changing the culture of the organization to where they are first able to see that data can make a difference and then are able to use it. Then the strategy is to show how data can be effective; for example, by demonstrating how a manager can use data to make a better decision or a more effective business case. Conducting this strategy at a personal or organizational level requires a champion who can teach managers how to communicate data insights at the right level – 'too much tech talk', Dan says, 'will creep customers out, while making it too simple might give customers the impression the manager doesn't know what he is talking about. Finding the balance with all levels is the key.'

Dan summarizes the advice he would give other organizations that want to increase their data analytics maturity:

> Don't start with the data! Start with the question: what exactly is the problem to be solved? Where do you believe value could be found in your business? And then, what's the fastest, cheapest way for you to demonstrate a test to see if that value really exists? Do you need to develop an analytical model or can you simply create a set of simple hypotheses to test? If you don't even know where to start, you probably want to do some analysis, and simply become familiar with interpreting insights and applying them to your problem.

(Continued)

Questions to think about

1. How can an organization's technologist make it easier for managers to effectively use data analytics?
2. How would you describe the steps from having data to having some insights from the data? Define any environment constraints and assumptions if necessary.
3. What are some of the dangers of misusing analytics in a business context?

On the journey to more data-driven decision-making, managers point to the adoption of data-driven decision-making as a specific form of organizational maturity of analytics capability. *Analytics maturity refers to an organization's analytics capabilities, but also to the extent these capabilities are exploited for decision-making and anchored in the organizational culture.* While there may be other measures of an organization's data analytics maturity, for this book on management decision-making and big data we use this definition as a measure of organizational analytics maturity. This concept of maturity expands on the academic and practitioner literature's view on analytics capabilities (LaValle et al., 2011; Davenport and Harris, 2017). Case 7.1 helps illustrate how this can be understood at both the individual and organizational levels. Analytics maturity is considered so far-reaching and symbiotic in regard to the other factors found in the manager's decision-making environment that it was not added as another hierarchical level, but as a parallel influence

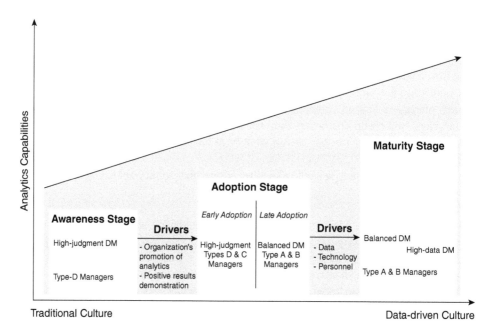

Figure 7.7 Data Journey to Analytics Maturity Model

on the decision-maker alongside the other factors of the ecological framework (Figure 7.2). Managers in our research confirmed this influence of the wider managerial decision-making environment when discussing conditions that affect decision-making.

Three stages of analytics maturity are evident when mapping the data journey of organizations. Figure 7.7 indicates the positioning of each stage in relation to the organization's analytics capabilities and its organizational culture. The stages reflect the organization's current relationship with analytics, namely stages of 'awareness', 'adoption' or 'maturity'.

Awareness Stage

The first stage of the data journey refers to the organization's 'awareness' and recognition of data analytics. Most organizations are aware to some degree of the potential of data analytics and possibly its value for decision-making. However, awareness does not equate with the actual use of data analytics. Organizations in the awareness stage have just recently embarked on their data journey. This pursuit of analytics maturity is not always a conscious decision but often triggered by an event in the wider environment, such as the sudden availability of a large new external data source. Such a data source could be from an industry-level source or the government. The organization may also hire an employee who turns out to be very experienced in the use of analytics and through this employee's efforts the organization begins its data journey. Presented with these sorts of opportunities an organization may start thinking about ways to take advantage of these resources.

In these early stages of the data journey it is important to get the buy-in of leadership, develop ideas for first use cases, and put together a team of skilled analysts. In terms of culture, organizations need to focus on showing employees that there is value to be gained from using data: this usually requires easy wins that demonstrate this value. From a technological point of view, the starting point is good data quality, as negative decision outcomes are often attributed to poor data. Poor data quality is often discovered early on in the awareness stage, when organizations look deeper at their available data. This can also unearth errors in previous projects that relied on data.

In the early stage of awareness, one usually finds managers making high-judgment decisions and belonging to Type D, i.e. the old-fashioned decision-makers. A marketing agency that contributed to our research was used to advising their customers on their data use and was able to work with big data on behalf of their clients. However, the agency itself barely used data, and executives almost exclusively relied on their judgment for decision-making.

Many non-profit organizations are also considered to be in this stage. Characteristically for their industry, non-profits tend not to have extensive exposure to data useful for their own decision-making. However, with the growing interest from funders in data-backed reports and decisions, non-profit organizations are now starting to adopt more data-driven cultures as well.

Adoption Stage

Adoption is the next stage on the journey to analytics maturity and it reflects an organization's intent to become more data-driven and take the first steps in actualizing this intent. Such organizations may have already hired analytic talent, intensified their data collection efforts, and/or employed additional IT systems. Industry-level influences may also be a significant factor in pushing an organization towards analytics maturity. While organizations may strive for more data-driven decisions, limited access to and experience with data often means high-judgment, experience-driven decisions are still the norm. Over time and with greater familiarity and competence with data, more balanced decisions are likely to be made. The adoption stage is likely to see a variety of decision-maker types. Type D, old-fashioned, and Type C, insecure, managers, may predominate in the early stages of transition. Type As, i.e. analytics-bent, will become more prominent in the early stages and grow in number and influence as the organization matures. Finally, all-rounder Type B managers will also become more prevalent with training and changing recruitment standards.

In the adoption stage organizations will often start to acquire technology in the form of data and information systems. Much can go wrong at this stage. Money may be spent on expensive systems without first laying the groundwork, which can include management training in the technology, appropriate information technologists as support staff, and an underlying strategy for using the technology in decision-making. Data might still be distributed among different silos. Individual decision-makers may still be showing resistance to data. The key objectives of organizations in this adoption stage are to increase their analytics capabilities and employ change management techniques to promote a more data-driven culture. This cultural shift is approached by building trust in data, tackling resistance, as well as sharing first successes and use cases.

Table 7.5   Evolving into a successful adoption stage

	Overall Strategies	Common Mistakes
Developing organizational culture	Sharing positive results and success stories	Lack of leadership support
		Not engaging resisting individuals
	Knowledge sharing	Not communicating the change
	Freedom to challenge	
Setting up data-driven workforce	Hiring and training staff who can understand and use analytics in decision-making	Not accounting for different skills and needs
		Hiring technical personnel without business understanding/people skills
	Bringing consultants on board on an as-needed basis	
		Provision and availability of analysts doesn't match business needs

	Overall Strategies	**Common Mistakes**
Acquiring technology	Technology that meets the near-term needs of the organization Systems that can grow as the organization's data capabilities grow	Capabilities of current technology are not understood or appraised, before additional technology acquisitions are made
		Big investments are made in new technology without an adequate business strategy in place and necessary personnel to make use of the technology
		Silo effect in both business and technology sides keeping data from being shared
Meeting industry standards	Making best use of industry-supplied data and industry best practice, e.g. data security	Ignoring or resisting industry standards
Environmental awareness	Keeping track of new laws and social attitudes on security, privacy and ethical use of data Preparing public relations to deal with security breaches and negative publicity	Information security incidents should be avoided Customers might perceive additional insights as invasion of privacy – tactful approach needs to be chosen

Having the appropriate data and related technology and actually using that data is often a common barrier to becoming an effective data-driven organization. There may be several reasons for the inefficient use of data and technology including organizational culture, the structure of the organization and inadequate human resources. An analyst at a large organization in the transport industry explains that her organization has several systems and data sources that would allow them to use additional data, but that they are not being used. The full potential of data insights was not being harnessed and the extent of data use for decision-making was still limited. For one, this was due to data being distributed among several locations, leading to data silos and difficult access to it. She explained:

There is the resource issue as well, because you have six or seven databases for one piece of input. Some of them are controlled by the guys at headquarters, some of them are looked after by the guys at Center X, some of them we look after. So it's just my time and people's time to obtain and collate the data.

The other reason this data is not being used is that while the systems and data sources are in place, the managers and other employees are not capable of accessing them or interpreting the insights:

Nobody does anything with the data we're getting in. It's not actively used all the time. Simply getting access to some of the systems and retrieving the required information is just really difficult.

Team and departmental-level factors are important in the adoption stage of analytics maturity. Similarly, the other levels of the ecological framework were found to play an essential role in affecting the analytics maturity of an organization. Having analysts on staff, as well as a supportive organizational culture are key components of data-driven decision-making. When asked about requirements for decision-making success, the CEO of an IT company described a team that was skilled, able to challenge data and human judgment, and an organizational culture that enabled knowledge exchange:

> You need a team of people who are smart, experienced, and able to challenge. So, you want a culture where challenging someone's view is acceptable rather than just saying, 'Oh, the boss said that, so that's all good.' So, if you have a collegial environment, where people are willing to help each other and share views and not be critical because of personality conflict or some other reason; then the chances are you might get a synthesis of a good answer.

Maturity Stage

Maturity is the final stage on the journey to analytics. In this stage, maturity comes with the gaining of experience and confidence with data sets and analytics, which in turn leads to an even greater understanding of and trust in data. Organizations that have reached the maturity stage are characterized as having in place their analytics teams and the required tools for data analysis. Their organizational culture is supportive of data-driven decision-making, yet open to the challenging of data results. A wide and readily available range of data sources is frequently accessed and harvested. Organizations in this stage may additionally have formal roles allocated for business intelligence, analytics and data: for example, Chief Data Scientist or Head of Business Intelligence. The primary objective in this stage is to further explore sophisticated data analysis techniques and new data sources, through experimentation. These organizations have a positive perception of data and consider it a critical organizational asset that improves their understanding of business problems and their ability to respond. This is exemplified by this manager who explained: 'What I've realized is that, if you operate between certain datasets and metrics every month, you just look at something, and then ... You know there is something not right.' With regard to decision-making, managers and organizations see the potential of data to explain phenomena and justify decisions.

These organizations, of course, make a great number of high-data decisions, but they are also capable of making highly successful balanced decisions by following the decision-making processes discussed in previous chapters. Managers in these organizations are likely to be both Type A managers, analytics-bent, and experienced Type B all-rounder decision-makers. In the analytics maturity stage, organizations have all the human and technological resources to heavily integrate data analytics into their operational, tactical and strategic decision-making processes. Data is used for scheduled reporting purposes, ad hoc discoveries, the piloting of new business segments, and as an embedded driver of the business model. In these organizations, the culture is such that analytics is part of the day-to-day work. However, even mature companies still have room to grow. Another characteristic of organizations in this stage is their awareness of their own limitations. They approach overcoming these limitations with a pragmatic attitude and experimentation.

Even mature organizations need to assess and reassess their abilities and limitations with data. The good ones do this on an ongoing basis, before problems crop up. This specialist advises this measured approach:

> So where exactly is your problem? Is it in reporting – well that's easy to solve: reports can be set up in a structured manner. They can be automated and are often entirely based on readily available internal data. The reports can be tested and changed incrementally. A lot of common KPIs that can be used on reports and examples of them can be found online.
>
> Is it analysis? Well that's a business-side function, so you need to get the right people focused on where they think the value could be. If you're looking for insights – do you have any idea of what's going on? Do you have any intuition that tells you the things you could test? If it's analytics, it means you start off with a hypothesis – fair enough, get operational research PhD people in to discover patterns, trends, just different ways to use your available data sources to create some valuable insights. That's what you need to do if you believe you've exhausted all of the insights that come from just asking your own people, 'What's going on?'

While analytics maturity contributes to the quality and sophistication of data-driven decision-making, reaching this maturity can be a slow process. To successfully move on from the stages of awareness and adoption, organizations need to address two primary drivers, which both relate to organizational culture. The first is the promotion of analytics by the organization's senior executives. Leadership is required in order to provide the necessary support, motivation and authority to switch to data-driven decisions. As one manager put it: 'It's got to be led by the absolute top of the organization. If it doesn't happen at the very, very top, it won't happen at all.' The second key driver is the demonstration of positive results, especially examples of significant wins that most likely would not have been achieved without the use of data driving decisions and action.

Even in the Internet-age start-ups that often start with the data and technology, tech-oriented Type A decision-makers engaging in data-driven decision-making can experience difficulties making it work for them in real-life business contexts. As often as not, this has to do with a lack of contextual knowledge around business. Many of these start-ups will fail without proper guidance. As we mentioned in Chapter 1, the ones that survive and prosper, like Google and Apple, have had to bring in top management expertise who understand how to make the data work in the real world.

CHAPTER SUMMARY

In this chapter we have looked at the environmental factors that can affect a manager's decision-making processes, particularly as they relate to the use of data and analytics. We have used the ecological framework as developed by Bronfenbrenner (1977, 1979) to illustrate the likely influences. Not surprisingly, the most significant influences on the individual manager are those at the team level, the colleagues that the manager works with. When it comes to the use of data analytics in decision-making, access to an analytics specialist is the biggest driver for managers to use and learn about data and analytics.

The next most significant factor affecting individual decision-making is the organizational culture that the manager works within. Culture includes the attitudes and expectations of the organization towards data-driven decisions, especially from senior management, but culture also includes the support systems, training and technology that facilitate the gathering and use of data in decision-making. If data is in silos that make it difficult or time-consuming for managers to access they may not use it. If data is of poor quality and leads to bad decisions, then managers similarly won't use it. Even if data is of high quality and easily available, technical support is required for managers to be able to use it. In all cases, organizational culture should support the training and up-skilling of manager competencies with data as well as the recruitment of those with the technical and business KSAs.

Industry and the larger societal influences were also discussed in this chapter. More and more, industry-level influences are driving data use, and these influences are rapidly affecting even data-averse organizations. The emphasis on STEM skills in universities is also leading to graduates with more technical skills. We can expect these influences to grow and increasingly affect both organizational and individual approaches to data-driven decision-making. Finally we touched upon the societal-level influences. These are significant and are covered in greater detail in Chapters 9 and 10.

We also introduced the concept of analytics maturity, linking this with the influences from the different levels in the ecological model. Analytics maturity is closely tied to all these levels: industry-level influences, i.e. data access; organizational-level influences in the form of organizational culture; and department-level influences, particularly in the form of available analysts. Given these influences, we consider analytics maturity the most critical component of the ecological framework affecting management decision-making and have tracked the evolution of analytics maturity with the Data Journey to Analytics Maturity Model (DJAMM).

In sum, the external influences on an individual manager's decision-making are significant. Along with the manager's own set of KSAs, the external influences shape the decision-making process, including if and how managers use data and analytics. In the next chapter, we look at how all the factors and influences discussed in this chapter, as well as in Chapters 5 and 6, affect a manager's decision-making.

KEY LESSONS

In this chapter we have introduced factors that influence organizational readiness to embrace data-driven decision-making. The most important takeaways can be summarized as:

1. Environmental factors can have a significant impact on organizational attitudes towards the use of data and analytics.
2. Organizational culture is the key to driving the evolution of organizational data analytics use and maturity.
3. Analytics maturity is a comprehensive concept that covers organizational culture, the availability of analysts and analytics skills, and the readiness to use analytics on a daily basis.
4. Industries face varying degrees of legal and regulatory restrictions that can affect individual data-driven decision-making, and which require organizational preparation.

8
INTEGRATING CONTEXTUAL FACTORS IN MANAGEMENT DECISION-MAKING

Contents

Consider This Box 8.1

Environmental Factors and the Complexity of Management Decision-Making

Management decision-making has never been easy. Trying to make the right decisions when decision situations are complex and when conditions within and outside of the organization are uncertain is challenging. These comments by managers are indicative of the complexities of modern-day decision-making.

General manager at a financial services organization:

Strategic decisions, honestly, they can take six months. You could be going back and forth, up and down that process for six months. And sometimes the problem with strategic decisions is that you are dealing with ambiguity and unknown market factors. And competitors, what are they doing, we don't necessarily know. And there's a whole range of unknown factors, like legislation kicks in, the environmental factors. So at some point in time, you do need to make a decision. You've got as much information as you're going to get ... for goodness sake make a decision and act on it. We're a pretty action-oriented organization, but I've been in corporates where that strategic discussion can go on and on to the point where a decision can't be made. There are too many conflicting views and no one is prepared to say: 'Well this is what we're going to do.'

CEO from a non-profit organization, recently transferred from a position on the board of directors:

From a governance role on the board to managing everyday operational activities as a CEO is a huge change when it comes to decision-making. From a governance perspective we were tracking monthly reports, against the requirements in our contracts. As a board member my interest was making sure that we are delivering what our contract requires us to. As a CEO, I need to be concerned as much with what the funder, our client, wants to know as with [what] the board wants to know. If we don't meet the funder's expectations we could lose some of the funding or in the worst case scenario, lose the contract.

So from a governance perspective I am looking at the overarching needs of the organiza- tion and hopefully providing some strategic advice, whereas as management I'm trying to implement that strategic plan that our board has created and updates every year. My job in management is to operationalize it and to look for opportunities to grow the business. Like most other NGOs in New Zealand, we are reliant on public funding; we have to adapt to changes in government policy. Changing government priorities can hugely affect our organization. Somehow we have to plan for these and be ready.

Questions to think about

1. What kind of decision-maker types do you think these managers are (refer to Chapter 6, Type A, B, C, D decision-makers)? Explain your answers.
2. Discuss the contextual factors that you identify in these decisions. Which ones do you think have the biggest impact on these decision-makers?
3. Discuss ways that the decision-makers in these cases can try to mitigate these contextual factors.

CHAPTER 8 KEY LESSONS

1. Management decision-making is a highly complex process.
2. The wider environment plays a significant role in the decision-making process.
3. Decision-makers must possess the necessary KSAs and organizations must possess the necessary capabilities for the effective use of data and analytics in decision-making.

INTRODUCTION

In the previous chapters we learned about management decision-making, the interlinking roles analytics and human judgment have in the decision-making process, the different decision-maker types, and the many environmental factors from team level to societal level that can affect data-driven decision-making. In this chapter, we integrate these insights together in a step-by-step approach. We then present case studies that illustrate how managers make decisions when faced with the kinds of everyday conditions managers face. This will provide students with valuable and practical guidance for better understanding decision situations and decision-making. We begin with a review of what we have learned so far.

THE MANAGEMENT DECISION-MAKING ENVIRONMENT IN THE AGE OF BIG DATA AND ANALYTICS

While decision-making has always been challenging, the recent developments of big data and analytics and their expected use in more and more decision situations has increased the complexity of decision-making from the time when decisions were made based mostly on experience, knowledge and human judgment. The exponential growth and availability of data and computing power inexorably affects decision-making. When and how to use data and analytics present new challenges for managers and organizations. There can be no single prescribed formula for using data and analytics in decision-making. But what can be done is for managers and organizations to understand as much as they can about data, analytics and decision-making and the factors that influence their use, and then develop principles and practices that suit their situations. In this section we review all the key factors.

In Chapter 4, we introduced decision-making processes and theory in some depth. We explained that decision-making becomes necessary when a decision situation is triggered. Decision situations may be obvious or hidden and the triggers can be anything from a 'loud' customer complaint broadcast on social media to 'hidden' patterns in a regular monthly data-driven report. Once the decision trigger is recognized, a manager usually initiates the decision-making process. We noted that various models suggest different numbers of decision-making stages and specific steps in the decision-making process and settled on a simplified three-stage decision-making process based on the work of Mintzberg et al. (1976): identification, development and selection (Figure 8.1). In the identification stage, managers find or are presented with situations in which to make decisions. In this book we call these decision triggers and as explained above these can be very obvious or involve in-depth searching. In the development stage, managers, often working with colleagues, develop and analyze potential consequences of alternatives that address the decision situation. Finally, in the selection stage, the manager makes the decision by choosing the best alternative. This can be a quick process if the manager has confidence in the results of the first two stages.

Figure 8.1 The three-stage decision-making process

We also reviewed several decision-making theories in Chapter 4, with a focus on dual process theory. This theory, we argued, best explains the way managers naturally make decisions in real life, by generally combining rational and non-rational ways of thinking that include step-by-step approaches based on data and information as well as heuristics and intuition. Figure 8.2 details the characteristics of high-data and high-judgment decision styles with System 1 and 2 processes from dual process theory.

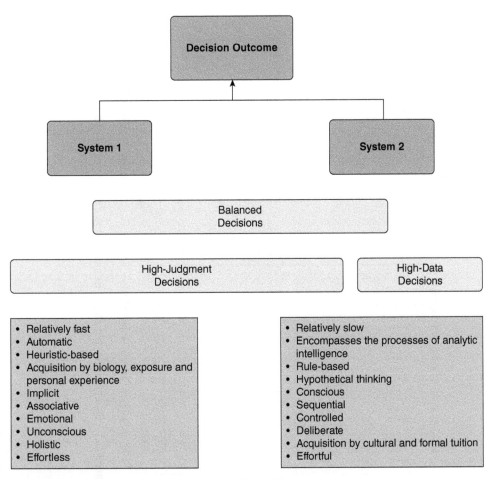

Figure 8.2 Dual process theory and decision styles

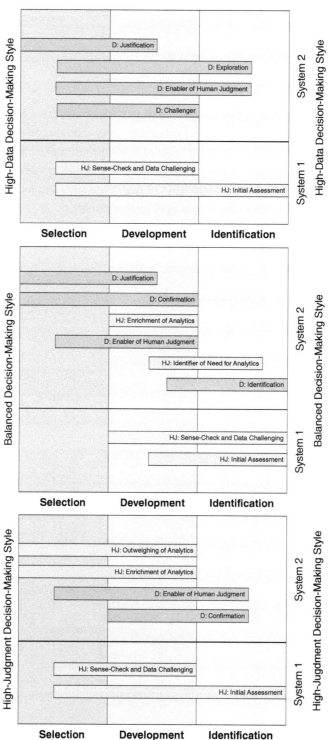

Figure 8.3 Decision-making steps, decision styles and roles of judgment and data and dual process theory

Data and analytics, as we pointed out, are tools that specifically support System 2 rational decision-making, but nevertheless as shown in Chapters 4 and 5, all decision styles – balanced, high-judgment and high-data – can include roles involving human judgment and data analytics in varying combinations throughout the decision-making process. Figure 8.3 illustrates the decision-making process of each style. We highlight the different decision steps and showcase the importance of the two systems and how the data and human judgment roles differ between the styles.

In Chapter 4 we also examined the types of decisions managers usually have to make. These include decisions that can be generically classified as operational, tactical and strategic, and that in terms of the decision situation can range from simple to complicated to complex. Operational decisions often operate within defined parameters and are usually automated based on incoming data and selected algorithms. Examples include factory floor machinery that self-regulates to common office tasks like applying for sick leave. Complicated decisions often have many data inputs, but these may be difficult to determine or collect data for while certain kinds of tactical decisions, especially those involving personal relationships, will require a manager's experience and knowledge. Examples of tactical decisions include setting next year's contract prices for old customers or spending this year's remaining advertising budget on new channels. Finally, long-term, complex strategic decisions will tend to involve a wide range of contextual factors that usually require both human judgment and data inputs. Examples of strategic decisions might include new product development or opening new international markets. Figure 8.4 captures the relationships between decision types and decision styles.

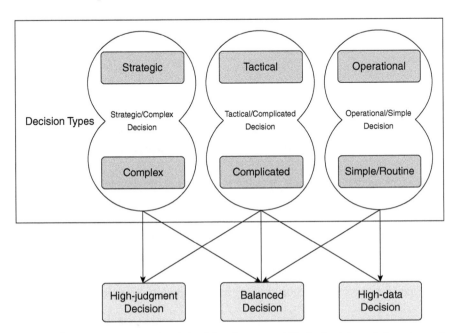

Figure 8.4 Common management decision types and likely decision-style approaches

In Chapter 5 we examined the role of analytics in decision-making. Based on our research we developed three kinds of management decision-making styles: balanced, high-judgment and high-data. Which style a manager uses often depends on a number of contextual factors that comprise the decision situation including: the decision trigger, the decision type, the availability of relevant data, the organizational culture and capabilities, and the manager's KSAs and personal decision-making styles – i.e. manager type (Figure 8.5).

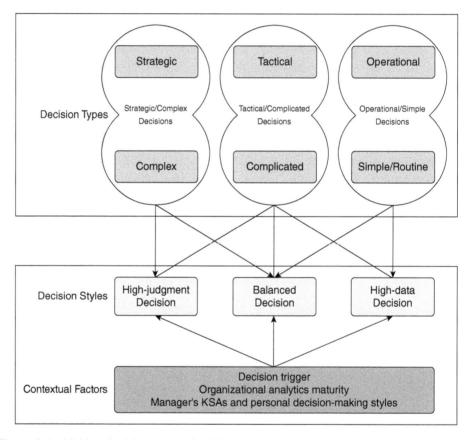

Figure 8.5   Linking decision types, decision styles and contextual factors

In Chapter 5, we also looked in detail at the role of human judgment and analytics in the decision-making process (Figure 8.6). We explained the five roles of human judgment and the seven roles of analytics in the decision-making process and how they work together in real-world decision-making as explained in dual process theory. We also explored how decision triggers, decision types and all of the other contextual factors influence how a manager uses analytics and judgment throughout the three stages of the decision-making process.

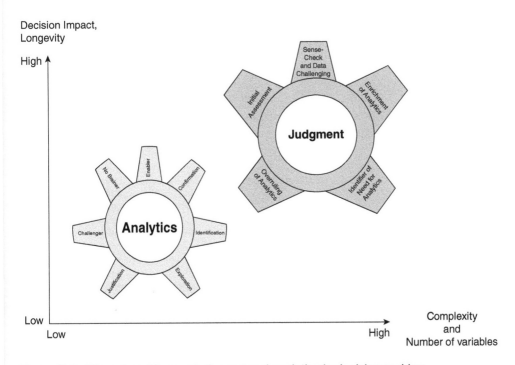

Figure 8.6   The roles of human judgment and analytics in decision-making

In Chapter 6, we developed a taxonomy of management decision-makers with four distinct types of decision-makers: Type A – Analytics-Bent; Type B – All-Rounder; Type C – Uncertain; and Type D – Old-Fashioned. Each of these decision-maker types favors a particular style of decision-making and uses data, information and analytics in different ways or sometimes not at all. These preferences are often shaped by their education, their work experience, their organization's culture and expectations, as well as their knowledge, skills and abilities. The key lesson of this book, and Chapter 6, is that data and analytics is increasingly seen as having a critical role in decision-making, and that both individuals and organizations need to take account of these different decision-making types of managers to optimize decision support policies and systems. Figure 8.7 highlights the central role managers play when making decisions while dealing with the influences of numerous contextual factors.

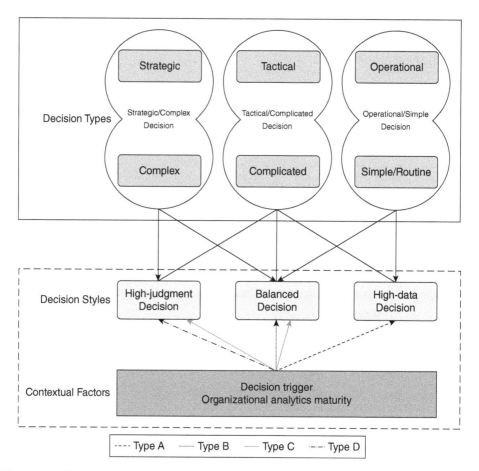

Figure 8.7   Manager types and contextual factors

In Chapter 7, we developed an ecological framework of management decision-making. We demonstrated how environmental factors can have a significant impact on organizational attitudes towards the use of data and analytics: for example, how customer expectations, industry best practice or government legal requirements can shape an organization's data collection and reporting. Equally important, we explained how individual data champions can initiate change in an organization by demonstrating and educating colleagues on the benefits of data in decision-making. In Figure 8.8 we bring together all of the contextual factors that can influence management decision-making.

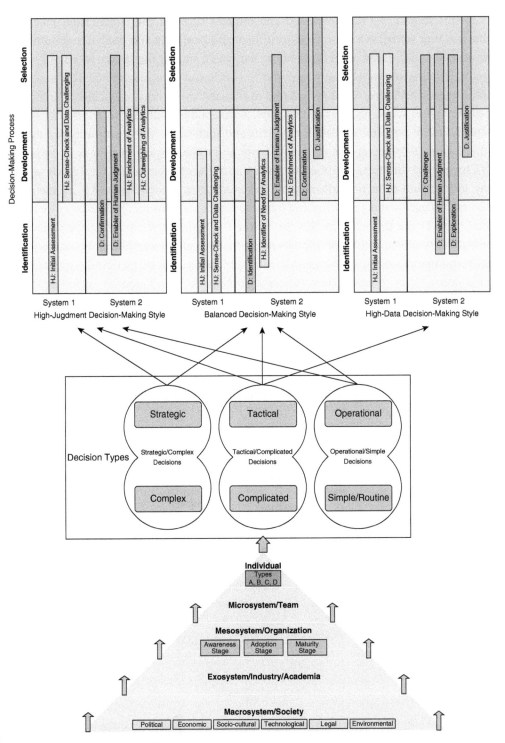

Figure 8.8 Influences of the ecological framework on management decision-making

In this section, we have reviewed and brought together the factors from previous chapters that we believe are critical in influencing how data and analytics are used in management decision-making, both at the individual and organizational levels. All these factors together and individually can drive the evolution of organizational data analytics culture and capabilities, which we referred to as analytics maturity in Chapter 7. Analytics maturity refers to an organization's analytics capabilities, but also to the extent these capabilities are exploited for decision-making and anchored in the organizational culture.

In Figure 8.9 we integrate analytics maturity into the ecological framework (introduced in Chapter 7) to illustrate how the various factors in the different hierarchical levels mutually interact and influence an organization's analytics maturity. Figure 8.9 represents a holistic management decision-making framework that accounts for all the factors we have introduced in the previous chapters. In a sense the figure represents the factors that are brought to bear in any given decision situation that a manager encounters. In most typical decision situations many of these factors, e.g. political factors, will be outside the immediate concern of the decision-maker. However, in many decision situations, including those that are strategic and complex, it will be relatively apparent that a number of these factors might need to be considered when making a decision (see Case Studies section). Next we discuss in some detail how these factors mutually influence each other and ultimately affect individual management decision-making and the use of analytics. To facilitate the discussion, we separate the framework into three parts: 1) the decision-maker, the decision type and the decision style; 2) colleagues and organizational culture; and 3) industry and society.

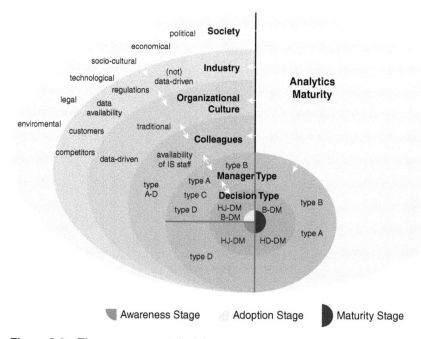

Figure 8.9 The management decision-making environment

The Inner Circles: The Decision-Maker, the Decision Type and the Decision Style

At the center of the model is the decision-maker, the decision type and the decision style. Assuming an ideal and fully (self-)aware decision-maker, the decision-maker will carefully consider the decision type (e.g. operational, tactical, strategic, simple, complicated, complex) and determine which decision-making style is most suitable. The decision style – balanced (B-DM), high-judgment (HJ-DM), or high-data (BD-DM) – will then determine the decision-making process that is followed by the manager: i.e. the relative use of judgment and data. Which decision style is used will depend in large part on the type of manager making the decision and their KSAs and decision-making preferences. A manager with high-judgment and high-data skills will have a much greater variety of options than an old-fashioned decision-maker with limited knowledge of analytics. The other directly important factors that will determine which decision style the manager chooses will include the availability of team support and data resources, as well as organizational and senior management preferences. Manager types and levels of team support, and organizational culture and data capabilities all reflect an organization's stage of analytics maturity.

Case Study 8.1

Wicked Problems, Analytics and Decision-Making

In Chapter 4, we looked at the different problem types from operational to strategic and simple to complex. Wicked problems are in a class of their own. In simple terms they are exceedingly complex problems that are often highly value laden due to the involvement of many stakeholders inside and outside of the organization and society as a whole (Intezari and Pauleen, 2019). In today's world of business, stakeholders include consumers (on social media), social organizations and governments demanding products and services (and ways of producing them) that are environmentally sustainable and socially responsible. In essence, with wicked problems, the whole of the decision-making environment (Figure 8.8) and all the factors that it contains become part of the decision situation and must be accounted for by the organization and the decision-maker.

An example of a wicked problem was the Deepwater Horizon oil spill that occurred in 2010 (Pauleen and Intezari, 2019). In this case, the problems that needed to be addressed at the time of the spill and afterwards were at many levels. Some of the questions that needed to be addressed immediately included among many others:

(Continued)

1. How did the spill occur?
2. How is it evolving from hour to hour?
3. How can it be stopped?
4. Who is in charge?
5. How can resources and people be coordinated?

Just addressing these few questions represented enormous complexity, involved multiple stakeholders, and would incur dire consequences if they could not be addressed. And, as nothing of this magnitude had occurred before, no one had the knowledge, experience, judgment or data to understand and deal with it.

Immediate follow-up questions needed to address the consequences of the spill on the physical and social environment of the Gulf of Mexico:

1. Who is responsible?
2. How can the environment be saved?
3. What about people's livelihoods?
4. Who will pay the costs?

Even years after the spill, the companies, governments, and social and environmental organizations still struggle to answer complex technical, financial, legal and ethical questions. Some may never be answered.

According to Intezari and Pauleen (2019), the Deepwater Horizon spill was wicked because:

1. the difficulty in formulating the problem was high
2. the cause–effect relationships of many of the issues were unknown
3. the unpredictability and uncertainty of the situation were high
4. the dynamism of the situation was high
5. the multidimensionality and interconnectedness of the factors were high
6. multiple stakeholders were involved and social responsibility and involvement were high, and
7. the ethical burden was high.

Wicked problems are not well understood. The scale or impact of wicked problems cannot be predicted. They are novel problems, with no specific right or wrong answer, and they often involve issues of complex morality or ethics. There are no maps to follow when trying to stop a wicked problem (Holtel, 2016). However, Holtel recommends an approach to managing wickedness that includes: involving as many stakeholders as possible to get their input and buy-in, talking about and discussing different types of values, and focusing on multiple possible solutions while constantly adapting them.

Given the characteristics of wicked problems and the suggested ways to approach them, the question must be asked, what might be the role of big data and analytics in wicked decision situations? In the example of the Deepwater Horizon spill, one would have expected scientists, engineers and policy makers to consult whatever data sets they had available to model possible ways of shutting off the machinery or show the likely effect of the oil spill on the environment etc., and then to use these models in judgment-based decisions. As nothing of the magnitude of this spill had occurred before, available data on lesser spills would be used to best effect. After this spill, there were intensive research efforts to develop computational models and analytical frameworks of it, and as described by Nelson and Grubesic (2019: 129), 'Much of this work is dedicated to deepening our understanding of the interactions between oil, fragile ecosystems, and the environment, as well as the impacts of oil on human settlements which are vulnerable to spill events'. These models and frameworks would be extremely helpful resources in the event of another similar spill, and their availability might then render another otherwise wicked decision situation to a merely complex one. The problem remains, however, that at the moment it is difficult, perhaps impossible, to predict and model emergent wicked problems. Perhaps some of the new technologies discussed in Chapter 10 will be of use.

The Middle Circles: Colleagues, Team Members and the Organization

Managers do not act in a vacuum and their use of data-driven decision-making approaches is influenced by their environment. As can be seen in Figure 8.8, managers are directly influenced by their colleagues, who are, along with the manager, in turn influenced by the organizational culture. As discussed in Chapter 7, team-level access to analysts is a significant prerequisite to using data analytics in decision-making. The availability of analysts throughout the organization depends on the organizational culture and data capabilities, i.e. whether data-driven decision-making is valued, prioritized and supported. All of these factors at this level will come to bear on a manager's decision-making style. For example, if an organization is at a mature stage of analytics maturity, it is most likely that all decisions a manager makes will need to be supported by data.

The Outer Circles: Industry and Society

Whether an organization's culture is data-driven will depend on factors from outside of the organization. Organizations operate within a larger industrial and social environment that includes customers, competitors, and industrial and government entities. All of these entities exert influence on and shape expectations of the way the organization operates, strongly influencing organizational culture and capabilities and ultimately the analytics maturity of individual organizations; for example, organizations that belong to data-rich industries often follow suit and have a more data-driven culture. Technological change is sometimes supported by government (e.g. initiatives supporting 5G) and sometimes by industry (e.g. security protocols). Factors from the outer circles can also influence individual managers making decisions. Government laws and societal mores on ethics and data privacy may affect individual decision-making.

As can be seen in Figure 8.7, these influences are not unidirectional. While it is clear that the higher levels exert influence on the lower levels, influences may also be generated from below; for example, a manager acting as a data champion can change team processes and influence organizational culture, a highly innovative company can influence a whole industry, and industry associations are constantly lobbying governments. This reciprocity of influences is particularly clear when it comes to an organization's analytics maturity. This factor has a direct influence on managers but is also highly dependent on the influence of colleagues, organizational culture and industry. Analytics maturity therefore spans across multiple levels in the framework.

In this section we have given a detailed and integrated account of decision-making. While it may appear to be theoretical or conceptual, it is based on research with real managers, how they make decisions, and the factors that influence their decision-making. In the following section we present cases that highlight the influences that were found in managers' decision-making environments, highlight their significance, and further discuss their impact and relation to each other.

DECISION-MAKING IN PRACTICE: CASE STUDIES

In this section we present cases of decision situations that illustrate how the influences and relationships discussed above and featured in Figure 8.8 can affect individual managers' decision-making processes. The decision situations are often broader than a single decision and include decision situations that are essentially 'always on': for example, responding to changing environmental factors such as new government regulations, market changes and competitor initiatives. The focus, however, remains on how individual decision-makers use data and judgment in their decision-making. A series of questions are asked at the end of each case that require you to think about how the various contextual factors influence the manager's decision-making process and what managers can do to respond to these influences.

Case Study 8.2

Type A Manager in a Data-Driven Organization

Decision Parameters

Decision Situation: Ongoing support for senior-level decision-makers

Decision Trigger: Evaluation

Decision Type: Strategic

Decision Style: Data-driven

Manager Type: Type A – Analytics-Bent

Organizational Analytics Maturity: Mature

Industry Influences: Data-driven

Societal Influences: Regulated, legal reporting requirements, data security and privacy restrictions

John is a Type A, analytics-bent, managerial decision-maker. He is a business analyst working for a large financial services company. The company is New Zealand-based, but has important connections with international partners. John's bent for analytical thinking was strongly influenced by his university undergraduate studies in mathematics, and statistics during his Master's degree in Business. While he has had no formal training in data and analytics, he has five to six years of work experience with them. Currently he manages a small analytics team that often contributes to strategic decision-making in the organization. He explains:

> I report directly to the CEO and provide key analytics, key data, for making strategic decisions for the business. My group oversees all the business performance reporting on a day-to-day, week-to-week, and month-to-month schedule that guides the understanding of where the business is at.

By contributing these data insights, John is an integral part of his organization's strategic decision-making. The decisions he is involved with are usually high-data decisions, but also include balanced decisions with high data use. While this high-data decision-making process usually begins with using judgment as an initial assessment, it is quickly followed by the gathering of as much information and data as possible. John critically examines his initial assessment for any potential biases he might bring to the decision-making process and challenges them before beginning his analysis of the problem using data analytics. He reflects on this process:

> What's my preconceived idea about this? I'm not afraid to recognize and challenge it. I try and remind myself not to try to find only the information to prove my initial assessment. I think a lot of people use data that way; they think: 'Oh yes, I know what the answer is, let's find some data to support what I already believe.' I think that's how people misuse data. Better to ask what is the situation here? Can data bring clarity to it? If yes, how am I going to gather this data? And then I make a quality observation and analysis. It's like I follow an almost experimental methodology every time I use big data to make a decision.

(Continued)

John finds that using data is a balancing act and that even decision-makers with the ana-lytics bent have to be mindful of their extent of data use: 'I think there's always a danger of dismissing it or over-relying on it. There's always a fine line, even if someone is analytical.' As a last step in the decision-making process, he also consults others to sense-check his ana-lytics results: 'I usually bounce it off other people in my team.' His colleagues are open to this process. Furthermore, the analytics that John develops are used in organizational strategic decision-making, and are also checked and challenged by his superiors. John needs confi-dence and communication skills to defend them when this happens.

John emphasized that he has always had the analytics bent, and describes the influence of the company culture on his decision-making approach as a good fit rather than an influence. He explains: 'I'm not sure if the company culture influences me as much as it supports how I already think and work.' The financial services industry also relies heavily on data analytics: again a good match for his analytical personality.

Comment

The data-driven decision-making approach reflects John's educational and work experiences, and the data-driven environment encouraged by his company and the financial services indus-try. John is definitely an advocate of data and analytics and sees them as a way to challenge judgment and make stronger decisions, but he also recognizes some of their limitations and the way they can be misused or misunderstood.

Questions to think about

1.   Based on your experience and worldview, what are the strengths and weaknesses of John's approach to decision-making? How would you improve his decision-making process?
2.   What kinds of KSAs does John need to most effectively make successful decisions with his team members as well as senior and lower-level managers? Would these KSAs need to change to succeed in organizations that are in different stages of awareness, adoption and maturity?
3.   What kind of issues John might have when working with people who are not analytics-bent? How are the issues different when he works with those from executive management?
4.   How do you think the analytics maturity of the organization, the industry and society in general influence John in his use of analytics for decision-making?
5.   What are the pros and cons of using data-driven decision-making in strategic decisions?
6.   Discuss the impact of contextual factors on the decision-making John is involved in. Which factors do you think have the biggest impact on John's decision-making process? Explain why.

Case Study 8.3

Type B Manager in a Data-Driven Organization

Decision Parameters

Decision Situation: Ongoing decision-making in response to organizational initiatives and external factors

Decision Trigger: Evaluation, routine check, external

Decision Type: Tactical and strategic

Decision Style: Balanced

Manager Type: Type B – All-Rounder

Organizational Analytics Maturity: Mature

Industry Influences: Best practices, highly competitive, data-driven, but in some ways traditional and conservative

Societal Influences: Heavily regulated, legal reporting requirements, possibly pressure from consumer groups, etc.

An example of Type B decision-makers is Sarah. Sarah has been working for 20 years in the New Zealand subsidiary of an Australian-owned bank. She has extensive business understanding and domain experience and is now a senior manager in operations. Once very traditional and conservative, banking has become over the last 20 years or so a highly data-driven industry. Banking operates in a competitive environment and is subject to strict reporting requirements by governments. Since starting out in this data-driven company, Sarah has been using data and analytics in her decision-making, which have provided her with an appreciation of their value. While she never received any formal analytics training, she undertook several in-house and external management training courses, which taught her to analyze problems from different angles using various analytic techniques. Sarah's most recent role was as a leader of a team evaluating the operational model of her organization, which she considered a very data-driven task.

In this role, Sarah regularly takes part in tactical and strategic decisions for the bank, often involving other senior executives, business analysts and data analytics support staff. Many of the decisions Sarah makes rely to a high extent on data – up to 80 per cent – but they also incorporate significant human judgment. This matches her general decision-making type of all-rounder, especially as Sarah explains that the data itself is already full of assumptions, and therefore contains significant amounts of human judgment. She explained: 'You could have a 100 per cent data-driven decision, but it's 50 per cent based on assumptions.'

(Continued)

This awareness of the intertwining of data and judgment usually leads Sarah to follow a balanced decision-making approach. For Sarah this balanced approach begins with a thorough initial assessment involving both judgment and the acquisition of all relevant data and information, similar to Type A decision-makers. However, once the decision-making process reaches the step of developing alternatives, Sarah follows a different approach. While she relies on data experts during this step to conduct the actual analysis of the data, she engages her judgment to sense-check and challenge the data results. As she explains:

> I know what questions to ask, I have a sixth sense in being able to understand if the data is accurate from my questions and from what I hypothesize in my head.

Sarah's business understanding and experience play a significant part in this step of the decision-making process. For the selection step, she then takes advantage of her excellent communication skills to convey the analytics results to other stakeholders:

> I know how to format and present data so that it helps to tell a story. So, I have people that find and create data. I have specialists that then turn data into insights, and then I have people that create insights that support business cases and presentations. I can work with all levels or areas, but I particularly like to work on the presentation end, in the sense of: 'I can show meaningful insights and tell you all a story.'

Comment

This well-rounded and balanced decision-making approach incorporates both Sarah's analytics skills and her judgment. The data-driven environment provided by the industry and company, in combination with the management training courses she attended, certainly supported her in becoming an all-rounder. After 20 years with the company, she identifies with their values and approaches. She shows a high appreciation for data and its potential, but she also understands that accessing and analyzing data are often time-consuming processes and are considered deterrents to data-driven decision-making by many. Sarah also recognizes the potential biases built into data sets and analysis. She recognizes these and other limitations of data analytics and therefore values the balance provided by human judgment when decisions need to be made.

Questions to think about

1. Based on your experience and worldview, what are the strengths and weaknesses of Sarah's approach to decision-making? How could it be improved?
2. What kind of issues might Sarah have when working with people who are not all-rounders? How can she manage these issues?
3. What are the prerequisites or enablers of successful decision-making for all-rounder types?

4. Sarah's organization is at a high level of analytics maturity. How do you think this, as well as the reporting and legal requirements of the banking industry and government, influence Sarah in her use of analytics for balanced decision-making?
5. What are the pros and cons of using balanced decision-making in strategic decisions?
6. Discuss the impact of contextual factors on the decision-making Sarah is involved in. Which factors do you think have the biggest impact on her decision-making process? Explain why.

Case Study 8.4

Type C Manager in an Adoption-Stage Organization

Decision Parameters

Decision Situation: Ongoing in response to internal directives and external customer reports

Decision Trigger: Evaluation, external

Decision Type: Operational/tactical/strategic

Decision Style: High-judgment to balanced

Manager Type: Type C – Uncertain

Organizational Analytics Maturity: Adoption

Industry Influences: Industry has rapidly become more data-driven over the last 20 years; industry can be cooperative but also highly competitive

Societal Influences: Highly government regulated

Mike is a good example of an uncertain decision-maker. Mike has been making decisions in a professional capacity for nine years, supported in part by analytics. Through his previous work engagements and his past five years working in the highly competitive and regulated international transport industry, he has acquired a vast amount of experience and domain knowledge. His decisions tend to be influenced by both, depending on the decision context and circumstances. Mike has attended several management workshops and two short introductions to specific software tools in his previous company. His current company has not provided any additional training.

(Continued)

For the past two years, in his role as manager of his company's support and services team, Mike is often involved in strategic and tactical decisions concerning customer satisfaction and retention. While Mike is used to well-organized and System 2-type structured decision-making, the use of data is not a common component. When he does encounter a decision requiring a relatively high amount of data, he needs the support of team members who are familiar with data analytics. What makes these situations work for Mike is the leadership support and encouragement he and the support teams receive. Particularly the role of leadership was deemed crucial for the positive outcome of this decision, as previous efforts had not been successful. Mike explains:

> I found the leadership role in the organization to be the key. I had tried some elements of the data-supported approach with a previous manager, but that wasn't successful, because he wasn't communicating the expectation (to use data) back to his staff or explaining its value in the decision-making process. But when a new manager started two years ago, I just saw a change overnight in the team's attitude and support – wanting to work together to improve our business.

Comment

In the past Mike's decision-making process matched the organizational culture, resulting in high-judgment decisions predominantly influenced by his extensive domain experience. However, as the organization evolved into a more data-driven culture, Mike also began to incorporate data into his decision-making. He saw the organizational culture as a definite influence on his own decision-making.

Questions to think about

1. What are the strengths and weaknesses of Mike's decision-making style?
2. What roles that you think experience/knowledge and data/analytics play in his decision-making?
3. How can Mike use his current set of KSAs to effectively work with colleagues who are different manager types?
4. What kinds of challenges will he face if his organization continues to evolve in analytics maturity? What kinds of KSAs will Mike need to develop?
5. What can Mike's organization do to help uncertain managers evolve into Type B?

Case Study 8.5

Type D Manager in an Awareness-Stage Company

Decision Parameters

Decision Situation: Owner of business; responsible for all decisions

Decision Trigger: Anecdotal, routine check, external

Decision Type: All types

Decision Style: High-judgment

Manager Type: Type D – Old-Fashioned

Organizational Analytics Maturity: Awareness

Industry Influences: Creative; highly competitive with large international companies

Societal Influences: Technological – Internet, social media, mobile, etc.

Michelle is an example of an old-fashioned decision-maker. For the past five years she has been the 'final' decision-maker as the owner and founder of a small marketing agency. She is involved in all strategic decisions, as well as more tactical and operational ones. For the past two years, analytics has become more relevant for her, as the company grew and allowed for more performance and project data to be collected and analyzed. Furthermore, their clients started having access to more and more data, and requested insights and advice from the agency. These trends are due to the increasing use of social media and other technology-based channels in marketing. Michelle has not had any formal management or analytics training, but through working with her clients' as well as her company's growing amounts of data, she has become more familiar with it. Nevertheless, Michelle mostly relies on her intuition in her decision-making, as she is suspicious of overly relying on or misunderstanding data results. Success with her decisions since the founding of her company gives her confidence and trust in her own judgment. Michelle's decisions follow a high-judgment decision-making approach, based on experience rather than data. As she explains:

> Basically all of my decisions are made based on my experience. I can pull reports and I use those to some extent, but essentially I 'gut feel' over the top of them.

For Michelle, the role of data analytics is limited to exploration or enabler of judgment, which are usually only of relevance for analyzing the results of marketing strategies. These data-based reports somewhat surprisingly only have a small impact on her decision outcomes, tending to be used for enriching her judgment: often she uses her judgment to overrule analytics. Along with her intuition, experience and domain knowledge Michelle also canvasses the perspectives of colleagues and peers. Collaborating with others is a valuable part of her decision-making process. She explains:

> I talk. I talk to a lot of people and I get different opinions on what they would do in this situation.

Competitors in her field provide her with valuable insights as well. From these contacts she learns more about common business models in her industry, which is mostly driven by maximizing profit margin by keeping employee salaries low. Michelle rejects this business model. As she explained:

(Continued)

One of my first decisions when I started this business was to follow my values and judgment instead of going with the numbers and data.

Although the company is small, Michelle reports to a 'board' of financial investors, which approves or rejects key decisions. For this board, data is an essential requirement to provide objective reasoning for new proposals. Michelle therefore concedes the use of the bare minimum of data to justify these decisions in front of the board, but rarely relies on it for her own decision-making.

Comment

Michelle is the founder and owner of her company. It is successful because of her existing KSAs. She trusts her knowledge and experience, and so far so good. But as the company grows she may need to meet customer expectations on the use of data and analytics in analyzing marketing strategies, as well as board demands for quality data to back up her projects and proposals.

Questions to think about

1. Michelle's high-judgment decision-making style is working for her. Should she change it? Why or why not?
2. What kind of decisions are more likely to be made more effectively in Michelle's organization?
3. Considering her KSAs, what are Michelle's relative strengths and weaknesses as the founder and director of her business?
4. How can Michelle respond to environmental factors, such as customers asking for more data-driven marketing strategies or her board asking for more data-supported decision-making?
5. What if the company needs to move up the analytics maturity model in response to contextual factors? How will Michelle be able to manage these changes?

CHAPTER SUMMARY

In this chapter, we have reviewed all the key materials from Chapters 4 to 7. We have recounted the key factors that influence the use of data and analytics in management decision-making. These include: the KSAs and decision-making preferences that most obviously influence a manager's decision-making processes; the organization's analytics maturity level, which often implicitly or explicitly spells out organizational preferences for decision-making; and the industry and societal factors that, while much more indirect than the manager's decision-making type and the organization's decision-making culture, nevertheless often have an effect on the decision-making process by either motivating or constraining certain decision-making behaviors. All of these factors play important roles when an individual manager encounters a decision situation and is required to make a decision.

The relative novelty of big data and analytics and the complexity presented by the factors reviewed in this chapter emphasize the points we made in Chapter 1 when we argued for basic KSA competencies for both managers and information technologists that would allow them to develop shared mental models. We realize now how important it is for managers and information technologists to be able to work together at the team level when incorporating data and analytics into decision-making: i.e. that they understand where each side is coming from and that they are able to ask relevant questions, understand the answers and appropriately use data and analytics.

What we also now understand is that the development of these shared mental models rests with an organization's senior management and top executives. It is they who must take into account the wider environment by recognizing industry leaders, reading the academic research, and following the laws and sentiments of society. It is the organization leaders that set the direction of the organization, decide on the appropriate level of analytics maturity for the organization, and develop the organizational culture and analytics capabilities that guide the development of these shared mental models, which lead to the effective use of data and analytics by individual managers making everyday decisions.

The material presented in this chapter, including the case studies, should help students become aware of the interrelationship and influences of all these factors. There is plenty to keep in mind as you hone your decision-making skills and grow your contextual knowledge of the complex world organizations operate within. In the chapters so far, we have only mentioned some of the wider issues that affect organizations and individual managers. In the next two chapters, we look in greater detail at the deeply relevant security, legal, privacy and ethical issues of data-driven decision-making as well as the emergence of technologies that are very likely to affect decision-making in the near future.

KEY LESSONS

In this chapter we have brought together all of the contextual factors that can influence management decision-making. The most important takeaways can be summarized as:

1. Management decision-making is a highly complex process.
2. The wider environment plays a significant role in the decision-making process.
3. Decision-makers must possess the necessary KSAs and organizations must possess the necessary capabilities for the effective use of data and analytics in decision-making.

9

MANAGING THE ETHICS, SECURITY, PRIVACY AND LEGAL ASPECTS OF DATA-DRIVEN DECISION-MAKING

Contents

Highlight Box 9.1

Summaries of Privacy Policies of Well-Known Organizations

More and more, organizations are being pressured by governments and consumer groups to institute meaningful privacy protections for those users who sign up for their services. Since many of these organizations profit from the collection, analysis and use of this data, they may be reluctant to comply and often make it difficult for consumers to protect their data. Table 9.1 contains summaries of current organizational policies on data and privacy as well as notes on how these policies play out in real life. Keep in mind that these policies are constantly being updated, often in response to new laws and consumer pressure.

Table 9.1 Privacy policies of well-known organizations

Google	Google Safety Centre – Data Privacy (https://safety.google/privacy/data/) • Lists all data that Google collects as you use their services, including search, clicks, history, location (IP), browser information and personal information from Google accounts (including names, password, photos, important dates, comments, etc.). • Google uses this data to optimize services for you in terms of speed and convenience (among other things). • While personal information is not directly sold, it is used to target ads and other messages given to them by advertising agents (either on Google's site, or other sites). • AdSense is the main vehicle, almost anyone with a website can put the code on their page, take a cut of the advertiser payout, and Google gets the rest. • Very clear about not selling data, what data they collect and how they make money via advertising. Note: • There are so many options for users to choose from to control much of what is and is not recorded, or kept for a long time. The vast majority of people will not change the default settings, so default settings matter (Watson et al., 2015).
Facebook	Facebook Data Policy (www.facebook.com/policy.php) • Openly collects all information that gets put on the platform or associated platforms (i.e. messenger, games). Everything gets stored (users can download their data profiles). • Collects all meta data associated with the content provided (i.e. phone/camera type, location of photos, game IDs, Wi-Fi and other connected devices, Bluetooth data, cookies, etc.). • Other sites using Facebook Business Tools (such as the LIKE plugin) provide Facebook with your browsing activities off Facebook platforms. These other sites are responsible for meeting the European Union's new General Data Protection Regulation (GDPR) requirements. Note: • The Court of Justice of the European Union ruled on 29 July 2019 that operators of websites with Facebook 'Like' buttons need to get consent from users to pass that information to Facebook (note that regardless of whether the button has been clicked or not, Facebook gets information of the page view) (Curia, 2019).

(Continued)

Table 9.1   (Continued)

Amazon	Privacy Notice – August 2017 (www.amazon.com/gp/help/customer/display.html?nodeId=468496)

- Amazon stores all information you give it on the site: search, wish list, purchases, addresses, payment, reviews, email addresses of people you buy things for, etc.
- Uses cookies, information from mobile apps, and data from joint ventures with other companies.
- Can get information from third party websites, which host Amazon add-ons and plugins (links to Amazon).
- Shares data with third parties for business purposes, which can include targeting you with ads for Amazon products/services.

Amazon Web Services – Privacy (https://aws.amazon.com/compliance/data-privacy-faq/)

- Amazon is a huge provider of cloud storage (AWS) (https://aws.amazon.com/products/?nc2=h_ql_prod). Unlike Amazon retail, the AWS policy clearly states: 'As a customer, you maintain ownership of your content, and you select which AWS services can process, store, and host your content. We do not access or use your content for any purpose without your consent. We never use customer content or derive information from it for marketing or advertising.'

Note:

- Privacy is seen as very important in the data storage business.

Merck	Data Privacy Policies (www.msdprivacy.com/us/en/transparency-and-privacy.html)

- Has separate documents for different stakeholders: contractors, consultants and other external partners; healthcare professionals; Canadian health care professionals; employment privacy and data protection; us patients, consumers and caregivers; Internet privacy statement; retirees and beneficiaries.
- Global Privacy Principles: respect/trust/prevent harm/comply.
- Self describes adherence to APEC Cross-Border Privacy Rules certification, Privacy Shield, etc.
- States primary data activities: research and manufacturing, commercial research, corporate and HR services, healthcare service delivery.

Web Policy (UK) (www.merckgroup.com/uk-en/privacy-statement.html)

- Similar to a lot of other large EU website policy pages.
- Describes how data is collected, what it will be used for, and the Data Protection Officer details.

Note:

- Pharmaceutical companies deal with huge amounts of medical data, which in many countries has specific laws regarding its handling due to its sensitive nature (privacy and identifiability). Because of the special treatment of medical data (and established laws in many countries for this, unlike more recent types of big data), multinational pharmaceuticals are likely to have more considered and detailed privacy policies.

Toyota	Europe Policy (www.toyota-europe.com/legal/data-privacy-policy) vs Global Policy (https://global.toyota/en/privacy-notice/) vs NZ Policy (www.toyota.co.nz/-/legal-privacy-policy/)

- Different texts – the EU text is formatted more in line with the GDPR requirements.
- Content between the policies appear similar, although formatting is different and reference to relevant legislation is different.

Note:

- The automobile industry is rapidly becoming a hub of sensitive data collection due to new connectivity technologies in cars. Almost every new car comes in with built-in, always-connected technology, recording location and state of the vehicle, as well as music being played, phone contacts, etc.

Samsung	Global Policy (www.samsung.com/nz/info/privacy/)

- Describes collection of information (personal info, device info, operation logs, location, voice recordings, which may go to third party for transcription, keyboard info with predictable text, viewing history, etc.).
- Describes use of third party analytics and who they share information with.
- Describes purposes for which information is used.
- Highlights rights (consistent with GDPR rights).

Note:

- Software recording what and when viewers watch: manufacturers are installing microphones and cameras to potentially record users viewing the TV. These are potentially hackable (Doffman, 2019).

Proctor & Gamble	Global Consumer Privacy (www.pg.com/privacy/english/privacy_statement.shtml)

- Data privacy policy in line with GDPR. States what data is collected, how and for what purpose, reasonable use, connection apps, who they share data with, etc.
- Note that the GDPR rights only seem 'accessible' if you live in an area covered by the GDPR (i.e. right to amend/be forgotten).

Questions to think about

1. Do you read company data use policies before signing up with a company? Why or why not?
2. List and discuss the top five risks of data being collected by social media apps (you can choose one you are familiar with).
3. In what ways, if any, do company data use policies change your behavior with regard to the data you generate?
4. Do you feel companies are entitled to collect and use data in exchange for the services they provide users? Explain your position.
5. Who should profit from customer data: companies or customers? Explain.

CHAPTER 9 KEY LESSONS

1. Issues of ethics, privacy, security and legality of data collection and use are increasingly important for organizations to take into account.
2. These issues are interlinked, complex and fluid. Sophisticated, dedicated organizational responses are required.
3. Senior management and organizational directors will need to take responsibility for the ongoing management of these issues. This will require a 'whole of organization' response.

INTRODUCTION

One of the most important aspects of the use of big data and analytics in management decision-making concerns the issues around the ethical, security, privacy and legal aspects of the acquisition, storage and use of data. These are different but interrelated issues that are gaining broad attention at all levels of society with government, industry, academia, non-government organizations (NGOs), business and individual citizens, including the consumers and end-users of technology. The numerous and deeply concerning issues around the ethical, security, privacy and legal aspects of the acquisition, storage and use of data are worthy of their own books, articles and websites and there are many available (see Further Reading). In this chapter we will focus primarily on explaining and relating these issues to organizational-level data acquisition and use in management decision-making, including decision-making about how to address these issues. We begin this chapter by first discussing the key issues in general terms, then look in more detail at ethics and privacy, legal requirements and finally organizational and management issues related to data security and use. Throughout the chapter we link these issues to the ecological model of management decision-making and the organizational analytics maturity model (Chapter 7).

Private companies and governments now have access to increasing amounts of personal data generated by the moment-to-moment activities of Internet users captured by a wide range of technologies and data sources (Intezari and Pauleen, 2019). If data is potential knowledge and knowledge is power, then unbridled access to data may lead to various kinds of inequalities with serious implications for organizations accessing, owning, aggregating and using large data sets (Boyd and Crawford, 2012). From a narrow management perspective, companies and government agencies are faced with the question of how to best utilize growing amounts of 'big data' (Davenport and Harris, 2017), but from the wider perspective informed by the ecological framework of management decision-making discussed in Chapter 7, it is increasingly clear that organizations must also address issues of privacy, consent and security of people's personal data. Expediting the need to address organizational systems and ethics are the rapidly developing technologies constituting social and wearable media, the Internet of Things, smart homes, wearable devices, robotics, and augmented and virtual reality (Livingstone et al., 2018). Arguably, an organization's analytics maturity is reflected in how well it develops appropriate policies and practices to effectively secure and respectfully use data from customers, employees, third parties, business and supply chain partners, etc.

While issues of ethics, security, privacy and legality of data use in management decision-making involve governments as well as organizations, in this chapter we focus primarily on how these issues affect organizational use of data, which of course includes government laws that may restrict and regulate how organizations can use data. In general, lessons regarding how these issues apply to management decision-making in organizations are also likely to apply to management decision-making in government.

The Issues

For our purposes, there are four levels of consideration when contemplating the ethical, privacy, security and legal aspects concerning the use of data in relationship to management decision-making – industry, the organization, the individual decision-maker and the organization's customers. Most public and academic attention is focused on the consumer and the organizational levels (government is being considered in the chapter primarily as an environmental influence, e.g. writing and enforcing laws around data collection and use). Industries set the tone in the collection and use of data. This is seen most clearly in the technology and tech-based industries, particularly those that revolve around the Internet, social media and mobile devices. The big companies in these industries, such as Amazon, Google and Facebook, derive huge amounts of value from the data they collect and this data plays a fundamental role in all aspects of their decision-making from operational to strategic. But many companies, large and small, from Uber to those providing free or low-cost apps for mobile devices, are collecting and then using or selling data. Other industries, especially those that are 'connected' through various kinds of telecommunications and computer networks, are also collecting the data that passes through their networks. These include financial services such as banking, retail, marketing and transportation. Many industries and businesses, large and small, are now using web pages and web-based apps to generate and collect data. In almost all these situations, much of the data that is collected is from individual 'users' of the services being offered, and this data is being used in management decision-making.

In an interconnected world, where information systems are embedded in the activities of daily life, all types of data are being generated in vast amounts in real time (Chapter 2). This data is being vacuumed up by organizations, analyzed and used, often without the knowledge of those who create the data, e.g. end-user consumers. Even when users 'give consent' for the collection and use of their data, they are unaware of the true scope or implications of the use of this data. As this situation has grown and the consequences of unbridled data collection and use become more apparent, consumers become more concerned and eventually governments step in to regulate this data market. Organizations are affected and must respond. Of course, consumers and consumer groups also directly attempt to pressure organizations. Social media has proved to be an effective channel for relaying consumer grievances, often forcing organizations to respond in real time to ethical and security issues raised by consumers.

In general, 'users' in today's socio-technical discourse of these issues refers to individuals, usually thought of as consumers, who generate data in their daily technology-enabled activities, such as surfing the web, shopping online, and using (and simply carrying) their mobile phones. With the emergence of new technologies, these users are increasing data generation though the use of smart homes, smart cars, the Internet of Things, etc. (see Chapter 10). All of this data is being captured and used, much of it by organizations such as private corporations. These organizations can also be considered 'users' of data, but more accurately can be understood as collectors, consolidators and analyzers of data, which they then use to achieve organizational goals that include supporting management decision-making. The issues around the ethical, security, privacy and legal aspects discussed in this chapter concern the generation, acquisition and use of this data and are summarized in Table 9.2

Table 9.2 Issues around data generation, acquisition and use

Context	Issues
Privacy and Ethics	Consumer uncertainty • Who is collecting data? • How is data being collected? • What is the purpose of data being collected? • What is being done with the collected data? How is it used? • What type of data is being collected? • Is data being shared with other parties? • Has user consent for the use of data been received? • Who owns the data? • Is there any policy around data?
Security	Consumer uncertainty • About data security Business uncertainty • About data security, including technical and managerial issues
Legal	Business uncertainty • What is the legal environment around data collection and use? • How to assure consistency for different countries in terms of data storage, transmission and integration, etc. • How to address the use and impact around new emerging technologies

PRIVACY AND ETHICS OF DATA ACQUISITION AND USE

The issues of privacy and the ethics of data acquisition and use are interlinked and the views about them are varied. On the one hand, there is a view that there is a quid pro quo in the provision of services by companies such as Facebook, which offer a free service to their users in exchange for the collection and use of their data. Users 'agree' to this exchange when they sign up for Facebook. On the other hand, most users do not read the full consent agreement and even if they do, these consent agreements are often written in a way that can be difficult to understand. Users are often startled by the use of their data, and given a better understanding of the consequences they might not have given their consent (Matzner, 2014). In this regard, it is argued by some (e.g. Mantelero and Vaciago, 2015) that users are not in fact providing informed consent. This ambiguity around consent can be considered an ethical, and increasingly a legal, issue. Since the issue of whether consent is freely and knowledgeably given is uncertain, it follows that the obligations inherent in the consent – i.e. ownership and use of data – are also uncertain.

In addition to the question of consent and ownership, there is the question of what the organizations that are collecting this data are doing with it (Matzner, 2014). In his work on big data ethics, Zwitter (2014) refers to this lack of awareness about the collection and use of data as an ethical disadvantage related to a lack of knowledge on the part of the user and hence a lack of genuine free will in choosing to give consent. Big data is considered a threat to the user's privacy, in particular because of its variety dimension, enabling the integration of data sets from multiple sources (Lodha et al., 2014). Anonymized data sets in their original context might not pose any privacy threats for users, but through combination with other data sets collected for different purposes they might reveal the user's identity or other private information. An example of this is provided by Boyd and Crawford (2012) in their critical article on big data. Harvard researchers had released anonymized social media data from students to the public, which was then partially deanonymized by other researchers exploring the data set. This privacy breach affected the students, who had no knowledge of their data being collected.

Velocity is another dimension that bears scrutiny. Because data can now be collected and analyzed in real time, users can be tracked wherever and whenever they are generating data, which can be as innocuous as carrying or wearing a mobile device. Such data generation allows companies to target users anytime with marketing pitches, but it can also allow hackers with malicious intent to follow and track people (Mao et al., 2017). One might well ask what legal or ethical responsibility a company bears if their product is in some way responsible for a user being harmed.

Consider This Box 9.2

The Case of Privacy, Ethics and Social Media

Social media data is a particularly interesting part of the privacy debate, with public posts marking a new territory for ethical considerations, as Boyd and Crawford (2012: 762) point out:

> Very little is understood about the ethical implications underpinning the Big Data phenomenon. [...] What if someone's 'public' blog post is taken out of context and analyzed in a way that the author never imagined? What does it mean for someone to be spotlighted or to be analyzed without knowing it? Who is responsible for making certain that individuals and communities are not hurt by the research process? What does informed consent look like?

Questions to think about

1. What are the most common social media sites/apps you use in your daily and business life?
2. In your opinion, who owns a 'public post' on the Internet: the writer or the hosting site? Can anyone or any company take the content and re-use it for any purpose? What, if any, are the ethical implications for doing so?
3. In what ways, if any, is your behavior on social media influenced by knowing that your data could be used for various purposes?
4. Several famous people have been called out for posts (often historic) on social media. Would you consider this 'cancel culture' a positive or negative development? Explain.

Social media companies, such as Twitter or WhatsApp, are often under scrutiny, as their privacy policies do not clearly specify the current and future use of the data shared on their platforms as well as other collected data about the user (Alharthi et al., 2017). From an ethical point of view, organizations should carefully consider the use of social media data. Simply having access to the data does not justify the analysis of it. This ethical challenge extends beyond the case of social media to other forms of big data as well, for example, personal health-related data generated by wearable devices.

Privacy has become a global issue, making it important for governments and businesses to address digital rights issues and develop effective policy frameworks around issues of consent, profiling and big data analytics. The recent EU General Data Protection Regulation (GDPR), which aims to give all Internet users knowledge and control over their personal data, has at the same time provided a somewhat simplistic regulatory guide for businesses when collecting and holding personal data but does not necessarily provide safeguards and protections for Internet users. Many Internet users remain unaware of how their personal information, digital activities and choices are collected by organizations (Goggin et al., 2017) and desire more transparency around personal data collection and use. As it stands, consumers have few avenues to access information about third-party use of personal information, and find out who these third parties are (Marwick and Boyd, 2014). With few options other than opting out of services, consumers are making trade-offs that may not be in their best interests.

Consider This Box 9.3

What Does Ethical Online Retail Behavior Look Like?

In this chapter, we are considering the issues of ethics, privacy, security and legality in organizational data management. But what is the relationship of these issues and how do they manifest in the real world for organizations and consumers?

In a study of e-retailing ethics (Elbeltagi and Agag, 2016), researchers surveyed Egyptian students to determine what factors the students considered important in order for an e-retailer to demonstrate ethical conduct. Five factors were considered essential:

1. Security – the safety of transaction/payment
2. Privacy – the degree to which information is passed on/sold to third parties
3. Non-deception – not feeling deceived by retailer marketing
4. Fulfillment/reliability – getting the product they wanted, in the time frame expected
5. Service recovery – the efforts made by the retailer to 'fix' problems that may occur.

The study found that the five factors were strongly predictive of consumer satisfaction, and that consumer trust, satisfaction and commitment were all positively associated with perception of a company's e-retail ethics. Customer satisfaction was also found to be mediated by trust and customer relationship. The online security of transactions was seen as the primary ethical concern of students.

Questions to think about

1. What can organizations that operate online take away from these findings, e.g. how can they apply these findings to their own data strategies and related business processes?
2. How important and in what ways are ethical data policies and practices linked to an organization's analytics maturity?
3. What is your understanding of the effects of these five factors on ethical behavior in online business? Would these factors be relevant in other types of online activity such as Facebook and Twitter? Explain.
4. This study surveyed Egyptian students. Do you think the results would be similar for students in your country? Would they extend to non-students as well? Explain your answers.

Organizations, particularly those that profit from the collection and use of data, but also those that include such data in their operational and strategic decision-making, should be concerned about ethical use of data as there can be substantial public relations consequences should lapses become public (e.g. Facebook and Cambridge Analytica). Even more importantly, organizations must take into account the legal ramifications of data use. There has been something of a 'wild west' attitude of 'anything goes' to the use of big data by organizations in the past, but this is rapidly changing as consumers and governments seek to regulate data collection and use. A critical part of an organization's analytics maturity is its policies and practices addressing the legal issues around data collection and use.

LEGAL OBLIGATIONS IN ORGANIZATIONAL DATA COLLECTION AND USE

For more than 20 years, organizations have had a more or less free ride from government when it comes to ensuring data privacy and security and their privacy policies tend to reflect this, usually allowing end users little choice when it comes to ensuring data privacy or security. Big data and analytics and enabling technologies like the Internet and mobile phones and telecommunications networks have become part of embedded information systems with very little discussion of how they affect individuals and society. Privacy laws that were promulgated more than 25 years ago often have little relevance in today's data-driven world, and even serious data breaches exposing tens of thousands of peoples' data can rarely be punished under these laws. However, this attitude of benign neglect is rapidly changing. Organizations have arguably overstepped ethical boundaries concerning data usage and have again and again proven unable to secure data (see Table 9.6 below). In response to consumer and citizen demands, governments are beginning to pass and enforce ever-stricter laws that will change the way organizations handle and use personal data. Highlight Box 9.4 highlights privacy laws from a number of countries. It's worth paying attention to the changing language and focus of the newer laws.

Highlight Box 9.4

Government Legislation on Data and Privacy

In Table 9.3 examples of legislation covering privacy are given. Privacy legislation tends to focus on personal consumer-oriented data and privacy vis-à-vis private and public organizations. Much of the legislation is old and does not address the realities of today's data-driven world. The most impactful legislation on data and privacy is the EU's GDPR of 2018. Consumer groups, such as Californians for Consumer Privacy, are currently pushing for stronger legal protections for consumers. In the United States, legislation seems to be gaining traction at the state level.

Table 9.3 Privacy legislation

	Legislation – Privacy
Australia	Primary Legislation: Federal Privacy Act 1988 (www.legislation.gov.au/Details/C2014C00076) Privacy Principles of the Act (www.oaic.gov.au/privacy/australian-privacy-principles/read-the-australian-privacy-principles/) Notifiable Data Breach scheme (www.oaic.gov.au/privacy/guidance-and-advice/data-breach-preparation-and-response/part-4-notifiable-data-breach-ndb-scheme/): • Part of the Privacy Act – IIIC, from February 2018 onwards. • Any entities that are public, in particular sectors (i.e. health, finance) or have over $3 million in annual revenue *and* have obligations under the Privacy Act have obligations to report data breaches publicly (to the Office of the Australian Information Commissioner). Federal legislation is limited, so states have their own varying privacy legislation, for example: • Information Privacy Act 2014 (Australian Capital Territory) (www.legislation.act.gov.au/a/2014-24/default.asp) • Information Act 2002 (Northern Territory) (https://legislation.nt.gov.au/en/Legislation/INFORMATION-ACT-2002) • Privacy and Personal Information Protection Act 1998 (New South Wales) (www.legislation.nsw.gov.au/#/view/act/1998/133) • Information Privacy Act 2009 (Queensland) (www.legislation.qld.gov.au/view/pdf/inforce/2017-06-05/act-2009-014) • Personal Information Protection Act 2004 (Tasmania) (www.legislation.tas.gov.au/view/html/inforce/current/act-2004-046) • Privacy and Data Protection Act 2014 (Victoria) (www.legislation.vic.gov.au/in-force/acts/privacy-and-data-protection-act-2014/025) Western Australia and South Australia do not have their own data protection legislation. Telecommunications and Other Legislations Amendment (Assistance and Access) Act 2018 (www.legislation.gov.au/Details/C2018A00148) provides law enforcement authorities with access to encrypted data for serious crime investigations, and in some cases provides technical capital to help. CDR (Consumer Data Right) (https://treasury.gov.au/consumer-data-right-bill) is (at time of writing) an amendment to the Competition and Consumer Act 2010. Targeted mostly at large banks, the CDR aims to empower customers to give their data only to third parties they approve. Note: The Telecommunications and Other Legislations Amendment Act (2018) passed in the last week of December, 2019.

(Continued)

Table 9.3   (Continued)

Legislation – Privacy

European Union	Charter of Fundamental Rights: Article 8 (https://eur-lex.europa.eu/legal-content/EN/TXT/?uri=CELEX:12012P/TXT) *Article 8* **Protection of personal data** • Everyone has the right to the protection of personal data concerning him or her. Data Protection Law Enforcement Directive (April 2016) (https://ec.europa.eu/info/law/law-topic/data-protection/data-protection-eu_en): • Sets rules for when personal data is used for 'prevention, investigation, detection or persecution of criminal offences'. General Data Protection Regulation (GDPR) (May 2018) (https://gdpr.eu/what-is-gdpr/): • Possibly the most impactful data privacy legislation to date, worldwide (see https://gdpr.eu/what-is-gdpr/ for details of this regulation).
New Zealand	Privacy Act 1993 (www.legislation.govt.nz/act/public/1993/0028/latest/DLM296639.html) Privacy Principles of the Act (https://privacy.org.nz/the-privacy-act-and-codes/privacy-principles/): • Data breach notification is not mandatory, but it is likely new amendments to the Privacy Act (Privacy Bill 34) (www.legislation.govt.nz/bill/government/2018/0034/latest/whole.html#contents) will introduce this requirement (www.privacy.org.nz/further-resources/knowledge-base/view/331).
United States	Unlike the EU, data privacy is not covered in all-encompassing federal law(s). Data usually belongs to whoever creates the record of it, not who or what the data signifies. The US has a number of sector-specific laws covering data privacy and security, for example: • Health Insurance Portability and Accountability Act (1996) (www.govinfo.gov/content/pkg/PLAW-104publ191/pdf/PLAW-104publ191.pdf) – allows identified users in medical data the ability to access and transfer information (and consent must be sought). • Fair Credit Reporting Act (1970) (www.ftc.gov/system/files/545a_fair-credit-reporting-act-0918.pdf) – credit reports, and limits to sharing credit/debt information. • Gramm Leach Bliley/Financial Services Modernization Act (1999) (www.govinfo.gov/content/pkg/PLAW-106publ102/pdf/PLAW-106publ102.pdf) – governs protection of personal information within the finance sector (they have to inform user of what is happening, but you often have to opt out to stop it). • Electronics Communications Privacy Act (1986) (https://it.ojp.gov/PrivacyLiberty/authorities/statutes/1285) – restrictions on wire-tapping and such activities. • Driver's Privacy Protection Act (1994) (https://epic.org/privacy/drivers/andwww.congress.gov/bill/103rd-congress/house-bill/3365) – covers information gathered by the Department of Motor Vehicle (DMV) like photos, social security and driver numbers, phone number, etc.

- Children's Online Privacy Protection Act (1998) (www.ecfr.gov/cgi-bin/text-idx?SID=4939e77c77a1a1a08c1cbf905fc4b409&node=16%3A1.0.1.3.36&rgn=div5) – prevents/restricts collection of online data from children under 13.
- Video Privacy Protection Act (1988) (https://epic.org/privacy/vppa/) – prevents wrongful disclosure of video/stream rentals.

Federal Trade Commission (FTC) Act (1914) (www.ftc.gov/sites/default/files/documents/statutes/federal-trade-commission-act/ftc_act_incorporatingus_safe_web_act.pdf):

- One of the larger acts in regard to enforcing data privacy, empowers the FTC to 'prevent … unfair or deceptive acts or practices in or affecting commerce' and 'prescribe trade regulations rules'.
- The FTC is the main enforcer/watchdog at the federal level.

Note: In 2019, the Federal Trade Commission fined Facebook $5 billion dollars for violating consumers' privacy rights in a case prompted by the Cambridge Analytica scandal.

While Federal law changes have been slow, a number of states have moved ahead with data privacy laws, bringing GDPR-like individual rights to state residents. These include California, Oregon, New Jersey, New York, Washington, Maine and Illinois in 2019.

California Consumer Privacy Act (CCPA) (2018, enacted 1 January 2020) (www.caprivacy.org/):

- Forefront of US legislation on data privacy legislation.
- Provides Californian residents with similar rights as the GDPR: right to know what is being collected, who the data is being sold to, right to refuse collection/sharing, right to be forgotten, etc.
- Sets conditions for opting-out of collection/sale, collection from minors, fines for violations.
- Defines personal data (i.e. personally identifiable data).

Note: The CCPA applies to companies operating in California. However, some companies, such as Microsoft, have already said they will extend these standards to all their US customers. For a summary chart of current US state data privacy laws, see US State Comprehensive Privacy Law Comparison at: https://iapp.org/news/a/us-state-comprehensive-privacy-law-comparison/.

Questions to think about

1. Is data privacy and security an issue in your country? What are the issues raised in relation to companies and consumers?
2. Review the legislation on data privacy in your country. Do you think it is appropriate? What could be changed to improve protection of personal data?
3. Where is the pressure for stronger data privacy legislation coming from in your country? Who are the players and what are the issues?
4. What kind of challenges and benefits would legislation bring to organizations?
5. Do you think is it possible and useful to have legislation at the global level? Discuss.

The strongest legislation in effect over the last few years has been the General Data Protection Regulation developed by the European Union (EU), which went into effect in 2018. The GDPR imposes obligations onto organizations anywhere if the organization targets or collects data related to people in the EU. As many organizations operate globally, even organizations headquartered outside of the EU must conform to the GDPR if they operate in the EU. Those companies that violate the GDPR privacy and security standards are subject to harsh fines and penalties reaching into the tens of millions of euros.

A number of well-known non-EU-based companies have already been targeted by the EU, including Facebook. In an October 2019 ruling, the EU's highest court ruled that Facebook could be ordered by member states to remove defamatory material worldwide, not just in EU member countries. In July 2019 the European Commission opened a formal investigation into Amazon to assess whether the e-retailer was complying with European rules on managing data from independent retailers. And in December 2019, the EU opened preliminary investigations into Google and Facebook's data practices, assessing whether the two US tech firms are complying with its rules in the region. These investigations are based on GDPR legislation and whether they are commercially or politically motivated attempts by the EU to contain dominant market players from other countries, they nevertheless clearly signal the EU's firm stance on data privacy and security at a time when more people are entrusting their personal data to cloud services, and breaches are a regular occurrence.

According to the GDPR.EU, 'the regulation itself is large, far-reaching, and fairly light on specifics, making GDPR compliance a daunting prospect, particularly for small and medium-sized enterprises (SMEs)'. And yet, for organizations wanting to operate in the EU, they must comply. If other countries (or important US states like California) adopt similar regulations, organizations will have to prioritize their data strategies to comply with these regulations. Legal compliance will become a significant indicator of an organization's analytics maturity as noted in Chapter 7.

The EU regulations and impending regulations from other government entities represent a huge change in the environment in which organizations have operated to this point – in which essentially there has been little or no regulation on data collection and use. Until this point, from a legal perspective, most organizations that have been processing user data rely on 'notice and consent' models, outlining the purpose of the collected data and the limitation of its use (Mantelero and Vaciago, 2015: 105) as shown in Highlight Box 9.1 at the beginning of this chapter. Clearly, new regulations will change this. Figure 9.1 highlights some organizational responses to the GDPR.

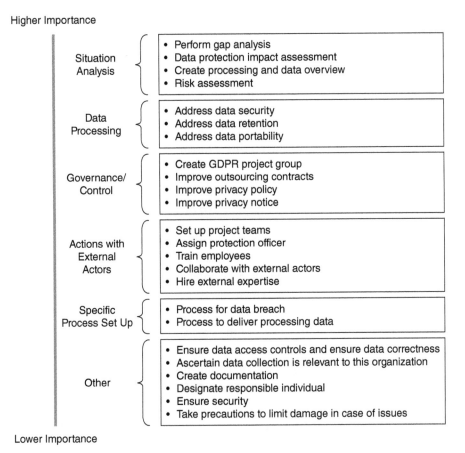

Higher Importance

Situation Analysis
- Perform gap analysis
- Data protection impact assessment
- Create processing and data overview
- Risk assessment

Data Processing
- Address data security
- Address data retention
- Address data portability

Governance/ Control
- Create GDPR project group
- Improve outsourcing contracts
- Improve privacy policy
- Improve privacy notice

Actions with External Actors
- Set up project teams
- Assign protection officer
- Train employees
- Collaborate with external actors
- Hire external expertise

Specific Process Set Up
- Process for data breach
- Process to deliver processing data

Other
- Ensure data access controls and ensure data correctness
- Ascertain data collection is relevant to this organization
- Create documentation
- Designate responsible individual
- Ensure security
- Take precautions to limit damage in case of issues

Lower Importance

Figure 9.1 How organizations comply with GDPR

Source: based on Seerden et al., 2018

When planning for the collection and use of big data, organizations need to account for these ethical and legal challenges in their data strategies to avoid controversies and financial repercussions (Motamarri et al., 2017). These are big challenges for organizations and it will entail sophisticated and dedicated efforts, which will be among the most significant challenges in achieving organizational analytics maturity. How to manage this process and these challenges is well beyond the scope of this book, but Kemp (2014: 491) offers this advice in his work on the legal aspects of managing big data:

A sound analytical legal model for understanding the rights and duties that arise in relation to Big Data in order to manage risk, and the development of a structured approach to legally compliant and software enhanced Big Data input, processing and output will be essential factors for successful Big Data projects and their governance and management.

However, the challenges for organizations may extend beyond meeting new legal requirements. This is because big data and analytics discover insights through integrating and analyzing different data sources. Along with constantly emerging new technologies (Chapter 10), it may be nearly impossible for organizations to disclose all possible uses at the point of data collection or even to know what the points of data collection will be. Organizations, consumers and regulators will all be asking the question: How can we 'trust an organisation with information when the organisation does not yet know how the information might be used in the future?' (Nunan and Di Domenico, 2013: 5).

Governments, Organizations and Big Data

While this chapter primarily focuses on organizational/business use of data, it is worth thinking about how governments use citizen data. As with most organizations, many governments are eager to exploit big data in order to improve efficiencies across government services and improve management decision-making. However, the use of data matching and analytics by governments, or private agencies contracted by governments, raises distinct questions about the power of the state and what kinds of personal information governments possess and how they use this data. For individuals there is little choice about providing personal information to governments (Goggin et al., 2017). A little bit of digging through the laws in Highlight Box 9.5 will show that governments tend to allow themselves wider latitude in the collection and use of data than they allow private industry, often for reasons of national security or law enforcement. Indeed, these laws often give governments legal access to an organization's customer data. As government information systems (from income tax to traffic cameras) are increasingly embedded in all areas of society, the opportunities for data collection by governments are wide and varied. With powerful analytics, governments are now capable of knowing just about anything about any individual citizen. Some find this a troubling proposition and seek to inform the public about it (e.g. the Electronic Frontier Foundation, www.eff.org).

Highlight Box 9.5

Governments, Big Data and National Security

While many governments have been somewhat slow to pass laws on consumer data privacy, they have been much more responsive to national data security by passing laws that often give governments access to citizen data in the name of national security. These laws may also require organizations to give the government access to the organization's customer data. This may involve forcing companies to, for example, turn over encryption keys, make user locations available, and build in 'backdoor' access to mobile devices. Once these laws and practices are established, they are unlikely to be reversed. Table 9.4 sources current security legislation from Australia, the EU, New Zealand and the United States.

Table 9.4   Current security legislation from Australia, the EU, New Zealand and the United States

	Legislation – Security
Australia	Australian Security Intelligence Organisation (www.asio.gov.au/) Australian Cyber Security Centre (www.cyber.gov.au/): • Interagency hub responsible for cyber security. • Intelligence monitoring online, encryption, security advice and services, response to cyber attacks. • Seems to have a broader mandate than NZ counterpart (provides a lot of general information for smaller enterprises).
European Union	European Union Agency for Cybersecurity (ENISA) (www.enisa.europa.eu/): • Originally European Network and Information Security Agency. EU Cybersecurities Act (17 April 2019, enacted 27 June 2019) (https://ec.europa.eu/digital-single-market/en/eu-cybersecurity-act): • Grants ENISA a permanent mandate within the EU, 15 years after initial founding, €23 million over a five- year budget. • Introduces EU-wide rules for cyber security certification.
New Zealand	Government Communications Security Bureau (GCSB) (www.gcsb.govt.nz/) National Cyber Security Centre (www.ncsc.govt.nz/): • Can be contacted after a cyber security incident involving 'nationally significant organisation'. • Administers IT equipment destruction/disposal. • Administers crypto registers and advises 'nationally significant organisations' on cryptosecurity, storage, cloud computing, etc.
United States	Cybersecurity and Infrastructure Agency Act (CISA) of 2018 (www.congress.gov/bill/115th-congress/house-bill/3359): • Amends the Homeland Security Act of 2002 to establish CISA. Cybersecurity and Infrastructure Agency (www.dhs.gov/CISA): • Cyber and communications protection for government (local, state, federal), private sector and international partners. • Infrastructure assessment. • Election security (voting systems, databases, storage, polling places), 'hometown security' (school and active shooter safety). • Cyber awareness education, training, warnings, detailed analysis of threats (www.us-cert.gov/ncas). • Specifically monitoring Chinese Malicious Cyber Activity (www.us-cert.gov/china.) US Cyber Strategy (www.whitehouse.gov/wp-content/uploads/2018/09/National-Cyber-Strategy.pdf)

(Continued)

Questions to think about

1. In your opinion, should governments be able collect and analyze citizen data? Should there be limits to this right? If so, what should the limits be and who should decide?
2. Even if laws force organizations to turn over customer data to governments, are there ethical reasons why organizations should not do so? Explain why or why not.
3. Are there inherent differences between the collection and use of data by business or government? What are they?

ORGANIZATIONAL STANDARDS FOR DATA SECURITY AND USE

Besides establishing a legal model and ensuring ethical conduct, security aspects need to be considered from both management and technical perspectives. The main technical issues are summarized in Table 9.5. In this section we will concentrate on some of the management issues around data security. These issues primarily concern the influences of the environment on management decision-making regarding security and their relation to organizational analytics maturity including:

- corporate governance and decision-making regarding data security
- extent of consumer control features allowed by organizations
- corporate data breaches and their effects on public relations
- hacking.

Corporate Governance and Decision-Making on Data Security

Corporate governance in the age of big data is subject to intense challenges. With large volumes of potentially highly valuable data being collected, organizations must be concerned with data security challenges, legal obligations, and policies on the fair and ethical use of data. We have already discussed the kinds of legal obligations and ethical issues that organizations are facing. Here we introduce some of the key data security issues that senior management must grapple with. These are highlighted in Table 9.5.

Table 9.5 Security issues and their management

General Sources of Security Issues	Type of Security Threat	Preventive and Mitigating Controls to Threats	Detection and Recovery Technical Controls to Threats
Lack of cyber security measures	Hacking	Authentication	Audit
	Social engineering	Authorization	Intrusion detection and containment
Lack of or limited understanding of cyber security risks	Intrusion	Access control	
	Unauthorized system access	Enforcement	Proof of wholeness
Lack of policy on cyber security		Non-repudiation	Restore secure state
	System penetration		Virus detection and eradication
Confusion between policy and compliance	System sabotage	Protected communications	
	Information theft and/or sale	Transaction privacy	
Malevolent insiders		Examples of solutions for security issues (i.e. on network security, Internet security, endpoint (device level) security, cloud security, application security):	
Policy on bring-your-own-device	Economic exploitation		
Lack of sufficient investment on cyber security resources	Malware and ransomware	Firewalls	
	Virus	Intrusion prevention system (IPS)	
Lack of training	Spyware	Data loss prevention system (DLP)	
Lack of recovery plan	Server or software vulnerabilities	Anti-spam/virus filters	
Emerging new risks	Cloud and mobility vulnerabilities	Cloud access service broker (CASB)	
		Web security gateway solutions, etc.	
	Fraud		
	Blackmail		

Source: Barker (2017); Bianculli (2019); Cisco (2019); Stoneburner et al., (2002)

As can be seen from Table 9.5, security related issues are diverse and involve a wide variety of human and technical factors to contain them. An in-depth analysis of these issues is beyond the scope of this book, but these are critical governance issues that senior management must deal with.

The Extent of Consumer Control Features Allowed by Organizations and Consumer Pushback

As we discussed in the chapter introduction, and as seen in Highlight Box 9.1, organizations have policies regarding user privacy and use of user data. As pointed out, the issues around these policies and consent agreements are whether they are understandable and practicable from the user's point of view. In many cases, it seems that organizations are intentionally obfuscating these agreements to make it difficult for users to, in fact, give informed consent. Moreover, many organizations have adopted 'opt in' forms of security management for users, meaning that when users sign up on organizations' websites or download apps, the users are automatically assigned settings optimally set for organizational data collection and use. Opting out of these settings often requires significant effort on the part of users to find and adjust these settings. These decisions to optimize data collection and use at the expense of user privacy and security are decided by senior management. The fact that governments are now creating and enforcing regulations on end-user privacy and security demonstrate just how problematic these organizational policies have become. Organizations will be legally enforced to comply with these new and changing laws.

Moreover, consumer rights groups are also demanding more meaningful privacy policies and more secure data protection including easier access to privacy control features. End-users getting paid for the data they produce and share has also been raised by consumer groups and academics (Lim et al., 2018). Going further, researchers are proposing automated personal technological solutions to protect users against increasingly hazardous and predatory behaviors and to ensure end-user data privacy. For example, the Exosoul project has developed a research framework that the authors expect will lead to a personal software exoskeleton, basically a digital interface between users and the digital world, which will protect users. The level of protection will be set by the users according to their own ethical preferences and the extent of data privacy they desire (Autili et al., 2019).

Organizations can expect that consumers and government will continue to push for more consumer rights when it comes to data privacy and security, and these are issues that management needs to consider when setting organizational data strategies and policies.

Corporate Data Breaches and Their Effects on Public Relations

Data security for organizations is a critical issue, and one that organizations seem to fail on a regular basis. Table 9.6 highlights just a few of the many and regularly increasing breaches of corporate data security. It is worth noting that the hack of Sprint took place through a compromised Samsung website and that the commentary regarding the Toyota hack focused on the fact that automakers have become attractive targets because cars have become hubs of data generation though the incorporation of in-car Wi-Fi, voice-based assistants, automated driver assist and other technologies. These interlinking business systems represent new and significant challenges for organizational data security systems.

Table 9.6 Examples of corporate data breaches in 2019 from around the world

Company	Breach	Company Response	Source
Air New Zealand	Personal Airpoints data of 112,000 customers leaked (2019)	The company waited nine days to notify customers	Foxcroft (2019)
Sephora (multinational beauty retailer)	Security breach of its online users' data, affecting customers from New Zealand, Australia, Hong Kong SAR and Southeast Asia	The company took precautionary action by canceling all existing passwords for customer accounts and have reviewed their security systems	Andelane (2019) Shaw (2019)
Capital One (bank)	A hacker gained access to more than 100 million Capital One customer accounts and credit card applications	The company stated it had fixed the vulnerability and said it is 'unlikely that the information was used for fraud or disseminated by this individual'	McLean (2019)
Sprint/Samsung	Threat actors gained unauthorized access to an undisclosed number of Sprint customer accounts via a compromised Samsung website	The company re-secured customer accounts as well as notified those affected that their account PIN may have been compromised and instructed them to change their PIN	Abel (2019)
Toyota	Toyota Motor Corporation has been the victim of a series of data breaches in Australia, Thailand, Vietnam and Japan; the last data breach in Japan was the most serious in nature, affecting the personal information of as many as 3.1 million customers	Toyota said the data breach has been contained, and that there is no evidence that cyber attackers have been able to exfiltrate any personal information for nefarious purposes	Ikeda (2019)

Hacking

Hacking is perhaps the most serious issue facing organizational data security. Just as organizations have found great value in collecting customer data, so have criminals and governments. As exemplified in Table 9.6, hacking company data can get criminals a great deal of personal and credit information, which can be used in identity and credit card theft, blackmail and other forms of crime. Hacking may also be done by corporate competitors and government agents looking for competitive advantages. The hacking of organizational data is a very common occurrence reported on a near-weekly basis in the press. We must also suspect that a great deal of successful hacks remain unreported in an effort to avoid public scrutiny. Most hacking is malicious and done by so-called black hat hackers. Those called white hat hackers also hack but usually for more altruistic motives. Table 9.7 highlights most of the key factors concerning hacking including different types of hackers, why they hack, how they hack, consequences of hacks, and organizational responses to hacking.

Table 9.7 Hackers and organizational responses

Type of hacker	White Hat Hackers – Ethical Hackers	Grey Hat Hackers	Black Hat Hackers – Crackers
Role	Authorized/certified hackers, intrusion detection specialists, or security professionals and freelancers working for organizations or governments They usually get some type of permission from the system owner	Somewhere between white and black hat hackers	Very skilled individuals or groups trying to gain unauthorized access to a system to harm it
Motivation	Finding and fixing security issues, strengthening the systems Educational purposes	Not legally authorized as hackers and some are not fond of some laws Might have both good and bad intentions	A 'cause' or money Greed Fear Curiosity, vandalism, hacktivism, industrial espionage, extortion or fraud and information warfare
Common Technique(s)	Penetration techniques	They use any technique they are familiar with, depending on their intentions	Various techniques including: • accessing gaps in security patch • social engineering • SQL injection • session hijacking • forms of trolling (i.e. denial of service, political Jujitsu, various Sockpuppet applications (i.e. astroturfing), algorithmic gaming, brigading, etc.)

Type of hacker	White Hat Hackers – Ethical Hackers	Grey Hat Hackers	Black Hat Hackers – Crackers
Organizational response	After a system's weaknesses are discovered, the organization makes adjustments	These hackers usually do not have permission from the owner of the system, so most organizations want to keep them out (Norton, 2019)	Risk mitigation Policies on use of technology Improved technical security with latest developments Training staff

Source: Barber (2001); Abraham and Chengalur-Smith (2010); Matthews and Goerzen (2019); Norton (2019); Thycotic (2019)

The ever present threat of hacking forces organizations to stay up to date with the latest security developments and to protect their information systems. For example, it is essential for organizations to maintain up-to-the-minute security patches as security update patch notes are a key source of information for hackers; i.e. if they see a vulnerability has been recently fixed, they often rush to exploit this window of opportunity before organizations have had a chance to install the patch. Hackers also often succeed in getting into organizational information systems through what are called social engineering strategies, such as phishing. Phishing is where employees of organizations are targeted by often highly sophisticated scams designed to reveal personal or network information (Henderson, 2017). As one reformed high-profile hacker, Kevin Mitnick, notes: 'Cybersecurity is about people, processes and technology – organisations need to bolster the weakest link – which is invariably the human element' (Gold, 2014: 77).

Highlight Box 9.6

The World of Hackers

While motivations vary among hackers and depend on the type of hackers, Madarie (2017) identified ten different motivations a hacker might have: 'universalism', 'benevolence', 'conformity', 'tradition', 'security', 'power', 'achievement', 'hedonism', 'stimulation' and 'self-direction'. Seebruck (2015) clusters hacker motivations into five categories: prestige, ideology, profit, revenge and recreation.

Besides black hat, white hat and grey hat hackers, other types of hackers mentioned on the GeeksforGeeks.org website (2019) and by Arrington (2019) include:

Script kiddies: Usually unskilled young people using scripts or tools from other hackers to attack systems to impress others.

(Continued)

Green hat hackers: Amateur hackers who want to learn about hacking through tutorials and online communities.

Blue hat hackers: Amateur hackers seeking revenge after being challenged or angered. Not much interest in learning but more in applying already available techniques to attack for revenge.

Red hat hackers: Vigilantes of the hacking world. They seek to shut down black hat hackers.

State/nation sponsored hackers: Hackers used by governments to get confidential information from other countries while at the same time defending their country's system from similar intentions – also called 'information warfare specialists' (Barber, 2001: 16).

Hacktivists: Hackers acting as online protesters/activists trying to gain access to government files for social, ecological, ethical or political causes.

Malicious insiders: An insider acting or aiming to harm the organization or government they work for.

Whistle-blowers: An insider reporting their knowledge of an existing illegal activity within their organization or government for ethical or monetary reasons.

Social media hackers: Hackers attacking social media accounts with unlawful or immoral intentions.

Suicide hackers: Hacker who hacks for the sake of destruction knowing that they will likely get caught. Motivated by chance at fame or just to harm the other side.

Data security represents one of the most profound issues facing twenty-first century organizations. Organizations face pressure from governments, customers and other organizations to not only use data ethically and legally, but also to secure it against a variety of internal and external threats. These pressures and threats are increasing and changing almost on a daily basis. Organizations must effectively respond to these challenges. This requires state-of-the-art technology and knowledgeable, well-trained and committed managers, technologists and general staff. Organizational data security must be thorough, coherent and fluid in order to respond to changing consumer expectations, government laws and motivated hackers.

CHAPTER SUMMARY

This chapter discusses some of the most important matters of concern raised in this book regarding big data and analytics for managers and organizations. It is not uncommon for the critical social implications of new technologies to be ignored at the time these technologies are developed and commercialized (Dalal and Pauleen, 2018). It is only when the effects of these technologies become apparent that society sits up and takes notice. This lag in public awareness can take a generation or more before it emerges. This has been the case with the Internet, social media, mobile technologies, and the cumulative effects of data generation, integration, analysis and use on areas of social concern such as ethics, privacy and security. Technology developers and organizations that use these technologies have had a free ride over the last 20 or 30 years when it comes to collecting and using personal end-user data. This era is perhaps coming to an end. The GDPR and other legislation as well as the emergence of significant consumer pushback means that organizations and management decision-makers will sooner or later likely have to accommodate their data practices to align with social and ethical norms and legal obligations. We would argue, perhaps somewhat naively, that doing so would be a sign of organizational analytics maturity.

Mature policies and practices would recognize the competing interests that involve the creation and use of data. Great competitive advantage and efficiencies may come to organizations that exploit data and analytics and incorporate them into their decision-making processes, but management should also keep in mind the perspectives of their customers, business associates, and society as a whole, as well as legal requirements, when setting data policy. In a sense, it is a question of trade-offs. More and more we can expect to see end-users demanding more transparent policies around ownership of their data. Implementing socially responsible organizational policies around data would seem to make sense, possibly leading to other forms of competitive advantage for organizations.

For example, while the big social media companies, such as Facebook and Google, have essentially demanded user data in exchange for their services, they are slowly coming to realize that they risk losing customers if they do not change. Moreover, by not making adjustments in data privacy and use policies, they risk losing out to those companies that will make it a point of difference to implement such policies. It is likely that soon some companies will be offering business models that entail exchanging cash or other incentives for user data.

With more transparency, organizations and end users might agree that data can be a valuable tool for improving society and work together in making this happen. Without a doubt, health research would benefit greatly from accessing data in real time from users wearing mobile health-related devices. However, for users to agree to this, they may want in return assurances that this data leads to benefits for everyone, not just profits for companies. Moreover, they would want absolute assurances that the data will not be transferred to third parties, such as insurance companies, who might then penalize their customers based on the data.

In sum, achieving responsible analytics maturity is likely going to involve trade-offs between organizations and those who generate the data. Transparent and ethical practices will likely be rewarded in a competitive marketplace where concern about personal data is growing. Regardless of whether or not organizations choose an ethical path, increasingly strict legal requirements will have to be met in any case. While Facebook may be able to shrug off a $5 billion fine (Nuñez, 2019), not all organizations will be able to do so. For this reason alone, it is good practice and responsible governance for organizations to implement sound data policies. The issue of data security is much more problematic. This requires significant investment in technical and human resources, good governance and constant vigilance on the part of system administrators and organizational employees. The costs to organizations of data breaches can be high if they lose proprietary knowledge, but to date when customer data is stolen, the costs to the organizations have been minimal. This also seems likely to change with new legislation.

KEY LESSONS

In this chapter we have introduced the ethical, security, privacy and legal aspects of data-driven decision-making. The most important takeaways can be summarized as:

1. Issues of ethics, privacy, security and legality of data collection and use are increasingly important for organizations to take into account.
2. These issues are interlinked, complex and fluid. Sophisticated, dedicated organizational responses are required.
3. Senior management and organizational directors will need to take responsibility for the ongoing management of these issues. This will require a 'whole of organization' response.

10

MANAGING EMERGING TECHNOLOGIES AND DECISION-MAKING

Contents

Highlight Box 10.1

Emerging, Converging and Disruptive Technologies

Technology is one of the most impactful factors in today's world. Throughout history, new technologies have shaped society, human culture and the environment. Technologies and technology-induced change are apparent in all aspects of our daily life from the food we eat to the way we communicate. In this book we are focused on information-driven technology, particularly data and how it is generated, collected, analyzed and applied in organizational contexts, especially management decision-making. Many terms are used to describe new technologies and here we briefly review three of the most common terms: emerging technologies, convergent technologies and disruptive technologies.

(Continued)

Emerging technology is the term used to describe technologies at the beginning of their life-cycle. These technologies open new ground in a particular field and have the potential to displace current technologies and significantly shift organizational (and social) processes and culture. Current examples of emerging technologies are the decentralized web, edge computing and augmented intelligence.

Converging technologies describe technologies that develop when different technologies or systems evolve towards similar objectives. These convergences can lead to efficiencies and even completely new ways of doing things. For example, the convergence of telephony and computers led to the development of the Internet. It may be that an emergent technology allows the convergence of other technologies; for example, 5G networks will lead to a greater variety of applications of the Internet of Things.

Disruptive technologies is the term used to describe innovations that displace previous technologies, disrupt current markets and create new markets. The term is commonly used to describe new technologies that have the potential to shift organizational and social processes and outcomes.

In this chapter we use the term 'emerging technologies' as we are focusing on new technologies that are likely to be developed in the coming years. Of course, these new technologies may result in convergence of other technologies and will have the potential to greatly disrupt current ways of doing things, including how managers make decisions.

Questions to think about

1. Can you give examples of emerging, converging and disruptive technologies in your recent life experience? How have they affected the way you do things?
2. After thinking about question 1, compare your experiences with those younger and older than you to gain perspective on how technologies affect people across different generations.
3. After discussing your observations with others, can you find evidence that technologies are emerging more rapidly and are having 'disruptive' effects on people and society or do the changes seem gradual and evolutionary? Explain your views.

CHAPTER 10 KEY LESSONS

1. Technological change can be both incremental and disruptive.
2. All aspects of the information environment are undergoing significant change.
3. These changes will affect organizational structures and processes, including management.
4. Individual managers need to stay informed and be ready for and capable of change.

INTRODUCTION

Over the past decades, constant incremental technological developments as well as significant innovations have been steadily changing society. While much technology development is driven by the needs and demands of markets and society, other more innovative technologies, such as gene splicing and quantum computing, have the potential to 'propel' business and society in radically new directions. The pace of development of these new and revolutionizing technologies seems to be rapidly increasing. A great proportion of these emerging technologies, both incremental and innovative, are related to information and computer technologies, in the form of hardware, software and systems (Srinivasan, 2008).

Emerging information-based technologies possess certain characteristics that make them different from general information technology. Novelty, speed of growth, type of impact, coherence, uncertainty, cost, network effect and limited research are among the most common characteristics of emerging technologies (Rotolo et al., 2015). All or some of these characteristics may be present at the emergence of the technology or may appear as the technology develops. Some of the most significant of these characteristics are listed in Table 10.1.

Table 10.1 Characteristics of emerging technologies

Characteristic	Definition
Radical novelty	Functioning based on different principles from other technologies
High speed of growth	Faster growth rate compared to other technologies
Coherence	Having already achieved some identity and momentum
Impact	Changing the composition of and interaction among actors and institutions as well as the process of knowledge creation
Uncertainty and ambiguity	Processes and outcomes with higher uncertainty
Cost	High ownership cost
Network effect	Value of the technology increases as the number of users/adopters increases
Need for investigation	Require further investigation as not much academic or scientific research exists

Source: Srinivasan (2008); Halaweh (2013); Rotolo et al. (2015)

While emerging technologies can be defined by their different characteristics, the ones we focus on in this book have overlapping capabilities and applications, which result in an 'environment' where ever greater varieties and amounts of real-world data are generated and collected constantly and in real time (see Chapter 2, 3Vs). Technologies that have emerged over the last decade such as smartphones and mobile networks as well as the apps – such as social media apps – that populate them, continue to evolve. Meanwhile, new emerging technologies continue to appear. Some of these newer technologies, such as the Internet of Things (IoT), cloud computing, artificial intelligence (AI) and machine learning (ML) have already started shaping our lives. New Internet architectures, such as Web 3.0, will host such technologies, paving the way for livestream analytics.

These technologies, based on their inherent characteristics and intended use, are emerging sources of data generation, collection, storage, analysis and use. Massive amounts of data generation and collection via these emerging technologies such as IoT devices and sensors allow for rapid improvements in analysis via ML and AI. Deep Learning and Neural Networks are going to be a big part of ML and AI in the near future. Big data analyzed in real time by highly developed AI and ML will promote the use of AI and AI algorithms as the primary source of environmental intelligence.

These technologies are evolving towards knowing more about actual human behaviors, reactions and feelings, and based on these, they will be able to make recommendations and decisions. Healthcare, politics, insurance, finance, even trust, privacy, freedom, and the nature of knowledge and the role of humans in its generation will be affected by these technologies. Whether these technologies and algorithms will be used in tandem with human decision-making or as sole decision-makers is yet to be determined. Either way, these technologies have the potential to significantly change the way organizations do business and managers make decisions. In this chapter, we will discuss some of these emerging technologies and provide a perspective on their likely effects on management decision-making.

EMERGING TECHNOLOGIES

'Emerging technology' is a popular term these days, embraced by technology researchers and practitioners. Despite its extensive use, there is no consensus about what constitutes emerging technologies. Rotolo et al. (2015: 1828) offer a comprehensive definition of emerging technology as:

> a radically novel and relatively fast growing technology characterized by a certain degree of coherence persisting over time and with the potential to exert a considerable impact on the socio-economic domain(s) which is observed in terms of the composition of actors, institutions and patterns of interactions among those, along with the associated knowledge production processes. Its most prominent impact, however, lies in the future and so in the emergence phase is still somewhat uncertain and ambiguous.

Srinivasan (2008: 633) defines them more simply as 'science-based innovations with the potential to create a new industry or transform an existing one'.

Emerging technologies usually appear as a result of either evolution, in which the technology is developed over time with the incorporation of technological features, such as the development of film cameras into digital cameras, or as a revolution by application, in which the technology is developed for its high potential for the market. Examples include the development of web browsers that opened up an infinite number of opportunities in computing and communications (Srinivasan, 2008), as well as wireless communication technology that has brought radical changes to many domains (Adner and Levinthal, 2002). In significant ways, these technologies affect the value chain, cause digitization of goods, and bring new perspectives to innovation.

The Gartner Hype Cycle (Gartner, 2020c), released annually, is a well-known reporter of emerging technologies. Gartner not only lists the emerging technologies, but also categorizes them into five phases: Innovation Trigger, Peak of Inflated Expectations, Trough of Disillusionment, Slope of Enlightenment and Plateau of Productivity (Figure 10.1)

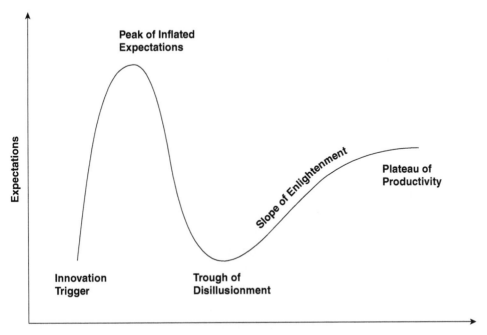

Figure 10.1   The Gartner Hype Cycle of Emerging Technologies

Each emerging technology is placed under one of these phases, starting with the first phase – Innovation Trigger – until it becomes a mainstream technology (the final phase) with a specific time estimate. For example, in the Hype Cycle for Emerging Technologies, 2019, Flying Autonomous Vehicles, Decentralized Web, Nanoscale 3D Printing, AR Cloud, Adaptive ML and Emotion AI were currently considered to be just kicking off (Innovation Trigger phase), with the first three technologies estimated to reach their Plateau of Productivity in more than 10 years and the last three between five and 10 years (Gartner, 2019b).

Emerging technologies such as Edge AI, Edge Analytics and 5G are in the second phase of Peak of Inflated Expectations with an estimation of two to five years to reach the plateau stage and become mainstream technology. While some emerging technologies will take a longer time to plateau, some, like Augmented Intelligence, are estimated to be mainstream in less than five years, even though it is still listed under the Innovation Trigger phase (Gartner, 2020c).

While the Gartner Hype Cycle illustrates the rise and mainstreaming of emergent technologies, it does not capture the synergies and effects these technologies have on each other and the cumulative effects on technology development as well as society. Individual technologies can have significant effects but together they may have far-reaching and unanticipated consequences. Chapter 9 looked at some of the ethical and legal implications of these effects: here we focus on the possible impacts on organizations and management decision-making.

The individual and cumulative effects of emerging technologies and the data they generate and analyze is making big data analytics available to a greater number of firms and organizations in a wider variety of industries. As the technologies mature, the costs go down and they become even more available to more organizations. These technologies have the potential to change the structure of organizations and many management processes including decision-making. As we have seen throughout this book, data and information are integral parts of the management decision-making process and their influence will continue to grow as more cost-effective data becomes available and more managers become more familiar with and educated about its potential and use. Examples of emerging technologies that may change organizational structures and processes include blockchain which may lead to Decentralized Autonomous Organizations (DAOs), open source entities located in the cloud which offer opportunities for competitive advantage (Kypriotaki et al., 2015), and decentralized decision-making (Christidis and Devetsikiotis, 2016; Atzori, 2017). Similarly, technologies like augmented technology, which use data generated by increasingly automated and intelligent analytics, will become increasingly prevalent in all kinds of organizational decision-making.

While it is obvious that data, emerging technologies and the relationships among them will play a big role in organizations and society, the question of what these relationships will lead to in the future is an interesting one. To provide some answers to this question, we are going to look at how industry and academia explain and predict what is coming next.

EMERGING TECHNOLOGIES AND MANAGEMENT DECISION-MAKING

We are not claiming to be seers. Which technologies will emerge and become part of organizations and society is not perfectly clear. The future is unpredictable and circumstances can change rapidly and in unexpected ways. The changes may come from social or environmental pressures. Only time will tell. However, assuming relative continuity of the current global environment, we can expect technological advances to continue and organizations and society to adapt to them. With this supposition in mind, in this section we discuss some of the most likely future near-term technologies that we believe will affect organizations and management decision-making.

Internet of Things

The Internet of Things can be defined as a system of interconnected devices and everyday things which collect and share data over a network (and then usually to the Internet) without human involvement. It is a dynamic global network in which all 'things' are interconnected (Botta et al., 2016). Two types of IoT – consumer IoT and industrial IoT – have emerged (Palattella et al., 2016) based on the technology and the use of it by organizations. Consumer IoT refers to all types of consumer devices and their virtual connectivity in environments such as homes, workplaces and even cities. Industrial IoT refers to interactions among machines and it focuses on the connectivity between operational technology and information technology. While consumer IoT helps to improve the quality of life of individuals, being economical, through saving time and money, industrial IoT focuses on improving business services through the monitoring and organizing of processes and systems.

With new consumer and industrial technologies becoming a more ordinary part of our everyday lives, we suggest that the IoT paradigm is going to revolutionize the way we live and work. Examples of such technologies are numerous. For example, smart home systems have been developed and are in high demand by homeowners. These systems are designed to message your phone, for example to inform owners of the temperature of the house and to allow the owner to turn on the heat or air-conditioning before they arrive home. They can also alert authorities in emergencies such as unauthorized entry or fire. In a smart home, a toaster can send information to a health app on your smartphone to record how much toast you consumed to calculate the calories.

In industrial applications, IoT will have significant effects. For example, connected devices and systems in transport, supply chain and logistics will potentially fully automate the transport process (Atzori et al., 2010) such as informing managers of the exact location and condition of a shipment. Applications and the impact of IoT on medicine and health will be enormous. For instance, constant monitoring of health data through IoT devices such as wearables (i.e. FitBit and ResearchKit from Apple) allows increased personalization of health care, advice or insurance powered by continuous data collection, leading to new 'health coaching' industries (Dimitrov, 2016).

In addition to the benefits and opportunities that IoT devices provide, they pose some potential risks and issues as well. One significant set of risks concerns the reliability, security, consent and privacy of these systems (Botta et al., 2016). This becomes a major concern if the devices collect sensitive data, such as places visited, health conditions, etc. As the technology is relatively new, the security concerns about the devices have not been fully resolved. A huge number of these devices are still unsecured and easy to access. Furthermore, there is still a lack of standards that will allow various IoT devices to integrate easily (Palattella et al., 2016).

We suggest that IoT will be integral in 'large system' decision-making. In such systems, IoT devices will generate data, and sub-systems will consolidate and perform preliminary analysis on data to be used in decision-making in real time. Operational decisions will be automated and part of the system. Traffic control systems that operate on these principles are already in operation; they record car numbers, traffic flows, accidents, etc. and adjust traffic lights, warning signs and other parts of the system automatically. These kinds of systems are also found in organizations on factory floors and in supply chain management. In the future, it is possible that we may see IoT devices and networks, powered by AI and ML, as part of automated real-time strategic decision-making platforms in organizations.

Dimitrov (2016) identifies the main characteristics of IoT platforms that will allow analysis and presentation of results for decision-making from the generated data. An IoT platform needs to provide easy access to connect different devices or data sources to collect data from. In such a platform, all connected devices should be easy to manage. Data from the connected devices should be captured and stored in such a way that it can be processed and analyzed easily. Finally, the platform with all devices and data should be protected from various technical and non-technical risks or threats.

IoT and Related Technologies

The data generated by IoT devices needs to be stored and processed before it is analyzed and used for decision-making. In operational systems with set parameters, like traffic management over a predetermined stretch of road, this is already being done. More and more, however, we will see the development of more complex, real-time information-based systems where various issues such as the real-time transferring, securing, cleaning and analyzing of data will need to be addressed. These various new technologies that are coming online will help address some of these issues. One of these technologies is

5G (see Figure 10.2). 5G is the next generation of mobile connectivity and will act as a catalyzer in IoT systems as it provides high bandwidth, mass coverage and low network latency for the connected devices. With 5G, the potential of IoT system platforms grows significantly; however, realizing the benefits of IoT – even with the help of 5G – will not be completely possible without resolving issues around data privacy and trust (Palattella et al., 2016) as discussed in Chapter 9.

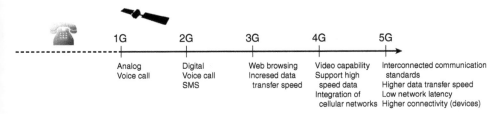

Figure 10.2   Evolution of 5G technology

Sources: Gohil et al., 2013; Ericsson, 2019; Segan, 2019

Blockchain technology could interface with IoT to create a marketplace of services between devices. Blockchain also helps solve trust issues between devices as all the blocks of a blockchain are linked with a special cryptography. Building IoT platforms using blockchain technology will help secure and decentralize the data, which can help solve some of the ethical, privacy and security issues with IoT. It is worth noting that using blockchain technology can be costly (Christidis and Devetsikiotis, 2016) as it is computationally demanding, which drains power and slows processing speeds. In addition, the privacy of the devices can be difficult to sustain since all transactions are open. Data will be available to anyone who can read the device data in the blockchain.

Cloud computing also brings complementary features to IoT. The National Institute of Standards and Technologies defines cloud computing as:

> a model for enabling ubiquitous, convenient, on-demand network access to a shared pool of configurable computing resources (e.g. networks, servers, storage, applications, and services) that can be rapidly provisioned and released with minimal management effort or service provider interaction. (Mell and Grance, 2011: 2)

Cloud computing brings unlimited processing and storage capability to IoT devices. While cloud computing is – at its core – highly centralized, IoT is highly decentralized. Cloud computing is a cheap and effective solution to connect all IoT devices while also offering opportunities to store all the data collected from various devices for long periods. Combining these two technologies' features and potential, cloud and IoT could form the Internet of the future (Botta et al., 2016)

Summary descriptions of these key IoT-related technologies are included in Table 10.2.

Table 10.2   Key IoT-related technologies

Technology	Definition	Characteristics	Challenges	Relation to Decision-making
5G	Next generation of mobile connectivity with standards	One standard bandwidth Mass coverage Low latency Supports wearable devices and AI capabilities Energy efficient	Allowing all different technologies and devices to work together smoothly	Provides the infrastructure for higher speed and efficiency for transferring data from 'things' to be processed for decision-making
Blockchain	'[A] distributed data structure that is replicated and shared among the members of a network' (Christidis and Devetsikiotis, 2016: 2293)	Decentralization Persistence Anonymity Auditability Trust through transparency Data integrity (verification by peers and cryptography) Immutability Decentralization through privacy Reliability (automation and redundancy) Versatility	Scalability Privacy of transactions A level of security (i.e. 'selfish mining' of blocks) Cost Reduced processing power	Helps with the transparent, trusted and improved exchange of (real-time) information among all parties, or all devices
Cloud (computing)	'Disruptive technology with profound implications for the delivery of Internet services as well as for the IT sector as a whole' (Botta et al., 2016: 687)	Service orientation Fault tolerant Easy to use TCP/IP based Security Virtualization Loose coupling Existing business model Less effort required for implementation Reliable Efficient infrastructure utility Scalable performance	High security and privacy Potential downtime of the service	Data produced by various devices (i.e. IoT) can be stored, transferred and processed outside the organization with security for decision-making

Source: Gong et al., 2010; Jadeja and Modi, 2012; Chin et al., 2014; Seebacher and Schüritz, 2017; Zheng et al., 2017

Web 3.0

While still not universally defined, Web 3.0 is often mentioned in the academic and professional literature. Web 3.0 refers to a worldwide linked data storage system and can be defined as 'an integrated web experience where the machine will be able to understand and catalogue data in a manner similar to humans' (Rudman and Bruwer, 2016: 132). Web 3.0 is about exploring vast amounts of linked and widely readable data sets, including real-time and real-world data. These data sets are not centralized but rather spread everywhere and anywhere and are readable to humans and other devices. This opens potentially new and significant options in linking previously isolated data sets.

Web 1.0, also known as the static web, had isolated web pages, Uniform Resource Identifiers (URIs), Hypertext Transfer Protocol (HTTP), and the Hypertext Markup Language (HTML) (Bizer, 2009), developed by individuals or groups of authors. Web 2.0, known as the dynamic web, contains fixed data sources for specific purposes. Typical content of Web 2.0 was generated by users via social media. Table 10.3 highlights the major characteristics of Web 1.0, 2.0 and 3.0.

Table 10.3   Selected characteristics of Web 1.0, Web 2.0, and Web 3.0

Web 1.0	Web 2.0	Web 3.0
'Read-only' web	'Read-write' web or social web	'Read-write-execute' web – portable and personal web – semantic web
Static content	Dynamic content	Personalized content through AI and learning web
Allows content mainly published by companies and used by people	Allows content published by people and used by people where companies produce environment allowing people to publish content	People develop applications for interaction and companies develop environment for people publishing services
Information sharing, online presence with limited interaction and content by the user	Improved interaction with other users and content contribution by the user	High-quality content and services by experienced/gifted users – immersion
Homepages	Social software, weblogs, wikis, podcasts, RSS, mashups, games, etc.	Live streams
Resource Identifiers (URIs), Hypertext Transfer Protocol (HTTP), and the Hypertext Markup Language (HTML)	Extensible Markup Language (XML), Really Simple Syndication (RSS)	Resource Description Framework (RDF), Resource Description Framework Schema (RDFS), Web Ontology Language (OWL)
Connecting information	Connecting people	Connecting knowledge

Source: based on Shivalingaiah and Naik, 2008; Sharma, 2019

Web 3.0 has major implications for business and society. Along with IoT, more data will be created and made available, with greater capability to reliably search and identify relevant data. Content of Web 3.0 will be readable to various devices and applications other than web browsers. This will affect all sectors of the economy and academia including media, art (e.g. data collection on global music consumption), sciences (bigger data sets), publishing, and even governance and elections. It will create new opportunities for business intelligence, reduce IT infrastructure costs (e.g. by outsourcing analytics), increase flow of analytics, and decrease time of processing. It will allow utilization of AI and learning (Shivalingaiah and Naik, 2008) and also improve decision-making due to the increased efficiency and accuracy of collecting relevant and good quality data from multiple sources (Rudman and Bruwer, 2016).

In addition to the usual privacy, security and ethical issues found with other emerging technologies, hyper-targeted marketing will be an issue with Web 3.0. It will also inevitably result in the development of new types of business models, which will mean entirely new and unpredictable challenges for organizations and management.

Consider This Box 10.2

Open Standards

Open standards (McKendrick, 2018) is a broad term used to refer to publicly available standards, and in the context of emerging technologies, formats and processes. The Open Data Institute (TODI, 2019) defines open standards for data as 'reusable agreements that make it easier for people and organisations to publish, access, share and use better quality data'. While the number of open standards is in the thousands, TODI (2019) categorizes them based on sharing vocabularies, sharing data and providing guidance. Open standards on vocabulary helps people and organizations to communicate over standards on 'concepts', 'words', 'attributes', 'relationships', 'models', 'identifiers' and 'units of measure'. Open standards on data exchange help standardize data 'formats', 'types', 'transfers', 'rules' and 'maps'. Finally, open standards for guidance help with understanding the document flow and data models through standardization of 'units of measure', 'processes' and 'codes of practice' (TODI, 2019).

For example, one of the current issues with big data is that much of the data is either unstructured, or fixed to particular software packages. Having public standards would make it easier to distribute and share the data and create ecosystems for data production, publishing, acquisition, aggregation and linkages. An example of such open standards is JSON (JavaScript Object Notation) (McKendrick, 2018). JSON uses human-readable text to transmit data straight to a browser rather than running through Flash plugins etc. While open standards provide a framework/structure and flexibility for applications and enterprises, selecting the right standards as well as gaining traction vis-à-vis competing standards will be an issue that needs to be resolved in the near future.

1. Discuss the challenges of developing open standards. What are the roles of govern-ments and industries in developing standards?
2. In what ways can organizations and end users benefit from open standards?
3. In what ways can open standards lead to better organizational decision-making?

Data as a Service and Analytics as a Service (DaaS + AaaS)

Emerging technologies have the potential to supercharge the 3Vs of big data – volume, variety and velocity (Chapter 2) – and continue to drive up the value of data. To remain competitive, many organizations will need to collect and process huge amounts of data (Demirkan and Delen, 2013). Although new technologies and economies of scale have lessened the cost of storing and processing data, it still remains an important issue. Storing and processing (transforming, sharing, utilizing, etc.) big data, and more specifi-cally distributed data, requires sophisticated hardware and high processing power that is not achievable for many small or even medium-sized companies. An example of such high power capability is IBM's Watson, which provides access to analytics through natural language processing. While the use of the system may not be very complicated, access to it is still costly for many organizations.

Data as a Service (DaaS) and Analytics as a Service (AaaS) provide more cost-efficient solutions for organizations looking to resolve issues around using data and analytics as a service. DaaS and AaaS are service-oriented concepts related to Software as a Service (SaaS) but about data or analytics provided on demand (Delen and Demirkan, 2013). DaaS is an Application Programming Interface (API) that allows data to be separated from specific software platforms. It is cost effective and results in a better quality product. With DaaS, customers can move quickly since aggregated data is simplified and readied for analytics. AaaS, also known as Agile Analytics, provides a general purpose analytics platform for processing a wide range of data at speed (Demirkan and Delen, 2013). AaaS is related to stream analytics, which provides real-time analytics.

In general, service-oriented business processes, architectures or infrastructures create an environment where the location of data or analytics is not important for the organiza-tion (Demirkan and Delen, 2013). With DaaS and AaaS, the organization can make sense of data, whether it is stored locally or in the cloud, using analytics whether the tools are local or in the cloud. With these services, data can be integrated, stored, cleaned, trans-formed, utilized, shared by other systems and visualized in any location in real time, making it an excellent information resource for organizations and management decision-making. These services are now being used in finance and credit services, e-retailing and consumer profiling.

Each of these technologies adds new capabilities to the technology ecosystem and can benefit management decision-making. The scalability and grid computing (processing power) of these services mean they can be integrated with the volume and variety of data collected through IoT, stored in the cloud over a high bandwidth infrastructure (5G), analyzed by tools located in server farms and displayed in desktop visualizations (AaaS) to be made available to managers for decision-making. Of course, the same downsides regarding data apply to DaaS as well, including the security risks of centralizing data. Challenges around AaaS include data encryption workarounds.

Edge Computing

As IoT, cloud computing, Web 3.0 and the other technologies discussed above become more established, new paradigms are emerging based on them.

One of these paradigms, developed in response to the centralized nature of cloud computing, is edge computing. Edge computing is about processing the data where it is generated: at the edge. Edge computing reduces the latency in applications that require very low response times, such as e-health and gaming (Caprolu et al., 2019). Edge computing has also been used in video analytics, smart homes and smart cities. Edge computing is mainly designed to deal with the data from large numbers of IoT devices at the 'edge' of a network, which could strain network bandwidth if it had to be moved into centralized cloud storage for processing. Moving the computation towards the edge of the network diffuses bandwidth demand, as edge computation is done using the processing power of IoT and mobile devices.

Moving computations and data closer to the edge requires more powerful devices. With the pull from the industry for such technology, under 5G, combined edge devices, installed along wireless gateways, will have the computational power of a server from 10 years ago (Mao et al., 2017). The emergence of such powerful devices has created a subset of edge computing, Mobile Edge Computing (MEC). Face recognition apps are an example of software relying on MEC servers. MEC reduces battery drain on IoT devices, allowing offloading of computing tasks to MEC devices nearby. MEC also opens up more efficient green energy use, as the individual devices are smaller and require less power than the big central cloud machines – also energy used can be optimized across the grid.

There will be some challenges with using edge devices (Mao et al., 2017), including security. Having many devices at the edge makes current authentication processes inadequate. Different standards and more sophisticated authorization for security will need to be developed and implemented to prevent digital interventions. MEC server security is also an issue as their widespread physical locations make them more susceptible to tampering. As many emerging technologies affect individuals and organizations, new regulations and legal considerations should accompany this new system as well. Finally, MEC or edge computing will work together with other technologies such as cloud, 5G, Web 3.0 and virtualization technologies. A comprehensive and flexible framework for managing these technologies will be needed to resolve challenges.

Edge computing, along with IoT, cloud, Web 3.0, 5G, and more advanced analytics will form the next version of the Internet. While big data will be generated by various devices and in various formats, it will be collected in the cloud but increasingly processed at the edge. With advanced analytics at the edge, managers will be able to have timely access to accurate and reliable information derived from not only organizational data but also external and IoT data.

Artificial Intelligence

The concept of artificial intelligence was first introduced in 1956. Recent technological advancements in computer power and data have boosted interest in AI. Since its inception, AI has been applied in various domains, and termed 'expert systems, knowledge-based systems, intelligent decision support systems, intelligent software agent systems, intelligent executive systems' among others (Duan et al., 2019: 67).

AI will soon appear in nearly every aspect of our lives. According to Holtel (2016), AI will bring a total transformation of society by utilizing the enhanced cognitive capabilities of machines. The recent acceleration of interest in and use of AI did not happen overnight or in isolation. Technological synergies with big data and analytics are driving AI (Duan et al., 2019). Big data enables AI, and AI makes sense of and obtains insight from big data. New algorithms using big data have created big data analytics, now considered a pillar of AI.

Organizational AI is the term we use to refer to current and potential applications of AI in an organizational context. AI is having a significant impact on organizational and management decision-making. This impact will continue to grow. As explained in Chapters 2 and 3, the growth of big data and advances in analytics are driving the use of analytics in organizations and as seen in Chapter 5, analytics is becoming a fundamental part of management decision-making. Managers now have access to an increasing variety of analytics that can assist decision-making, including: descriptive analytics, diagnostic analytics, predictive analytics, prescriptive analytics, and increasingly autonomous analytics, which is an advanced form of analytics using AI and cognitive technologies, like ML, to create models that are continuously learning from data (Davenport and Harris, 2017). Autonomous analytics makes it easier to get deeper insights from the data, which can assist decision-makers in making more informed decisions. Industrial applications of autonomous analytics include self-driving cars, traffic control and various areas of the healthcare system.

In addition to decision-making, organizational AI can be applied in different organizational domains. Davenport and Ronanki (2018) identify three categories of AI applications: cognitive process automation for back office and finance activities; cognitive insights for detecting and interpreting organizational and environmental patterns; and cognitive engagement which can, for example, improve relationships with customers and employees. The techniques used for the applications include robotic automation, ML based on statistics, natural language processing and more advanced ML (Duan et al., 2019). In combination with the emerging technologies in communication and data technologies discussed above, a new role for AI has emerged: decision augmentation, in which AI is designed to assist humans in decision-making situations, but in which humans remain in control of the final decision. Decision augmentation has direct applications for management decision-makers. In decision augmentation, AI applications shift from mechanical tasks towards more analytical thinking (Huang et al., 2019). In this application humans deal with interpersonal, emotional and empathic tasks while AI does the hard thinking.

Consider This Box 10.3

Decision-Making, Uncertainty and AI

Decision-making involves dealing with the challenges of uncertainty, complexity and equivocality (Jarrahi, 2018). Uncertainty is associated with lack of information about alternatives and outcomes. Complexity is often associated with too much information. Equivocality refers to the existence of multiple possibly conflicting perspectives. In an organizational decision situation, these multiple perspectives come from various stakeholders.

Big data and analytics can reduce uncertainty by revealing relationships among different variables and factors (Jarrahi, 2018). AI possesses the power of reducing complexity through identifying causal relationships among a great number of factors (Jarrahi, 2018). AI can also help reduce equivocality though, for example, sentiment analysis of real-time big data. In all these situations AI and human decision-making abilities work together to optimize decision-making.

Questions to think about

1. Discuss the technical and practical challenges of using AI for decision-making.
2. What are the risks and advantages of humans using AI in management decision-making?

While big data enables the use of organizational AI, it also brings new challenges to organizations. We have discussed the big data challenges throughout this book and they include process and management challenges. The challenges of big data refer to the 3V characteristics of data. Process challenges include how big data is acquired, cleaned, combined, stored, processed and interpreted. Management challenges concern the privacy, security, ethicality and governance of data and in particular, the focus of this book: how to use big data and analytics in management decision-making (Sivarajah et al., 2017). Perhaps the biggest management and social concern is the belief among many that AI will replace human workers.

Highlight Box 10.4

The Future of AI – Emotional Artificial Intelligence and the Feeling Economy

The future of AI and its application rests with its three different 'intelligences': mechanical intelligence, thinking intelligence and feeling intelligence (Huang et al., 2019). AI systems with mechanical intelligence are designed to perform simple, repetitive and standardized tasks with no learning requirements. The objective is usually to improve output in terms of consistency and reliability. AI systems with thinking intelligence are designed to learn autonomously from data and perform complex, rule-based and systematic tasks. A typical example using thinking intelligence is autonomous vehicles that operate by themselves based on the data they collect through sensors. According to Huang et al. (2019), in the future, advanced versions of thinking intelligence might be an AI system fully mimicking human intuition and making decisions based on data and human judgment – an automated application to address bounded rationality.

Finally, feeling intelligence refers to a system that can understand, imitate and respond to human emotions, build relationships and understand experience. It focuses on measuring, recording and adapting to human emotions such as facial expressions, tone of voice, gestures and other expressions of non-verbal communication (Jarrahi, 2018). This type of system will perform social, emotional and interactive tasks. While current technologies like chatbots, i.e. Alexa and Siri, process natural language, intelligence able to react and make decisions based on human emotions will require further advances in natural language programs (Huang et al., 2019).

Feeling intelligence will lie at the heart of the new feeling economy. Huang et al. (2019) argue that the economy is shifting from a 'processing and problem-solving' economy towards a more empathetic 'feeling' economy and will complete this shift around 2036. In the feeling economy, both AI and human workers will work together on the same team, each complementing the capabilities of the other. The nature of work for humans will move more towards feelings, with the AI focusing on hard facts and data. Jobs will become increasingly people oriented with an emphasis on those with 'people skills'. With such technologies soon becoming available, organizations and managers will need to react to new strategies in hiring and managing customer interactions.

(Continued)

Questions to think about

1. What would be some of the advantages of implementing emotional intelligence programs in organizations? Where do you see them having the greatest value?
2. Is there a danger of these kinds of programs replacing employees, including managers? Explain your thoughts.
3. Understanding and replicating emotions may be the next necessary step to reach 'machine consciousness'. Do we want to go there? Why or why not?

Deep Learning

Deep learning (DL) is a branch of ML, a 'field of study that gives computers the ability to learn without being explicitly programmed' (Xin et al., 2018: 35366), based on artificial neural networks, which are connected node systems that mimic 'human-like' pattern recognition rather than specific set instructions (Figure 10.3). It is worth noting that although DL and ML are related, they differ on various levels including data and hardware dependency, problem-solving methods, execution time – because of the number of variables involved in each method – and interoperability (Xin et al., 2018). DL uses multiple layers of analysis to extract higher level features from raw input, simulating human learning/recognition. Being able to extract and conceptualize abstract thinking is a feature of DL. The abstractions 'learned' at each layer and passed on are not the product of human engineering, but are adapted from the environment by the program. Examples of DL (Litjens et al., 2017) include automatic speech recognition, image recognition and fraud detection.

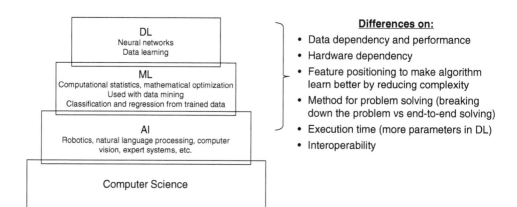

Figure 10.3   Comparison of main ML and DL features

Source: based on Xin et al., 2018

DL can provide useful information for decision-making as well as being able to process, analyze and recognize complex structures and patterns from different types of data, including unstructured data. DL analysis can produce real-time findings that can, for example, identify and match news, messages and other network-based data with customer interests. Applications of this sort can be useful for managers in making more efficient, accurate and faster tactical and strategic decisions. DL applications, along with augmented intelligence (discussed below) are also being proposed for super-efficient power grid management. On the darker side, DL will likely form the basis of facial recognition surveillance software, which will make it possible to track anyone anywhere.

Augmented Intelligence

Since the late 1950s, AI researchers have tried to mimic human intelligence by making machines understand, think and learn as humans do (Pan, 2016). In the earlier years the developments remained limited and isolated, but more recently the pace of AI development has quickened. Better algorithms, extensive data and data sources, and more powerful processors are the main reasons for this progress (Hebbar, 2017). With the existence of these prerequisites as well as demands from business and government, AI has found more application areas. Developments in AI are leading towards what is now called AI 2.0 (Pan, 2016). AI 2.0 will focus on intelligence, including:

- *Big-data-based AI*: AI that can handle large amounts of data to make efficiency gains. An example of this AI is DeepMind's AlphaGo that transforms big data into knowledge by developing human-like capabilities. The algorithm behind this Go game analyzes big data, learns and acts. The algorithm, using the big data, develops a strategy to make the next move and evaluates the chance of winning based on the move.
- *Internet crowd intelligence*: Examines crowd participation and networks in collective tasks. This technology emphasizes a new type of intelligence emerging from participation and interaction of huge crowds. Wikipedia and Zhihu Questions and Answers are examples of this technology.
- *Cross-media intelligence*: This intelligence is similar to the human capacity to draw information from very different sources. The basic argument of cross-media intelligence is that just as humans develop better understanding by combining different information such as text, voice, image and video, AI can develop 'intelligent behavior' by combining different sources from the external environment. Pokemon Go is an example of such an early stage technology, which integrates 3D graphics with real-time video on a device.
- *Autonomous intelligence systems*: This branch of AI aims to reduce the need for and intervention of humans. In earlier times of AI, one focus area was building robots for this purpose. More recent applications include self-driving cars and medical bots.
- *Human–machine hybrid-augmented intelligence*: This intelligence refers to very different operations working together to learn from each other. Augmented intelligence aims to

improve human capacity by recognizing the role of human intelligence and emotion in AI development. Augmented intelligence is sometimes seen as a 'friendly' spin on AI, and sometimes seen as distinct from AI but having overlap with deep neural networks, a sub-field of machine learning whose primary objective is to teach machines to learn without being programmed (Hebbar, 2017).

Augmented intelligence aims to bring mathematics and computation together with visualization and context with the aim of improving human capabilities in a variety of tasks. The most prominent role of augmented intelligence in business or management is in digital transformation projects (i.e. call center overhaul, analytics systems) to support or enhance existing day-to-day business operations (Brock and von Wangenheim, 2019). These systems provide relevant and timely data-based information that can help people answer questions or analyze situations for more effective decision-making. Combining human knowledge with deep learning AI for analyzing medical scans more effectively (Jarrahi, 2018), or combining human experience with developments in emotional AI to assist in emotional or empathic areas like HR (Tambe et al., 2019) are becoming more common.

As with other emerging technologies, there are concerns and issues about augmented intelligence. One of the biggest is the belief that AI and its various permutations introduced here will result in making humans redundant and perhaps unnecessary. The benefits of AI could be substantial but so may the risks (Holtel, 2016). This is an issue that is unlikely to go away anytime soon.

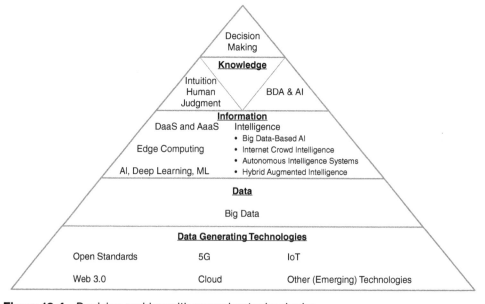

Figure 10.4   Decision-making with emerging technologies

Figure 10.4 illustrates how new decision-making-related technologies discussed in this chapter, along with changes in the analytics and information environments, are creating new decision-making environments.

CHAPTER SUMMARY

In this chapter, we have reviewed technologies in current states of emergence, development and use. All of these technologies are all related to the generation, gathering, analysis and use of data and information. The emergence of technological innovation will result in social and organizational change. At the same time, incremental technological development will be driven by market forces. This push–pull market dynamic will see demands for smart/intelligent things such as smart cities, smart homes and intelligent medicine, and these in turn will result in demands for new technologies. To address these needs, technologies such as big-data-based intelligence, 'Internet crowd intelligence', 'cross-media intelligence', 'autonomous intelligence', 'human–machine hybrid-augmented intelligence' (Pan, 2016: 411), thinking intelligence and emotional intelligence (Huang et al., 2019) will be developed.

If this technological trajectory continues unabated, both machines and humans will need to figure out how to work in complementary ways. For society in general, this represents an enormous challenge, far too large for us to make any meaningful predictions or draw conclusions at this time. As for the role of data and analytics in management decision-making, we feel more confident in predicting that in the near future the integration of human intelligence and artificial intelligence will be a reality and that this will certainly affect management decision-making.

As we argued in Chapter 1, managers need to become more familiar with data and information-based technologies and processes to accommodate technological change in organizations and to improve their decision-making capabilities. With an extended and more sophisticated set of KSAs, including a greater awareness of legal and ethical issues, managers and senior executives will be better able to manage the social and organizational changes that current and emerging technologies engender. Should a future unfold where human intelligence and artificial intelligence are integrated and where machines do the thinking and humans do the feeling, we will need to revisit Chapter 1 and instead emphasize that managers will need to work on their emotional and relationship skills, which would also be a good thing to do ... even now!

KEY LESSONS

In this chapter we have introduced emerging technologies in relation to management decision-making. The most important takeaways can be summarized as:

1. Technological change is both incremental and disruptive.
2. All aspects of the information environment are undergoing significant change.
3. These changes will affect organizational structures and processes, including management.
4. Individual managers need to stay informed and be ready for and capable of change.

GLOSSARY OF TECHNICAL TERMS

CHAPTER 1

AMOS Analysis of a Moment Structures, IBM's structural equation modeling software (www.ibm.com/nz-en/marketplace/structural-equation-modeling-sem).

Bayesian networks A type of probabilistic model using graphs (Soni, 2019).

Business analyst A person who is in charge of managing business processes and producing scheduled as well as ad hoc reports for decision-makers. They closely work with business managers and are often responsible for database design, ROI assessment, managing budgets and risks, and planning marketing and finance activities (Granville, 2013, 2014a, 2014b, 2014c; Mazenko, 2016; Schmarzo, 2018; DataFlair, 2019).

Data analyst Usually works with structured or organized data and converts the collected data, usually from enterprise systems, into different formats before conducting their analysis and creating visual representations of them to address business issues (Granville, 2013, 2014a, 2014b, 2014c; Mazenko, 2016; Schmarzo, 2018; DataFlair, 2019).

Data architect A person who possesses extensive knowledge of databases and data warehouses and focuses on developing the architecture for the data or data warehousing and data integration (Granville, 2013, 2014a, 2014b, 2014c; Mazenko, 2016; Schmarzo, 2018; DataFlair, 2019).

Data engineer A person who possesses extensive knowledge of databases, data warehouses, and software engineering and focuses on developing the architecture for the data or data warehousing and data integration (Granville, 2013, 2014a, 2014b, 2014c; Mazenko, 2016; Schmarzo, 2018; DataFlair, 2019).

Data science A field possessing attributes from other fields such as computer science, software engineering, statistics, mathematics, data mining, machine learning, management science and operations research/industrial engineering (Granville, 2013, 2014a, 2014b, 2014c; Mazenko, 2016; Schmarzo, 2018; DataFlair, 2019).

Data scientist A person employed to explore data collected from different sources, gain insights and look for patterns to predict future events, usually excelling in statistics, mathematics, data engineering, machine learning, business, software engineering, visualization and spatial data. (Granville, 2013, 2014a, 2014b, 2014c; Mazenko, 2016; Schmarzo, 2018; DataFlair, 2019)

E-Views A statistical package commonly used for time series or related econometric analysis (www.eviews.com/home.html).

Hadoop 'The Apache Hadoop software library is a framework that allows for the distributed processing of large data sets across clusters of computers using simple programming models' (https://hadoop.apache.org/).

Hive 'The Apache Hive™ data warehouse software facilitates reading, writing, and managing large datasets residing in distributed storage using SQL' (https://hive.apache.org/).

HLM Hierarchical Linear Modeling (www.statcon.de/shop/en/software/statistics/hlm).

Java 'The Java™ Programming Language is a general-purpose, concurrent, strongly typed, class-based object-oriented language' (https://docs.oracle.com/javase/7/docs/technotes/guides/language/).

JavaScript 'JavaScript (JS) is a lightweight interpreted or just-in-time compiled programming language with first-class functions' (https://developer.mozilla.org/en-US/docs/Web/JavaScript).

Jira 'Jira is a family of products built to help all types of teams manage their work' (www.atlassian.com/software/jira/guides/getting-started/overview).

Lisrel A structural equation modeling analysis tool (www.ssicentral.com/index.php/products/lisrel/).

MatLab Matrix Laboratory 'is a programming platform designed specifically for engineers and scientists' (www.mathworks.com/products/matlab.html).

Microsoft Azure AI Microsoft's AI platform for AI (https://azure.microsoft.com/en-us/overview/ai-platform/).

Microsoft Azure ML Microsoft's service for machine learning (https://azure.microsoft.com/en-us/services/machine-learning-service/).

Minitab A data analysis tool (www.minitab.com/en-us/).

MLWin A multi-level modeling tool (www.bristol.ac.uk/cmm/software/mlwin/).

MPlus 'Mplus is a statistical modeling program that provides researchers with a flexible tool to analyze their data' (www.statmodel.com/features.shtml).

MySQL A database management system (www.mysql.com/).

NoSQL 'Next Generation Databases mostly addressing some of the points: being non-relational, distributed, open-source and horizontally scalable' (http://nosql-database.org/).

Perl   Perl is a family of languages 'suitable for both rapid prototyping and large scale development projects' (www.perl.org/).

Pig   'Apache Pig is a platform for analyzing large data sets that consists of a high-level language for expressing data analysis programs, coupled with infrastructure for evaluating these programs' (https://pig.apache.org/).

PLS   'Partial least squares regression is an extension of the multiple linear regression model' (www.tibco.com/products/data-science; https://warppls.com/).

Python   A high level programming language (www.python.org/; www.w3schools.com/python/python_intro.asp).

R   'R is a free software environment for statistical computing and graphics' (www.r-project.org/).

RATS   Regression Analysis of Time Series, a tool for econometrics and time series analysis (www.estima.com/).

Ruby   A high level, open source programming language (www.ruby-lang.org/en/).

SAS   Statistical Analysis System 'is an integrated software suite for advanced analytics, business intelligence, data management, and predictive analytics' (www.sas.com/en_nz/home.html).

Shazam   'SHAZAM is comprehensive software for econometrics, statistics and analytics' (www.econometrics.com/).

Spark   'Apache Spark is a unified analytics engine for big data processing, with built-in modules for streaming, SQL, machine learning and graph processing' (https://spark.apache.org/).

SPSS   'The IBM SPSS® software platform offers advanced statistical analysis, a vast library of machine-learning algorithms, text analysis, open-source extensibility, integration with big data and seamless deployment into applications' (www.ibm.com/analytics/spss-statistics-software).

SQL   'SQL is a standard language for storing, manipulating and retrieving data in databases' (www.w3schools.com/sql/).

Statistica   'The STATISTICA line of software consists of a fully integrated line of analytic solutions' (www.tibco.com/products/data-science).

Statistician   A person excelled in designing surveys or conducting experiments to collect data, then analyzing and interpreting the data by applying statistical theories, methods, techniques and analysis, before applying visualization techniques to present the results.

Tableau   A popular data visualization tool (www.tableau.com/).

Toad   'Toad Software is a database management toolset from Quest that database developers, database administrators and data analysts use to manage both relational and non-relational databases using SQL' (www.quest.com/toad/).

Trello   A collaborative project management tool (https://trello.com/en).

XML   eXtensible Markup Language 'is a software- and hardware-independent tool for storing and transporting data' (www.w3schools.com/xml/xml_whatis.asp).

CHAPTER 2

Big data   Huge volumes of data collected from different sources and in different formats that can be analysed in real time.

Value   Refers to economic benefits that result from the use of big data.

Variety   Refers to types of data captured and stored from diverse data sources.

Velocity   Refers to the speed of data generation and being processed in (near) real time.

Veracity   Reflects how credible a data source is and how well the data suits the organization to provide reliable results.

Volume   Refers to data sets exceeding the capacity of DBMS and traditional analytics tools.

CHAPTER 3

Artificial intelligence   'Artificial intelligence is a subpart of computer science, concerned with how to give computers the sophistication to act intelligently, and to do so in increasingly wider realms' (Nilsson, 1980: 1). Applications: customer support; smart cars; surveillance.

Cloud computing (1)   'an information technology service model where computing services (both hardware and software) are delivered on-demand to customers over a network in a self-service fashion, independent of device and location. The resources required to provide the requisite quality-of-service levels are shared, dynamically scalable, rapidly provisioned, virtualized and released with minimal service provider interaction. Users pay for the service as an operating expense without incurring any significant initial capital expenditure, with the cloud services employing a metering system that divides the computing resource in appropriate blocks' (Marston et al., 2011: 177). Serves\ businesses as: Software as a Service (SaaS); Platform as a Service (PaaS); Infrastructure as a Service (IaaS).

Cloud computing (2) 'a model for enabling ubiquitous, convenient, on-demand network access to a shared pool of configurable computing resources (e.g. networks, servers, storage, applications, and services) that can be rapidly provisioned and released with minimal management effort or service provider interaction' (Mell and Grance, 2011: 2).

Dashboards An 'application that provides multiple views of a large dataset' (McKeon, 2009: 1082). Applications: collaboratively developing knowledge for decision-making about various contexts; student performance monitoring/improvement.

Data mining A step in knowledge discovery from databases and 'is the application of specific algorithms for extracting patterns from data' (Fayyad et al., 1996: 39). Applications: investment decision; fraud detection; predicting problems or defects in manufacturing.

Information visualization An inductive method used for developing insights from data. It is about 'exploiting the dynamic, interactive, inexpensive medium of graphical computers to devise new external aids that enhance cognitive abilities' (Card, 1999: 5).

IoT The Internet of Things, 'Internet of Everything or the Industrial Internet, is a new technology paradigm envisioned as a global network of machines and devices capable of interacting with each other' (Lee and Lee, 2015: 431). Commonly used IoT technologies include: RFID, wireless sensor networks (WSN), middleware, cloud computing, and IoT application software. Applications: monitoring smart homes for security and savings; information sharing for customer engagement and promotions.

IoT platform 'a multi-layer technology that enables straightforward provisioning, management, and automation of connected devices within the Internet of Things universe. It basically connects your hardware, however diverse, to the cloud by using flexible connectivity options, enterprise-grade security mechanisms, and broad data processing powers' (Kaa Project, 2020). Applications: cost optimization from sensor data to help real-time production; monitoring patients remotely for treatment purposes.

Machine learning 'Machine learning is a data analytics technique that teaches computers to do what comes naturally to humans and animals: learn from experience. Machine learning algorithms use computational methods to 'learn' information directly from data without relying on a predetermined equation as a model' (MathWorks, 2019). Applications: credit scoring; face recognition; drug discovery.

Visualisation 'The use of computer-supported, interactive, visual representations of data to amplify cognition' (Card, 1999: 6). Applications: all sorts of aggregated information, reports, etc.

CHAPTER 4

Bounded rationality Explains that a decision-maker's use of rationality is bounded by the complexity of problems and the decision-maker's mental (in-)capacity to process all available information and alternatives.

Chaotic decision Decisions defined by turbulence and without underlying cause-and-effect relationships.

Complex decision Unpredictable decisions that rely on probing and experiments.

Complicated decision Several potential solutions to a decision require thorough analysis and expertise.

Decision trigger The first step in the decision-making process leading to the identification of decision situations.

Decision trigger as anecdotal Concerns, often longstanding, based on employees' perceptions that require a decision.

Decision trigger as evaluation An internally triggered, intentional review of current practices, or an evaluation of future opportunities.

Decision trigger as external trigger An external impulse, i.e. opportunity or problem, prompting a decision.

Decision trigger as routine check An ad hoc problem identified during a routine check or review.

Disorder decision No other decision type or context is predominant.

Dual process decision-making Refers to addressing the moment of decision in one of two ways, through reasoning or intuition.

Naturalist decision-making Approach aiming to understand how decisions are actually made in practice.

Non-rational decision-making An umbrella term for factors such as intuition, experience, insight and judgment.

Operational decision Mostly routine, well-defined decisions regarding the immediate future.

Rational decision-making Normative and prescriptive decision-making where expected outcomes and probabilities are evaluated against objective (rather than subjective) criteria.

Simple/routine decision Decisions or problems are assessed, categorized and responded to with established practices.

Strategic decision Important, high-level, long-term decisions that influence the organization's goals and objectives.

System 1 Refers to intuition, which is described as a holistic, time-efficient, emotional, but non-conscious process that relies on learning from experience.

System 2 Set of systematic procedures that allow decision-makers to consciously gather and evaluate information and engage in abstract reasoning and hypothetical thinking.

Tactical decision Medium-term decisions regarding the organization's efficiency.

CHAPTER 5

Balanced decisions Decisions that display high levels of data analytics and human judgment use.

Challenger of judgment Case where initial assessments and cognitive biases are challenged with the assistance of data analytics.

Confirmation Case where data is used to confirm initial assessments.

Enabler of judgment Case where data is applied to choices that are too complex to determine without analytics.

Enrichment of analytics Human judgment adds valuable insights and additional aspects to the data analytics results.

Exploration Case where data sources are explored for trends explaining a phenomenon, or for potential solutions to problems.

High-data decisions Decisions that are characterized by high levels of data analytics, and low levels of human judgment use.

High-judgment decisions Decisions that involve high levels of judgment, and only low to moderate levels of data use.

Identification Case where analytics (e.g. reporting) identifies a previously unknown problem or opportunity that requires a decision.

Identifier of need for analytics Decision-makers recognize the need for additional, more sophisticated decision-making support.

Initial assessment Human judgment is used by managers to create an initial impression of the situation.

Justification Case where data analytics results are used as objective validation to justify decisions during the selection stage.

No-brainer Case where data analytics results are so certain that they are the sole basis of a decision.

Overruling of analytics Factors such as relationships, intuition and cultural aspects can outweigh fact-based analytics results.

Sense-check and data challenging The analysis results are challenged and run through a sense-check.

CHAPTER 6

Type A – Analytics-Bent Managers who are quite adept at and experienced in using data and analytics and tend to have more faith in data than in human judgment, which leads to mainly high-data decisions.

Type B – All-Rounders Managers who are comfortable with the use of analytics and have accumulated a significant amount of contextual and domain experience, which enables them to make balanced decisions.

Type C – Uninformed or uncertain Managers who are mostly lacking analytics training and experience, which leads to skepticism and avoidance and adopting various decision styles, depending on the extent of collaboration with others.

Type D – Old-Fashioned
Managers who mostly trust in their own experience and judgment and are most likely to hold positions in companies that are not very data-driven. They have either not been exposed to data or are data-averse.

CHAPTER 7

Adoption stage Refers to the organization's intent to become more data-driven and take the first steps in actualizing this intent towards maturity.

Awareness stage Refers to the organization's recognition of data analytics and possibly its value for decision-making.

Maturity stage Refers to the organization's stage that comes with the gaining of experience and confidence with data sets and analytics, which in turn leads to an even greater understanding of and trust in data.

CHAPTER 9

Blue hat hackers   Amateur hackers seeking revenge after being challenged or angered. Not much interest in learning but more in applying already available techniques to attack for revenge.*

Green hat hackers   Amateur hackers who want to learn about hacking through tutorials and online communities.*

Hacktivist   Hackers acting as online protesters/activists trying to gain access to government files for social, ecological, ethical or political causes.*

Malicious insider   An insider acting or aiming to harm the organization or government they work for.

Red hat hackers   Vigilantes of the hacking world. They seek to shut down black hat hackers.*

Script Kiddies   Usually unskilled young people using scripts or tools from other hackers to attack systems in order to impress others.

Social media hacker   Hacker attacking social media accounts with unlawful or immoral intentions.*

State/nation sponsored hackers   Hackers used by governments to get confidential information from other countries while at the same time defending their country's system from similar intentions. Also called 'information warfare specialists' (Barber, 2001: 16).

Suicide hacker   Hacker who hacks for the sake of destruction knowing that they will likely get caught. Motivated by chance at fame or just to harm the other side*.

Whistle-blowers   An insider reporting their knowledge of an existing illegal activity within their organization or government for ethical or monetary reasons.

*(GeeksforGeeks.org and Arrington, 2019)

CHAPTER 10

5G   Considered as the next generation of mobile connectivity that can act as a catalyzer in IoT systems as it provides high bandwidth, mass coverage and low network latency for the connected devices.

AaaS   A general purpose analytics platform for processing a wide range of data at speed (Demirkan and Delen, 2013).

Algorithm '[M]ath formulas and/or programming commands that inform a regular non-intelligent computer on how to solve problems with artificial intelligence. Algorithms are rules that teach computers how to figure out on their own' (Gans and Christensen, 2019: 10).

Augmented intelligence A conceptualization of AI that aims to bring mathematics and computation together with visualization and context with the aim of improving human capabilities in a variety of tasks (Brock and von Wangenheim, 2019).

Big-data-based-AI AI that can handle large amounts of data to make efficiency gains (Pan, 2016).

Blockchain '[A] distributed data structure that is replicated and shared among the members of a network' (Christidis and Devetsikiotis, 2016: 2293).

Cloud (computing) 'Disruptive technology with profound implications for the delivery of Internet services as well as for the IT sector as a whole' (Botta et al., 2016: 687).

Cross-media intelligence AI that can develop 'intelligent behavior' by combining different sources from the external environment (Pan, 2016).

DaaS An Application Programming Interface (API) that allows data to be separated from specific software platforms (Demirkan and Delen, 2013).

Deep learning A branch of machine learning, a 'field of study that gives computers the ability to learn without being explicitly programmed' (Xin et al., 2018: 35366).

Edge computing Refers to processing the data where it is generated: at the edge.

Emotional intelligence system Refers to a system that can emulate and respond to human emotions, build relationships and understand experience.

Internet crowd intelligence Collaborative intelligence enabled by crowd participation and networks in collective tasks (Pan, 2016).

Internet of Things A system of interconnected devices and everyday things, which collect and share data over a network (and then usually to the Internet).

Machine learning '[T]he process by which an AI uses algorithms to perform artificial intelligence functions' (Gans and Christensen, 2019: 10).

Natural language processing 'AI ... trained to interpret human communication' (Gans and Christensen, 2019: 11).

Neural network Type of AI 'designed to be very similar to the human nervous system and brain ... using stages of learning to give AI the ability to solve complex problems by breaking them down into levels of data' (Gans and Christensen, 2019: 10).

Open standards   Refer to publicly available standards, and in the context of emerging technologies, formats and processes (McKendrick, 2018).

Web 1.0   Read-only, static content web.

Web 2.0   Read-write web or social web with dynamic content.

Web 3.0   '[A]n integrated web experience where the machine will be able to understand and catalogue data in a manner similar to humans' (Rudman and Bruwer, 2016: 132).

REFERENCES

CHAPTER 1

Alharthi, A., Krotov, V. and Bowman, M. (2017) 'Addressing barriers to big data', *Business Horizons*, 60(3): 285–292.

Bholat, D. (2015) 'Big data and central banks', *Big Data & Society*, 2(1): 1–6.

Bumblauskas, D., Nold, H., Bumblauskas, P. and Igou, A. (2017) 'Big data analytics: Transforming data to action', *Business Process Management Journal*, 23(3): 703–720.

DataFlair (2019) 'Data scientist vs data analyst – the hot debate for a promising career'. Retrieved from: https://data-flair.training/blogs/data-science-vs-data-analytics/ (accessed 18 April 2020).

Davenport, T.H. and Dyché, J. (2013) 'Big data in big companies'. Retrieved from: https://docs.media.bitpipe.com/io_10x/io_102267/item_725049/Big-Data-in-Big-Companies.pdf (accessed 18 April 2020).

Granville, V. (2013) 'Job titles for data scientists'. Retrieved from: www.datasciencecentral.com/profiles/blogs/job-titles-for-data-scientists (accessed 18 April 2020).

Granville, V. (2014a) 'Data scientist versus business analyst'. Retrieved from: www.data-sciencecentral.com/profiles/blogs/data-scientist-versus-business-analyst (accessed 18 April 2020).

Granville, V. (2014b) 'Data scientist versus data engineer'. Retrieved from: www.data-sciencecentral.com/profiles/blogs/data-scientist-versus-data-engineer (accessed 18 April 2020).

Granville, V. (2014c) 'Six categories of data scientists'. Retrieved from: www.datascience-central.com/profiles/blogs/six-categories-of-data-scientists (accessed 18 April 2020).

Gressel, S. (2020) 'Management decision making in the age of big data – An exploration of the roles of analytics and human judgment', PhD thesis, Massey University.

Holden, N. (2002) *Cross-Cultural Management: A Knowledge Management Perspective*. Harlow: Financial Times Prentice Hall.

Intezari, A. and Gressel, S. (2017) 'Information and reformation in KM systems: Big data and strategic decision-making', *Journal of Knowledge Management*, 21(1): 71–91.

Intezari, A and Pauleen, D. (2019) *Wisdom, Analytics and Wicked Problems: Integral Decision Making in the Data Age*. London: Routledge.

Janssen, M., van der Voort, H. and Wahyudi, A. (2017) 'Factors influencing big data decision-making quality', *Journal of Business Research*, 70: 338–345.

Mazenko, E. (2016) 'What's the difference between data science roles?'. Retrieved from: www.betterbuys.com/bi/comparing-data-science-roles/ (accessed 18 April 2020).

McAfee, A. and Brynjolfsson, E. (2012) 'Big data: The management revolution', *Harvard Business Review*, 90(10): 60–66.

McCarthy, E.D. (1996) *Knowledge as Culture: The New Sociology of Knowledge*. London: Routledge.

Pauleen, D., Rooney, D. and Holden, N. (2010) 'Practical wisdom and the development of cross-cultural knowledge management: A global leadership perspective', *European Journal of International Management*, 4(2): 382–395.

Pauleen, D. and Wang, W (2017) 'Does big data mean big knowledge? KM perspectives on big data and analytics', *Journal of Knowledge Management*, 21(1): 1–6.

Rooney, D. and Schneider, U. (2005) 'A model of the material, mental, historical and social character of knowledge', in D. Rooney, G. Hearn and A. Ninan (eds), *Handbook on the Knowledge Economy*. Cheltenham: Edward Elgar. pp. 19–36.

Sathi, A. (2012) *Big Data Analytics: Disruptive Technologies for Changing the Game*. Boise, ID: MC Press.

Schmarzo, B. (2018) 'Updated: Difference between business intelligence and data science'. Retrieved from: www.datasciencecentral.com/profiles/blogs/updated-difference-between-business-intelligence-and-data-science (accessed 18 April 2020).

Shah, S., Horne, A. and Capellá, J. (2012) 'Good data won't guarantee good decisions', *Harvard Business Review*, 90(4): 23–25.

Simon, H.A. (1960) *The New Science of Management Decision*. New York: Harper.

Taskin, N., Pauleen, D., Intezari, A. and Scahill, S. (2019) 'Why are leaders trusting their gut instinct over analytics? And what to do about it?', *New Zealand Management Magazine*, April: 10. Retrieved from: https://management.co.nz/article/why-are-leaders-trusting-their-gut-instinct-over-analytics-and-what-do-about-it (accessed 18 April 2020).

Watson, H. (2016) 'Creating a fact-based decision-making culture', *Business Intelligence Journal*, 21(2): 5–9.

Watson, H. and Marjanovic, O. (2013) 'Big data: The fourth data management generation', *Business Intelligence Journal*, 18(3): 4–8.

Wirth, N. and Wirth, R. (2017) 'How to meet the four key challenges to turn big data into smart data-driven solutions', *Research World*, 64: 31–36.

CHAPTER 2

Abbasi, A., Sarker, S. and Chiang, R. (2016) 'Big data research in information systems: Toward an inclusive research agenda', *Journal of the Association for Information Systems*, 17(2): i–xxxii.

Ackoff, R. (1989) 'From data to wisdom', *Journal of Applied Systems Analysis*, 16: 3–9.

Agarwal, R. and Dhar, V. (2014) 'Editorial – Big data, data science, and analytics: The opportunity and challenge for IS research', *Information Systems Research*, 25(3): 443–448.

Alavi, M. and Leidner, D. (2001) 'Review: Knowledge management and knowledge management systems: Conceptual foundations and research issues', *MIS Quarterly*, 1(10): 107–136.

Alharthi, A., Krotov, V. and Bowman, M. (2017) 'Addressing barriers to big data', *Business Horizons*, 60(3): 285–292.

Ardelt, M. (2003) 'Empirical assessment of a three-dimensional wisdom scale', *Research on Aging*, 25(3): 275–324.

Ardolino, M., Rapaccini, M., Saccani, N., Gaiardelli, P. and Crespi, G. (2018) 'The role of digital technologies for the service transformation of industrial companies', *International Journal of Production Research*, 56(6): 2116–2132.

Bholat, D. (2015) 'Big data and central banks', *Big Data & Society*, 2(1): 1–6.

Bumblauskas, D., Nold, H., Bumblauskas, P. and Igou, A. (2017) 'Big data analytics: Transforming data to action', *Business Process Management Journal*, 23(3): 703–720.

Chen, H., Chiang, R. and Storey, V. (2012) 'Business intelligence and analytics: From big data to big impact', *MIS Quarterly*, 36(4): 1165–1188.

Colombo, P. and Ferrari, E. (2015) 'Privacy aware access control for big data: A research roadmap', *Big Data Research*, 2(4): 145–154.

Cox, M. and Ellsworth, D. (1997) 'Application-controlled demand paging for out-of-core visualization', paper presented at the 8th ACM Conference on Visualization, Arizona.

Davenport, T.H. (2018) 'From analytics to artificial intelligence', *Journal of Business Analytics*, 1(2): 73–80.

Davenport, T.H. and Dyché, J. (2013) 'Big data in big companies'. Retrieved from: https://docs.media.bitpipe.com/io_10x/io_102267/item_725049/Big-Data-in-Big-Companies.pdf (accessed 18 April 2020).

Davenport, T. and Harris, J. (2017) *Competing on Analytics: Updated, with a New Introduction: The New Science of Winning.* Boston, MA: Harvard Business Press.

Davenport, T. and Prusak, L. (1998) *Working Knowledge: How Organizations Manage What They Know.* Boston, MA: Harvard Business Review Press.

Domo (2018) *Data Never Sleeps 6.0.* Retrieved from: https://web-assets.domo.com/blog/wp-content/uploads/2018/06/18_domo_data-never-sleeps-6verticals.pdf (accessed 18 April 2020).

Duan, Y., Edwards, J. and Dwivedi, Y. (2019) 'Artificial intelligence for decision-making in the era of big data – Evolution, challenges and research agenda', *International Journal of Information Management*, 48: 63–71.

Faucher, J.-B., Everett, A. and Lawson, R. (2008) 'Reconstituting knowledge management', *Journal of Knowledge Management*, 12(3): 3–16.

Firestone, J.M. (2003) 'The new knowledge management: A paradigm and its problems'. Retrieved from: www.kmci.org/media/Firestone-tnkmparadigm.pdf (accessed 18 April 2020).

Frické, M. (2009) 'The knowledge pyramid: A critique of the DIKW hierarchy', *Journal of Information Science*, 35(2): 131–142.

Gandomi, A. and Haider, M. (2015) 'Beyond the hype: Big data concepts, methods, and analytics', *International Journal of Information Management*, 35(2): 137–144.

Gressel, S. (2020) 'Management decision making in the age of big data – An exploration of the roles of analytics and human judgment', PhD thesis, Massey University.

Intezari, A. and Gressel, S. (2017) 'Information and reformation in KM systems: Big data and strategic decision-making', *Journal of Knowledge Management*, 21(1): 71–91.

Intezari, A. and Pauleen, D.J. (2017) 'The past-present-future conundrum: Extending time-bound knowledge', *International Journal of Knowledge Management*, 13(1): 1–15.

Intezari, A. and Pauleen, D. (2019) *Wisdom, Analytics and Wicked Problems: Integral Decision Making in the Data Age*. London: Routledge.

Jagadish, H., Gehrke, J., Labrinidis, A., Papakonstantinou, Y., Patel, J., Ramakrishnan, R. and Shahabi, C. (2014) 'Big data and its technical challenges', *Communications of the ACM*, 57(7): 86–94.

Kaisler, S., Armour, F., Espinosa, A. and Money, W. (2013) 'Big data: Issues and challenges moving forward', paper presented at the 46th Hawaii International Conference on System Sciences (HICSS).

Kuang, C. (2015) 'Disney's $1 billion bet on a magical wristband'. Retrieved from: www.wired.com/2015/03/disney-magicband/ (accessed 18 April 2020).

Laney, D. (2001) '3D data management: Controlling data volume, velocity, and variety'. Retrieved from: www.bibsonomy.org/bibtex/742811cb00b303261f79a98e9b80bf49 (accessed 18 April 2020).

Laskowski, N. (2013) 'Ten big data case studies in a nutshell', *The Data Mill*. Retrieved from: http://searchcio.techtarget.com/opinion/Ten-big-data-case-studies-in-a-nutshell (accessed 18 April 2020).

The Leadership Network (2016) 'How Disney creates digital magic with big data'. Retrieved from: https://theleadershipnetwork.com/article/disney-digital-magic-big-data (accessed 18 April 2020).

Marr, B. (2017) 'Disney uses big data, IoT and machine learning to boost customer experience'. Retrieved from: www.forbes.com/sites/bernardmarr/2017/08/24/disney-uses-big-data-iot-and-machine-learning-to-boost-customer-experience/ (accessed 18 April 2020).

McAfee, A. and Brynjolfsson, E. (2012) 'Big data: The management revolution', *Harvard Business Review*, 90(10): 60–66.

Mishra, D., Luo, Z., Jiang, S., Papadopoulos, T. and Dubey, R. (2017) 'A bibliographic study on big data: Concepts, trends and challenges', *Business Process Management Journal*, 23(3): 555–573.

Moore, J. (2017) 'Data visualization in support of executive decision making', *Interdisciplinary Journal of Information, Knowledge, and Management*, 12: 125–138.

Niesen, T., Houy, C., Fettke, P. and Loos, P. (2016) 'Towards an integrative big data analysis framework for data-driven risk management in Industry 4.0', paper presented at the 49th Hawaii International Conference on System Sciences (HICSS).

O'Leary, D. (2013) 'Artificial intelligence and big data', *IEEE Intelligent Systems*, 28(2): 96–99. doi:10.1109/MIS.2013.39.

Pauleen, D. (2017) 'KM and big data: An interview with David Snowden', *Journal of Knowledge Management*, 21(1): 12–17.

Pauleen, D. and Wang, W. (2017) 'Does big data mean big knowledge? KM perspectives on big data and analytics', *Journal of Knowledge Management*, 21(1): 1–6.

Petter, S., DeLone, W. and McLean, E. (2012) 'The past, present, and future of "IS success"', *Journal of the Association for Information Systems*, 13(5): 341–362.

Phillips-Wren, G., Iyer, L.S., Kulkarni, U. and Ariyachandra, T. (2015) 'Business analytics in the context of big data: A roadmap for research', *Communications of the Association for Information Systems*, 37(1): 448–472.

Reinsel, D., Gantz, J. and Rydning, J. (2018) *The Digitization of the World: From Edge to Core*, IDC White Paper. Retrieved from: www.seagate.com/files/www-content/our-story/trends/files/idc-seagate-dataage-whitepaper.pdf (accessed 18 April 2020).

Ross, J.W., Beath, C.M. and Quaadgras, A. (2013) 'You may not need big data after all', *Harvard Business Review*, 12. Retrieved from: https://hbr.org/2013/12/you-may-not-need-big-data-after-all (accessed 18 April 2020).

SAS (2020) 'Big data: What it is and why it matters'. Retrieved from: www.sas.com/en_nz/insights/big-data/what-is-big-data.html (accessed 18 April 2020).

Sathi, A. (2012) *Big Data Analytics: Disruptive Technologies for Changing the Game*. Boise, ID: MC Press.

Sivarajah, U., Kamal, M.M., Irani, Z. and Weerakkody, V. (2017) 'Critical analysis of big data challenges and analytical methods', *Journal of Business Research*, 70: 263–286.

Statista (2019) 'Number of e-mails per day worldwide 2017–2023'. Retrieved from: www.statista.com/statistics/456500/daily-number-of-e-mails-worldwide/ (accessed 18 April 2020).

Sumbal, M.S., Tsui, E. and See-to, E.W.K. (2017) 'Interrelationship between big data and knowledge management: An exploratory study in the oil and gas sector', *Journal of Knowledge Management*, 21(1): 180–196.

Terrific Data (2016) 'Big data at Macy's Inc.' Retrieved from: http://terrificdata.com/2016/06/30/big-data-at-macys-inc/ (accessed 18 April 2020).

Tole, A.A. (2013) 'Big data challenges', *Database Systems Journal*, 4(3): 31–40.

Wallace, D.P. (2007) *Knowledge Management: Historical and Cross-Disciplinary Themes*. Westport, CT: Libraries Unlimited.

Walmart (2012) 'Walmart announces new search engine to power Walmart.com', press release. Retrieved from: http://corporate.walmart.com/_news_/news-archive/2012/08/30/walmart-announces-new-search-engine-to-power-walmartcom (accessed 18 April 2020).

Watson, H. and Marjanovic, O. (2013) 'Big data: The fourth data management generation', *Business Intelligence Journal*, 18(3): 4–8.

Wognin, R., Henri, F. and Marino, O. (2012) 'Data, information, knowledge, wisdom: A revised model for agents-based knowledge management systems', in L. Moller and J.B. Huett (eds), *The Next Generation of Distance Education: Unconstrained Learning.* New York: Springer. pp. 181–189.

CHAPTER 3

Akter, S., Wamba, S.F., Gunasekaran, A., Dubey, R. and Childe, S.J. (2016) 'How to improve firm performance using big data analytics capability and business strategy alignment?', *International Journal of Production Economics*, 182: 113–131.

Banerjee, A., Bandyopadhyay, T. and Acharya, P. (2013) 'Data analytics: Hyped up aspirations or true potential?', *Vikalpa*, 38(4): 1–12.

Bhatt, G. (2001) 'Knowledge management in organizations: Examining the interaction between technologies, techniques, and people', *Journal of Knowledge Management*, 5(1): 68–75. doi:10.1108/13673270110384419.

Bhidé, A. (2010) 'The judgment deficit', *Harvard Business Review*, 88(9): 44–53.

Bose, R. (2009) 'Advanced analytics: Opportunities and challenges', *Industrial Management & Data Systems*, 109(2): 155–172. doi:10.1108/02635570910930073.

Brynjolfsson, E., Hitt, L.M. and Kim, H.H. (2011) 'Strength in numbers: How does data-driven decisionmaking affect firm performance?. http://dx.doi.org/10.2139/ssrn.1819486.

Brynjolfsson, E. and McElheran, K. (2016) 'Data in action: Data-driven decision making in US manufacturing', US Census Bureau Center for Economic Studies Paper No. CES-WP-16-06.

Cao, G., Duan, Y. and Li, G. (2015) 'Linking business analytics to decision making effectiveness: A path model analysis', *IEEE Transactions on Engineering Management*, 62(3): 384–395.

Chen, H., Chiang, R. and Storey, V. (2012) 'Business intelligence and analytics: From big data to big impact', *MIS Quarterly*, 36(4): 1165–1188.

Danisch, R. (2011) 'Risk assessment as rhetorical practice: The ironic mathematics behind terrorism, banking, and public policy', *Public Understanding of Science*, 22(2): 236–251.

Davenport, T.H. (2006) 'Competing on analytics', *Harvard Business Review*, 84(1): 98–107.

Davenport, T. (2013) 'Analytics 3.0', *Harvard Business Review*, 91(12): 64–72.

Davenport, T. (2014) 'How strategists use "big data" to support internal business decisions, discovery and production', *Strategy & Leadership*, 42(4): 45–50.

Davenport, T.H. (2018) 'From analytics to artificial intelligence', *Journal of Business Analytics*, 1(2): 73–80.

Davenport, T. and Harris, J. (2017) *Competing on Analytics: Updated, with a New Introduction: The New Science of Winning.* Boston, MA: Harvard Business Press.

Davenport, T.H. and Prusak, L. (1998) *Working Knowledge: How Organizations Manage What They Know*. Boston, MA: Harvard Business School Press.

Delen, D. and Demirkan, H. (2013) 'Data, information and analytics as services', *Decision Support Systems*, 55(1): 359–363.

Elliott, T. (2013) 'Predictive is the next step in analytics maturity? It's more complicated than that!'. Retrieved from: https://timoelliott.com/blog/2018/04/predictive-is-the-next-step-in-analytics-maturity-its-more-complicated-than-that.html (accessed 20 April 2020).

Fan, W. and Gordon, M.D. (2014) 'The power of social media analytics', *Communication of ACM*, 57(6): 74–81.

FCIC (Financial Crisis Inquiry Commission) (2011) *The Financial Crisis Inquiry Report: Final Report of the National Commission on the Causes of the Financial and Economic Crisis in the United States*. Washington, DC: Financial Crisis Inquiry Commission.

Gandomi, A. and Haider, M. (2015) 'Beyond the hype: Big data concepts, methods, and analytics', *International Journal of Information Management*, 35(2): 137–144.

Gartner (2020a) 'Gartner Glossary: Analytics'. Retrieved from: www.gartner.com/it-glossary/analytics/ (accessed 20 April 2020).

Gartner (2020b) 'Gartner Glossary: Analytics and Business Intelligence (ABI)'. Retrieved from www.gartner.com/it-glossary/business-intelligence-bi/ (accessed 20 April 2020).

Ghosh, P. (2017) 'Fundamentals of descriptive analytics'. Retrieved from: www.dataversity.net/fundamentals-descriptive-analytics/ (accessed 20 April 2020).

Gressel, S. (2020) 'Management decision making in the age of big data – an exploration of the roles of analytics and human judgment', PhD thesis, Massey University.

Gupta, M. and George, J.F. (2016) 'Toward the development of a big data analytics capability', *Information & Management*, 53(8): 1049–1064.

Halo (2019) 'Descriptive, predictive, and prescriptive analytics explained'. Retrieved from: https://halobi.com/blog/descriptive-predictive-and-prescriptive-analytics-explained/ (accessed 20 April 2020).

Kaisler, S., Armour, F., Espinosa, A. and Money, W. (2013) 'Big data: Issues and challenges moving forward', paper presented at the 46th Hawaii International Conference on System Sciences (HICSS).

Kawas, B., Squillante, M., Subramanian, D. and Varshney, K. (2013) 'Prescriptive analytics for allocating sales teams to opportunities', in IEEE 13th International Conference on Data Mining Workshops. Dalla, TX: IEEE. pp. 211–218. doi:10.1109/ICDMW.2013.156.

LaValle, S., Lesser, E., Shockley, R., Hopkins, M. and Kruschwitz, N. (2011) 'Big data, analytics and the path from insights to value', *MIT Sloan Management Review*, 21: 21–32.

Lee, I. (2017) 'Big data: Dimensions, evolution, impacts, and challenges', *Business Horizons*, 60(3): 293–303.

Lodha, R., Jain, H. and Kurup, L. (2014) 'Big data challenges: data analysis perspective', *International Journal of Current Engineering and Technology*, 4(5): 3286–3289.

Loshin, D. (2013) *Big Data Analytics: From Strategic Planning to Enterprise Integration with Tools, Techniques, NoSQL, and Graph*. Amsterdam: Morgan Kaufmann.

McAfee, A. and Brynjolfsson, E. (2012) 'Big data: The management revolution', *Harvard Business Review*, 90(10): 60–66.

Pauleen, D. (2017a) 'KM and big data: An interview with Larry Prusak & Tom Davenport', special issue 'Big Data/Analytics and Knowledge Management', *Journal of Knowledge Management*, 21(1): 7–11.

Pauleen, D.J. (2017b) 'Dave Snowden on KM and big data/analytics: Interview with David J. Pauleen', *Journal of Knowledge Management*, 21(1): 12–17.

Pauleen, D., Rooney, D. and Intezari, A. (2016) 'Big data, little wisdom: Trouble brewing? Ethical implications for the information systems discipline', *Journal of Social Epistemology*, 31(4): 400–416.

Provost, F. and Fawcett, T. (2013) 'Data science and its relationship to big data and data-driven decision making', *Big Data*, 1(1): 51–59. doi:10.1089/big.2013.1508.

Rehman, M.H. ur., Chang, V., Batool, A. and Wah, T.Y. (2016) 'Big data reduction framework for value creation in sustainable enterprises', *International Journal of Information Management*, 36(6): 917–928.

Sivarajah, U., Kamal, M.M., Irani, Z. and Weerakkody, V. (2017) 'Critical analysis of big data challenges and analytical methods', *Journal of Business Research*, 70: 263–286.

Tamm, T., Seddon, P. and Shanks, G. (2013) 'Pathways to Value from Business Analytics'. Proceedings in Thirty Fourth International Conference on Information Systems, Milan.

Taskin, N., Pauleen, D., Intezari, A. and Scahill, S. (2019) 'Why are leaders trusting their gut instinct over analytics? And what to do about it?', *New Zealand Management Magazine*, April: 10. Retrieved from: https://management.co.nz/article/why-are-leaders-trusting-their-gut-instinct-over-analytics-and-what-do-about-it (accessed 18 April 2020).

Taskin, N., Pauleen, D., Intezari, A. and Scahill, S. (2020) 'Decision making with big data and analytics'. Unpublished raw data.

Watson, H. and Marjanovic, O. (2013) 'Big data: The fourth data management generation', *Business Intelligence Journal*, 18(3): 4–8.

CHAPTER 4

Ackoff, R. (1990) 'Strategy', *Systems Practice*, 3(6): 521–524. doi:10.1007/BF01059636.

Bazerman, M.H. (2006). *Judgment in Managerial Decision Making* (6th edn). Hoboken, NJ: John Wiley & Sons.

Bazerman, M. and Moore, D. (2013) *Judgment in Managerial Decision Making* (8th edn). Hoboken, NJ: Wiley & Sons.

Beach, L.R. and Connolly, T. (2005) *The Psychology of Decision Making: People in Organizations* (2nd edn). Thousand Oaks, CA: Sage Publications.

Betsch, T. and Glöckner, A. (2010) 'Intuition in judgment and decision making: Extensive thinking without effort', *Psychological Inquiry*, 21(4): 279–294. doi:10.1080/10478 40X.2010.517737.

Bhidé, A. (2010) 'The judgment deficit', *Harvard Business Review*, 88(9): 44–53.

Bryant, D.J. and Tversky, B. (1999) 'Mental representations of perspective and spatial relations from diagrams and models', *Journal of Experimental Psychology: Learning, Memory, and Cognition*, 25(1): 137–156. doi:10.1037/0278-7393.25.1.137.

Buchanan, L. and O'Connell, A. (2006) 'A brief history of decision making', *Harvard Business Review*, 84(1): 32–42.

Cabantous, L. and Gond, J.P. (2011) 'Rational decision making as performative praxis: Explaining rationality's éternel retour', *Organization Science*, 22(3): 573–586.

Carruthers, B. (2010) 'Knowledge and liquidity: Institutional and cognitive foundations of the subprime crisis', in M. Lounsbury and P. Hirsch (ed.), *Markets on Trial: The Economic Sociology of the U.S. Financial Crisis: Part A (Research in the Sociology of Organizations, Vol. 30 Part A)*. Bingley: Emerald. pp. 157–182. doi: 10.1108/S0733-558X(2010)000030A009.

Dalal, N. and Pauleen, D. (2018) 'The wisdom nexus in information systems: Guiding information systems research, practice and education', *Information Systems Journal*, 29(1): 224–244.

Dane, E. and Pratt, M.G. (2007) 'Exploring intuition and its role in managerial decision making', *Academy of Management Review*, 32(1): 33–54. doi:10.5465/AMR.2007.23463682.

Davenport, T., Barth, P. and Bean, R. (2013) 'How "big data" is different', *MIT Sloan Management Review*, 54(1): 42–47.

Dewey, J. (1933) *How We Think* (revised edn). Boston, MA: D.C. Heath.

Drucker, P.F. (1967) 'The effective decision', *Harvard Business Review*, 45(1): 92–98.

Drucker, P.F. (2006) *The Effective Executive: The Definitive Guide to Getting the Right Things Done* (Harperbusiness Essentials). New York: Collins.

Evans, J.S.B. (2003) 'In two minds: Dual-process accounts of reasoning', *Trends in Cognitive Sciences*, 7(10): 454–459.

Galotti, K.M. (2002) *Making Decisions That Matter: How People Face Important Life Choices*. London: Lawrence Erlbaum Associates.

Gibcus, P., Vermeulen, P.A.M. and Radulova, E. (2008) 'The decision-making entrepreneur: A literature review', in P.A.M. Vermeulen and P.L. Curşeu (eds), *Entrepreneurial Strategic Decisionmaking: A Cognitive Perspective*. Cheltenham: Edward Elgar Publishing Limited. pp. 11–40.

Gilhooly, K. and Murphy, P. (2005) 'Differentiating insight from non-insight problems', *Thinking & Reasoning*, 11(3): 279–302. doi:10.1080/13546780442000187.

Gressel, S. (2020) 'Management decision making in the age of big data – An exploration of the roles of analytics and human judgment', PhD thesis, Massey University.

Hammond, J.S., Keeney, R.L. and Raiffa, H. (1999) *Smart Choices: A Practical Guide to Making Better Life Decisions.* New York: Broadway.

Harrison, E.F. (1995) *The Managerial Decision-making Process* (5th edn). Boston, MA: Houghton Mifflin.

Harrison, F.E. (1999) *The managerial decision-making process* (5th edn). Boston: Houghton Mifflin Company.

Intezari, A. and Pauleen, D. (2019) *Wisdom, Analytics and Wicked Problems: Integral Decision Making in the Data Age.* Routledge: London.

Kahneman, D. (2003) 'A perspective on judgment and choice: Mapping bounded rationality. *American Psychologist*, 58(9): 697–720.

Khatri, N. and Ng, A. (2000) 'The role of intuition in strategic decision making', *Human Relations*, 53(1): 57–86. doi:10.1177/0018726700531004.

Klein, G., Calderwood, R. and Clinton-Cirocco, A. (2010) 'Rapid decision making on the fire ground: The original study plus a postscript', *Journal of Cognitive Engineering and Decision Making*, 4(3): 186–209.

Kudesia, R.S. (2019) 'Mindfulness as metacognitive practice', *Academy of Management Review*, 44(2): 405–423. doi:10.5465/amr.2015.0333.

Küpers, W. and Pauleen, D. (2015) 'The art of learning wisdom: Embodied approaches to management education', *Scandinavian Journal of Management*, 31(4): 493–500.

Lewin, K. (1951) 'Problems of research in social psychology', in D. Cartwright (ed.), *Field Theory in Social Science: Selected Theoretical Papers.* New York: Harper & Row. pp. 155–169.

Maddalena, V. and Canada, H. (2007) 'A practical approach to ethical decision-making', *Leadership in Health Services*, 20(2): 71–75.

Messick, D.M. and Bazerman, M.H. (2001) 'Ethical leadership and the psychology of decision making', in J. Dienhart, D. Moberg and R. Duska (eds), *The Next Phase of Business Ethics: Integrating Psychology and Ethics.* Oxford: JAI Elsevier. pp. 213–238.

Miller, S.J., Hickson, D.J. and Wilsdon, D.C. (2002) 'Decision-making in organizations', in G. Salaman (ed.), *Decision Making for Business: A Reader.* London: Sage Publications. pp. 74–92.

Mintzberg, H., Raisinghani, D. and Theoret, A. (1976) 'The structure of "unstructured" decision processes', *Administrative Science Quarterly*, 21(2): 246–275. doi:10.2307/2392045.

Nutt, P.C. (2002) *Why Decisions Fail: Avoiding the Blunders and Traps that Lead to Debacles.* San Francisco: Berrett-Koehler Publishers.

Patvardhan, S. (2017) 'Exploring imagination and its implications for strategic choice', *Academy of Management Proceedings*, 2017(1). doi: 10.5465/AMBPP.2017.10823abstract.

Porter, M.E. (1985) *Competitive Advantage: Creating and Sustaining Superior Performance.* New York: Free Press.

Rosanas, J.M. (2013) *Decision-making in an Organizational Context: Beyond Economic Criteria.* Basingstoke: Palgrave Macmillan.

Saaty, T.L. (1994) 'How to make a decision: The analytic hierarchy process', *Informs*, 24(6): 19–43.

Shah, S., Horne, A. and Capellá, J. (2012) 'Good data won't guarantee good decisions', *Harvard Business Review*, 90(4): 23–25.

Sheshasaayee, A. and Bhargavi, K. (2017) 'A study of automated decision making systems', *Research Inventy: International Journal of Engineering And Science*, 7(1): 28–31.

Shiloh, S., Koren, S. and Zakay, D. (2001) 'Individual differences in compensatory decisionmaking style and need for closure as correlates of subjective decision complexity and diffculty', *Personality and Individual Differences*, 30(4): 699–710.

Simon, H.A. (1957) *Models of Man: Social and Rational*. Oxford: Wiley.

Simon, H.A. (1960) *The New Science of Management Decision*. New York: Harper.

Simon, H.A. (1965) *The Shape of Automation*. New York: Harper and Row.

Simon, H.A. (1987) 'Making management decisions: The role of intuition and emotion', *The Academy of Management Executive*, 1(1): 57–64.

Snowden, D. (2000) 'Cynefin: A sense of time and space, the social ecology of knowledge management', in C. Despres and D. Chauvel (eds), *Knowledge Horizons: The Present and the Promise of Knowledge Management*. Oxford: Butterworth-Heinemann. pp. 237–266.

Snowden, D. and Boone, M. (2007) 'A leader's framework for decision making', *Harvard Business Review*, 85(11): 68–76.

Stanovich, K.E. and West, R.F. (2000) 'Individual differences in reasoning: Implications for the rationality debate?', *Behavioral and Brain Sciences*, 23(5): 645–665.

Taskin, N., Pauleen, D., Intezari, A. and Scahill, S. (2020a) 'Decision making with big data and analytics'. Unpublished raw data.

Taskin, N., Pauleen, D. and Mi, M. (2020b) 'Impact of rational and intuition on decision quality and organizational performance'. Unpublished raw data.

Tversky, A. and Kahneman, D. (1973) 'Availability: A heuristic for judging frequency and probability', *Cognitive Psychology*, 5(2): 207–232.

Tversky, A. and Kahneman, D. (1975) 'Judgment under uncertainty: Heuristics and biases', in *Utility, Probability, and Human Decision Making*. The Netherlands: Springer. pp. 141–162.

Wray, C. (2017) 'A proposed new psychological model for judgement and decision-making: Integrating the tri-partite model with hemispheric difference', *Leadership & Organization Development Journal*, 38(4): 549–563.

CHAPTER 5

Bazerman, M. and Moore, D. (2013) *Judgment in Managerial Decision Making* (8th edn). Hoboken, NJ: Wiley & Sons.

Bohanec, M. (2009) 'Decision making: A computer-science and information-technology viewpoint', *Interdisciplinary Description of Complex Systems*, 7(2): 22–37.

Calabretta, G., Gemser, G. and Wijnberg, N.M. (2017) 'The interplay between intuition and rationality in strategic decision making: A paradox perspective', *Organization Studies*, 38(3–4): 365–401.

Courtney, J. (2001) 'Decision making and knowledge management in inquiring organizations: Toward a new decision-making paradigm for DSS', *Decision Support Systems*, 31(1): 17–38. doi:10.1016/S0167-9236(00)00117-2.

Dijksterhuis, A. and Nordgren, L. (2006) 'A theory of unconscious thought', *Perspectives on Psychological Science*, 1(2): 95–109. doi:10.1111/j.1745-6916.2006.00007.x.

Dreyfus, S. and Dreyfus, H. (1980) *A Five-Stage Model of the Mental Activities Involved in Directed Skill Acquisition*. DTIC Document.

Gressel, S. (2020) 'Management decision making in the age of big data – An exploration of the roles of analytics and human judgment', PhD thesis, Massey University.

Gupta, M. and George, J.F. (2016) 'Toward the development of a big data analytics capability', *Information & Management*, 53(8): 1049–1064.

Harrison, E.F. (1995) *The Managerial Decision-making Process* (5th edn). Boston, MA: Houghton Mifflin.

Huber, G. (1990) 'A theory of the effects of advanced information technologies on organizational design, intelligence, and decision making', *Academy of Management Review*, 15(1): 47–71. doi:10.5465/AMR.1990.4308227.

Jagadish, H., Gehrke, J., Labrinidis, A., Papakonstantinou, Y., Patel, J., Ramakrishnan, R. and Shahabi, C. (2014) 'Big data and its technical challenges', *Communications of the ACM*, 57(7): 86–94. doi:10.1145/2611567.

Kaufmann, L., Wagner, C.M. and Carter, C.R. (2017) 'Individual modes and patterns of rational and intuitive decision-making by purchasing managers', *Journal of Purchasing and Supply Management*, 23(2): 82–93.

Khatri, N. and Ng, A. (2000) 'The role of intuition in strategic decision making', *Human Relations*, 53(1): 57–86. doi:10.1177/0018726700531004.

LaValle, S., Lesser, E., Shockley, R., Hopkins, M. and Kruschwitz, N. (2011) 'Big data, analytics and the path from insights to value', *MIT Sloan Management Review*, 52(2): 21–32.

Mintzberg, H., Raisinghani, D. and Theoret, A. (1976) 'The structure of "unstructured" decision processes', *Administrative Science Quarterly*, 21(2): 246–275. doi:10.2307/2392045.

Provost, F. and Fawcett, T. (2013) 'Data science and its relationship to big data and data-driven decision making', *Big Data*, 1(1): 51–59. doi:10.1089/big.2013.1508.

Shah, N., Irani, Z. and Sharif, A.M. (2017) 'Big data in an HR context: Exploring organizational change readiness, employee attitudes and behaviors', *Journal of Business Research*, 70: 366–378.

Simon, H.A. (1960) *The New Science of Management Decision*. New York: Harper.

Snowden, D. and Boone, M. (2007) 'A leader's framework for decision making', *Harvard Business Review*, 85(11): 68–76.

Stanovich, K.E. and West, R.F. (2000) 'Individual differences in reasoning: Implications for the rationality debate?', *Behavioral and Brain Sciences*, 23(5): 645–665.

Taskin, N., Pauleen, D., Intezari, A. and Scahill, S. (2019) 'Why are leaders trusting their gut instinct over analytics? And what to do about it?', *New Zealand Management Magazine*, April: 10. Retrieved from: https://management.co.nz/article/why-are-leaders-trusting-their-gut-instinct-over-analytics-and-what-do-about-it (accessed 18 April 2020).

Taskin, N., Pauleen, D., Intezari, A. and Scahill, S. (2020) 'Decision making with big data and analytics'. Unpublished raw data.

Wirth, N. and Wirth, R. (2017) 'How to meet the four key challenges to turn big data into smart data-driven solutions', *Research World*, 2017(64): 31–36.

CHAPTER 6

Boeker, W. (1997) 'Strategic change: The influence of managerial characteristics and organizational growth', *Academy of Management Journal*, 40(1): 152–170.

Cristofaro, M. and Cristofaro, M. (2017) 'Reducing biases of decision-making processes in complex organizations', *Management Research Review*, 40(3): 270–291.

Gressel, S. (2020) 'Management decision making in the age of big data – an exploration of the roles of analytics and human judgment', PhD thesis, Massey University.

Gupta, A.K. and Govindarajan, V. (1984) 'Business unit strategy, managerial characteristics, and business unit effectiveness at strategy implementation', *Academy of Management Journal*, 27(1): 25–41.

Hensman, A. and Sadler-Smith, E. (2011) 'Intuitive decision making in banking and finance', *European Management Journal*, 29(1): 51–66. doi:10.1016/j.emj.2010.08.006.

Hirsh, K. and Hirsh, E. (2010) *Myers-Briggs Type Indicator® Decision-Making Style Report*. Menlo Park, CA: CPP, Inc.

Shah, S., Horne, A. and Capellá, J. (2012) 'Good data won't guarantee good decisions', *Harvard Business Review*, 90(4): 23–25.

Shepherd, N.G. and Rudd, J.M. (2014) 'The influence of context on the strategic decision-making process: a review of the literature', *International Journal of Management Reviews*, 16(3): 340–364.

CHAPTER 7

Alharthi, A., Krotov, V. and Bowman, M. (2017) 'Addressing barriers to big data', *Business Horizons*, 60(3): 285–292.

Bandura, A. (1978) 'Self-efficacy: Toward a unifying theory of behavioral change', *Advances in Behaviour Research and Therapy*, 1(4): 139–161.

Bronfenbrenner, U. (1977) 'Toward an experimental ecology of human development', *American Psychologist*, 32(7): 513–531.

Bronfenbrenner, U. (1979) *The Ecology of Human Development: Experiments by Nature and Design*. Cambridge, MA: Harvard University Press.

Bumblauskas, D., Nold, H., Bumblauskas, P. and Igou, A. (2017) 'Big data analytics: Transforming data to action', *Business Process Management Journal*, 23(3): 703–720.

Chen, H.-M., Schütz, R., Kazman, R. and Matthes, F. (2017) 'How Lufthansa capitalized on big data for business model renovation', *MIS Quarterly Executive*, 16(1): 19–34.

Davenport, T. and Harris, J. (2017) *Competing on Analytics: Updated, with a New Introduction: The New Science of Winning*. Boston, MA: Harvard Business Press.

Goepfert, J. and Shirer, M. (2018) 'Revenues for big data and business analytics solutions forecast to reach $260 billion in 2022, led by the banking and manufacturing industries, according to IDC', press release. Retrieved from: www.idc.com/getdoc.jsp?containerId=prUS44215218 (accessed 12 May 2019).

Gressel, S. (2020) 'Management decision making in the age of big data – An exploration of the roles of analytics and human judgment', PhD thesis, Massey University.

Harrison, E.F. (1995) *The Managerial Decision-making Process* (5th edn). Boston, MA: Houghton Mifflin.

Hensman, A. and Sadler-Smith, E. (2011) 'Intuitive decision making in banking and finance', *European Management Journal*, 29(1): 51–66. doi:10.1016/j.emj.2010.08.006.

Keenan, C. (2015) 'Big data and predictive analytics: A big deal, indeed', *American Bankers Association. ABA Banking Journal*, 107(4): 32.

LaValle, S., Lesser, E., Shockley, R., Hopkins, M. and Kruschwitz, N. (2011) 'Big data, analytics and the path from insights to value', *MIT Sloan Management Review*, 52(2): 21–32.

Taskin, N., Pauleen, D. and Li, J. (2020a) 'Decision making with big data and analytics: A comparative study', unpublished raw data.

Taskin, N., Pauleen, D., Intezari, A. and Scahill, S. (2019) 'Why are leaders trusting their gut instinct over analytics? And what to do about it?', New Zealand Management Magazine, April: 10. Retrieved from: https://management.co.nz/article/why-are-leaders-trusting-their-gut-instinct-over-analytics-and-what-do-about-it (accessed 18 April 2020).

Taskin, N., Pauleen, D., Intezari, A. and Scahill, S. (2020b) 'Decision making with big data and analytics'. Unpublished raw data.

Wirth, N. and Wirth, R. (2017) 'How to meet the four key challenges to turn big data into smart data-driven solutions', *Research World*, 2017(64): 31–36.

CHAPTER 8

Holtel, S. (2016) 'Artificial intelligence creates a wicked problem for the enterprise', *Procedia Computer Science*, 99: 171–180.

Intezari, A. and Pauleen, D. (2019) *Wisdom, Analytics and Wicked Problems: Integral Decision Making in the Data Age.* London: Routledge.

Mintzberg, H., Raisinghani, D. and Theoret, A. (1976) 'The structure of "unstructured" decision processes', *Administrative Science Quarterly*, 21(2): 246–275. doi:10.2307/2392045.

Nelson, J. and Grubesic, T. (2019) 'Oil spill modeling: Computational tools, analytical frameworks, and emerging technologies', *Progress in Physical Geography: Earth and Environment*, 43(1): 129–143.

CHAPTER 9

Abel, R. (2019) 'Sprint customer data breached via Samsung website flaw'. Retrieved from: www.scmagazine.com/home/security-news/data-breach/sprint-is-notifying-customers-that-threat-actors-gained-unauthorized-access-to-an-undisclosed-number-of-customer-accounts-via-a-compromised-samsung-website/ (accessed 27 April 2020).

Abraham, S. and Chengalur-Smith, I. (2010) 'An overview of social engineering malware: Trends, tactics, and implications', *Technology in Society*, 32(3): 183–196.

Alharthi, A., Krotov, V. and Bowman, M. (2017) 'Addressing barriers to big data', *Business Horizons*, 60(3): 285–292.

Andelane, L. (2019) 'Sephora discovers online data breach, New Zealand customers could be affected'. Retrieved from: www.newshub.co.nz/home/money/2019/07/sephora-discovers-online-data-breach-new-zealand-customers-could-be-affected.html (accessed 27 April 2020).

Arrington, J. (2019) '10 types of hackers: The definitive guide'. Retrieved from: https://bestiphider.com/types-of-hackers/ (accessed 27 April 2020).

Autili, M., DiRuscio,D., Inverardi, P., Pelliccione, P. and Tivoli, M. (2019) 'A software exoskeleton to protect and support citizen's ethics and privacy in the digital world', *IEEE Access*, 7: 62011–62021.

Barber, R. (2001) 'Hackers profiled – who are they and what are their motivations?', *Computer Fraud & Security*, 2: 14–17.

Barker, S. (2017) '5 types of IT security threats facing businesses'. Retrieved from: www.rutternet.com/blog/5-types-of-it-security-threats-facing-businesses (accessed 27 April 2020).

Bianculli, L. (2019) '10 common IT security risks in the workplace'. Retrieved from: www.ccsinet.com/blog/common-security-risks-workplace/ (accessed 27 April 2020).

Boyd, D. and Crawford, K. (2012) 'Critical questions for big data: Provocations for a cultural, technological, and scholarly phenomenon', *Information, Communication & Society*, 15(5): 662–679.

Cisco (2019) 'What is IT security?'. Retrieved from: www.cisco.com/c/en/us/products/security/what-is-it-security.html (accessed 27 April 2020).

Curia (2019) 'Court of Justice of the European Union', Press Release No 99/19, Luxembourg1, 29 July. Retrieved from: https://curia.europa.eu/jcms/upload/docs/application/pdf/2019-07/cp190099en.pdf (accessed 27 April 2020).

Dalal, N. and Pauleen, D. (2018) 'The wisdom nexus in information systems: Guiding information systems research, practice and education', *Information Systems Journal*, 29(1): 224–244.

Davenport, T. and Harris, J. (2017) *Competing on Analytics: Updated, with a New Introduction: The New Science of Winning*. Boston, MA: Harvard Business Press.

Doffman, Z. (2019) 'Samsung's warning to owners of QLED Smart TVs is quickly deleted', *Forbes*. Retrieved from: www.forbes.com/sites/zakdoffman/2019/06/18/samsung-issues-then-deletes-warning-to-check-smart-tvs-for-malicious-software/#23806c25389b (accessed 27 April 2020).

Elbeltagi, I. and Agag, G. (2016) 'E-retailing ethics and its impact on customer satisfaction and repurchase intention: A cultural commitment-trust theory perspective', *Internet Research*, 26(1): 288–310.

Foxcroft, D. (2019) 'Customers could face long-term privacy issues after Air New Zealand data breach'. Retrieved from: www.stuff.co.nz/business/114913189/customers-could-face-longterm-privacy-issues-after-air-new-zealand-data-breach (accessed 27 April 2020).

GeeksforGeeks (2019) 'Types of hackers'. Retrieved from: www.geeksforgeeks.org/types-of-hackers/ (accessed 27 April 2020).

General Data Protection Regulation (GDPR) (2018) Retrieved from: https://gdpr.eu/what-is-gdpr/ (accessed 17 September 2020).

Goggin, G., Vromen, A., Weatherall, K.G., Martin, F., Webb, A., Sunman, L. and Bailo, F. (2017) *Digital Rights in Australia*. Sydney, NSW: University of Sydney.

Gold, S. (2014) 'Get your head around hacker psychology', *Engineering & Technology*, 9(1): 76–80.

Henderson, L. (2017) 'National infrastructure – the next step for seasoned hackers', *Network Security*, March: 8–10.

Ikeda, S. (2019) 'New Toyota data breach exposes personal information of 3.1 million customers'. Retrieved from: www.cpomagazine.com/cyber-security/new-toyota-data-breach-exposes-personal-information-of-3-1-million-customers/ (accessed 27 April 2020).

Intezari, A. and Pauleen, D. (2019) *Wisdom, Analytics and Wicked Problems: Integral Decision Making in the Data Age*. London: Routledge.

Kemp, R. (2014) 'Legal aspects of managing big data', *Computer Law & Security Review*, 30(5): 482–491.

Lim, S., Woo, J., Lee, I. and Huh, S.Y. (2018) 'Consumer valuation of personal information in the age of big data', *Journal of the Association of Science and Technology*, 69(1): 60–71.

Livingstone, S., Mascheroni, G. and Staksrud, E. (2018) 'European research on children's Internet use: Assessing the past and anticipating the future', *New Media & Society*, 20(3): 1103–1122.

Lodha, R., Jain, H. and Kurup, L. (2014) 'Big data challenges: Data analysis perspective', *International Journal of Current Engineering and Technology*, 4(5): 3286–3289.

Madarie, R. (2017) 'Hackers' motivations: Testing Schwartz's theory of motivational types of values in a sample of hackers', *International Journal of Cyber Criminology*, 11(1): 78–97.

Mantelero, A. and Vaciago, G. (2015) 'Data protection in a big data society: Ideas for a future regulation', *Digital Investigation*, 15: 104–109.

Mao, Y., You, C., Zhang, J., Huang, K. and Letaief, K.B. (2017) 'A survey on mobile edge computing: The communication perspective', *IEEE Communications Surveys & Tutorials*, 19(4): 2322–2358.

Marwick, A.E. and Boyd, D. (2014) 'Networked privacy: How teenagers negotiate context in social media', *New Media & Society*, 16(7): 1051–1067.

Matthews, J. and Goerzen, M. (2019) 'Black hat trolling, white hat trolling, and hacking the attention landscape', in Companion Proceedings of the 2019 World Wide Web Conference. New York: Association for Computing Machinery. pp. 523–528.

Matzner, T. (2014) 'Why privacy is not enough privacy in the context of "ubiquitous computing" and "big data"', *Journal of Information, Communication and Ethics in Society*, 12(2): 93–106.

McLean, R. (2019) 'A hacker gained access to 100 million Capital One credit card applications and accounts'. Retrieved from: https://edition.cnn.com/2019/07/29/business/capital-one-data-breach/index.html (accessed 27 April 2020).

Motamarri, S., Akter, S. and Yanamandram, V. (2017) 'Does big data analytics influence frontline employees in services marketing?', *Business Process Management Journal*, 23(3): 1–36.

Norton (2019) 'What is the difference between black, white and grey hat hackers?'. Retrieved from: https://us.norton.com/internetsecurity-emerging-threats-what-is-the-difference-between-black-white-and-grey-hat-hackers.html (accessed 27 April 2020).

Nunan, D. and Di Domenico, M. (2013) 'Market research & the ethics of big data', *International Journal of Market Research*, 55(4): 505–520.

Nuñez, M. (2019) 'FTC slaps Facebook with $5 billion fine, forces new privacy controls', *Forbes*. Retrieved from: www.forbes.com/sites/mnunez/2019/07/24/ftcs-unprecedented-slap-fines-facebook-5-billion-forces-new-privacy-controls/ (accessed 27 April 2020).

Seebruck, R. (2015) 'A typology of hackers: Classifying cyber malfeasance using a weighted arc circumplex model', *Digital Investigation*, 14: 36–45.

Seerden, X., Salmela, H. and Rutkowski, A.F. (2018) 'Privacy governance and the GDPR: How are organisations taking action to comply with the new privacy regulations in Europe?'. Proceedings of the 14th European Conference on Management, Leadership and Governance 2018. Sonning Common: ACPI.

Shaw, A. (2019) 'Sephora data breach: Customers' personal data for sale on the dark web'. Retrieved from: www.nzherald.co.nz/business/news/article.cfm?c_id=3&objectid=12254999 (accessed 27 April 2020).

Stoneburner, G., Goguen, A. and Feringa, A. (2002) *Risk Management Guide for Information Technology Systems*. Gaithersburg, MD: NIST Special Publication, pp. 800–830.

Thycotic (2019) 'Hackers & security professionals at Black Hat: Where they agree and where they differ'. Retrieved from: https://thycotic.com/resources/black-hat-2019-hacker-survey-report/ (accessed 27 April 2020).

Watson, J., Richter-Lipford, H. and Besmer, A. (2015) 'Mapping user preference to privacy default settings', *ACM Transactions on Computer–Human Interaction*, 22(6): Article 32.

Zwitter, A. (2014) 'Big data ethics', *Big Data & Society*, 1(2): 1–6.

CHAPTER 10

Adner, R. and Levinthal, D.A. (2002) 'The emergence of emerging technologies', *California Management Review*, 45(1): 50–66.

Atzori, L., Iera, A. and Morabito, G. (2010) 'The Internet of Things: A survey', *Computer Networks*, 54: 2787–2805.

Atzori, M. (2017) 'Blockchain technology and decentralized governance: Is the state still necessary?', *Journal of Governance and Regulation*, 6(1): 45–62.

Bizer, C. (2009) 'The emerging web of linked data', *Computer: IEEE Intelligent Systems*, Sept/Oct: 87–92.

Botta, A., de Donato, W, Persico, V. and Pescape, A. (2016) 'Integration of cloud computing and Internet of Things: A survey', *Future Generation Computer Systems*, 56: 684–700.

Brock, J. and von Wangenheim, F. (2019) 'Demystifiying AI: What digital transformation can teach you about realistic artificial intelligence', *California Management Review*, 61(4): 110–134.

Caprolu, M., Di Pietro, R., Lombardi, F. and Raponi, S. (2019) 'Edge computing perspectives: Architectures, technologies, and open security issues', in 2019 IEEE International Conference on Edge Computing (EDGE). Milan: IEEE. pp. 116–123.

Chin, W.H., Fan, Z. and Haines, R. (2014) 'Emerging technologies and research challenges for 5G wireless networks', *IEEE Wireless Communications*, 21(2): 106–112.

Christidis, K. and Devetsikiotis, M. (2016) 'Blockchains and smart contracts for the Internet of Things', *IEEE Access*, 4: 2292–2303.

Davenport, T. and Harris, J. (2017) *Competing on Analytics: Updated, with a New Introduction: The New Science of Winning*. Boston, MA: Harvard Business Press.

Davenport, T.H. and Ronanki, R. (2018) 'Artificial intelligence for the real world', *Harvard Business Review*, 96(1): 108–116.

Delen, D. and Demirkan, H. (2013) 'Data, information and analytics as services', *Decision Support Systems*, 55(1): 359–363.

Demirkan, H. and Delen, D. (2013) 'Leveraging the capabilities of service-oriented decision support systems: Putting analytics and big data in cloud', *Decision Support Systems*, 55(1): 412–421.

Dimitrov, D. (2016) 'Medical Internet of Things and big data in healthcare', *Healthcare Informatics Research*, 22(3): 156–163.

Duan, Y., Edwards, J. and Dwivedi, Y. (2019) 'Artificial intelligence for decision-making in the era of big data – Evolution, challenges and research agenda', *International Journal of Information Management*, 48: 63–71.

Ericsson (2019) 'Gearing up for 5G'. Retrieved from: www.ericsson.com/en/5g/what-is-5g (accessed 27 April 2020).

Gartner (2019a) 'Gartner Hype Cycle'. Retrieved from: www.gartner.com/en/research/methodologies/gartner-hype-cycle (accessed 27 April 2020).

Gartner (2019b) Smarter With Gartner '5 Trends Appear on the Gartner Hype Cycle for Emerging Technologies, 2019', 29 August. Available at: https://www.gartner.com/smarterwithgartner/5-trends-appear-on-the-gartner-hype-cycle-for-emerging-technologies-2019/ (accessed 8 July 2020).

Gartner (2020a) Gartner IT Glossary "Analytics." Available at: www.gartner.com/it-glossary/analytics/ (accessed 20 April 2020).

Gartner (2020b) Gartner IT Glossary "Analytics and Business Intelligence (ABI)." Available at: www.gartner.com/it-glossary/business-intelligence-bi/ (accessed 20 April 2020).

Gartner (2020c) Gartner Methodologies "Gartner Hype Cycle." Available at: www.gartner.com/en/research/methodologies/gartner-hype-cycle (accessed 27 April 2020).

Gohil, A., Modi, H. and Patel, S.K. (2013) '5G technology of mobile communication: A survey', in 2013 International Conference on Intelligent Systems and Signal Processing (ISSP). Gujarat: IEEE. pp. 288–292.

Gong, C., Liu, J., Zhang, Q., Chen, H. and Gong, Z. (2010) 'The characteristics of cloud computing', in 2010 39th International Conference on Parallel Processing Workshops. San Diego, CA: IEEE. pp. 275–279.

Halaweh, M. (2013) 'Emerging technology: What is it', *Journal of Technology Management & Innovation*, 8(3): 108–115.

Hebbar, A. (2017) 'Augmented intelligence: Enhancing human capabilities', in 2017 Third International Conference on Research in Computational Intelligence and Communication Networks (ICRCICN). Kolkata: IEEE. pp. 251–254.

Holtel, S. (2016) 'Artificial intelligence creates a wicked problem for the enterprise', *Procedia Computer Science*, 99: 171–180.

Huang, M.H., Rust, R. and Maksimovic, V. (2019) 'The feeling economy: Managing the next generation of artificial intelligence (AI)', *California Management Review*, 61(4): 43–65.

Jadeja, Y. and Modi, K. (2012) 'Cloud computing – concepts, architecture and challenges', in 2012 International Conference on Computing, Electronics and Electrical Technologies (ICCEET). Kumaracoil: IEEE. pp. 877–880.

Jarrahi, M. (2018) 'Artificial intelligence and the future of work: Human–AI symbiosis in organisational decision making', *Business Horizons*, 61(4): 577–586.

Kypriotaki, K., Zamani, E. and Giaglis, G. (2015) 'From bitcoin to decentralized autonomous corporations', in Proceedings of the 17th International Conference on Enterprise Information Systems. pp. 284–290. doi: 10.5220/0005378402840290.

Litjens, G., Kooi, T., Bejnordi, B.E., Setio, A.A.A., Ciompi, F., Ghafoorian, M., van der Laak, J.A.W.M., van Ginneken, B. and Sánchez, C.I. (2017) 'A survey on deep learning in medical image analysis', *Medical Image Analysis*, 42: 60–88.

Mao, Y., You, C., Zhang, J., Huang, K. and Letaief, K.B. (2017) 'A survey on mobile edge computing: The communication perspective', *IEEE Communications Surveys & Tutorials*, 19(4): 2322–2358.

McKendrick, J. (2018) '8 Game-Changing Data Technologies'. Retrieved from: www.dbta.com/Editorial/Think-About-It/8-Game-Changing-Data-Technologies-125503.aspx (accessed 27 April 2020).

Mell, P. and Grance, T. (2011) *The NIST Definition of Cloud Computing: Recommendations of the National Institute of Standards and Technology.* Special Publication 800-145. Retrieved from: https://nvlpubs.nist.gov/nistpubs/Legacy/SP/nistspecialpublication800-145.pdf (accessed 27 April 2020).

Palattella, M.R., Dohler, M., Grieco, A., Rizzo, G., Torsner, J., Engel, T. and Ladid, L. (2016) 'Internet of Things in the 5G era: Enablers, architecture, and business models', *IEEE Journal on Selected Areas in Communications*, 34(3): 510–527.

Pan, Y. (2016) 'Heading towards artificial intelligence 2.0', *Engineering*, 2(4): 409–413.

Rotolo, D., Hicks, D. and Martin, B.R. (2015) 'What is an emerging technology?', *Research Policy*, 44(10): 1827–1843.

Rudman, R. and Bruwer, R. (2016) 'Defining Web 3.0: Opportunities and challenges', *The Electronic Library*, 34(1): 132–154.

Seebacher, S. and Schüritz, R. (2017) 'Blockchain technology as an enabler of service systems: A structured literature review', in International Conference on Exploring Services Science. Cham: Springer. pp. 12–23.

Segan, S. (2019) 'What is 5G?', *PCMag*. Retrieved from: https://au.pcmag.com/cell-phone-service-providers/47717/what-is-5g (accessed 27 April 2020).

Sharma, M. (2019) 'Web 1.0, Web 2.0 and Web 3.0 with their difference'. Retrieved from: www.geeksforgeeks.org/web-1-0-web-2-0-and-web-3-0-with-their-difference/ (accessed 27 April 2020).

Shivalingaiah, D. and Naik, U. (2008) 'Comparative study of Web 1.0, Web 2.0 and Web 3.0'. 6th International CALIBER 2008. doi: 10.13140/2.1.2287.2961.

Sivarajah, U., Kamal, M.M., Irani, Z. and Weerakkody, V. (2017) 'Critical analysis of big data challenges and analytical methods', *Journal of Business Research*, 70: 263–286.

Srinivasan, R. (2008) 'Sources, characteristics and effects of emerging technologies: Research opportunities in innovation', *Industrial Marketing Management*, 37(6): 633–640.

Tambe, P., Capelli, P. and Yakubovich, V. (2019) 'Artificial intelligence in human resources management: Challenges and a path forward', *California Management Review*, 61(4): 15–42.

TODI (2019) 'Types of open standards for data'. Retrieved from: https://standards.theodi. org/introduction/types-of-open-standards-for-data/ (accessed 27 April 2020).

Xin, Y., Kong, L., Liu, Z., Chen, Y., Li, Y., Zhu, H., Gao, M, Hou, H. and Wang, C. (2018) 'Machine learning and deep learning methods for cybersecurity', *IEEE Access*, 6: 35365–35381.

Zheng, Z., Xie, S., Dai, H., Chen, X. and Wang, H. (2017) 'An overview of blockchain technology: Architecture, consensus, and future trends', in 6th IEEE International Congress on Big Data (Big Data Congress 2017). Honolulu, HI: IEEE. pp. 557–564.

GLOSSARY

Barber, R. (2001) 'Hackers profiled – who are they and what are their motivations?', *Computer Fraud & Security*, 2: 14–17.

Botta, A., de Donato, W, Persico, V. and Pescape, A. (2016) 'Integration of cloud computing and Internet of Things: A survey', *Future Generation Computer Systems*, 56: 684–700.

Card, M. (1999) *Readings in Information Visualization: Using Vision to Think*. San Francisco, CA: Morgan Kaufmann.

Christidis, K. and Devetsikiotis, M. (2016) 'Blockchains and smart contracts for the Internet of Things', *IEEE Access*, 4: 2292–2303.

Fayyad, U.M., Piatetsky-Shapiro, G. and Smyth, P. (1996) 'Knowledge discovery and data mining: Towards a unifying framework', *KDD*, 96: 82–88.

Gans, J.S. and Christensen, K. (2019) 'Exploring the impact of artificial intelligence: Prediction versus judgment', *Rotman Management Magazine*, 1 January, 7–11.

Kaa Project (2020) 'What is an IoT platform?'. Retrieved from www.kaaproject.org/what-is-iot-platform (accessed 8 May 2020).

Lee, I. and Lee, K. (2015) 'The Internet of Things (IoT): Applications, investments, and challenges for enterprises', *Business Horizons*, 58(4): 431–440.

Marston, S., Li, Z., Bandyopadhyay, S., Zhang, J. and Ghalsasi, A. (2011) 'Cloud computing: The business perspective', *Decision Support Systems*, 51(1): 176–189.

MathWorks (2019) 'What is machine learning?'. Retrieved from https://au.mathworks. com/discovery/machine-learning.html (accessed 8 May 2020).

McKeon, M. (2009) 'Harnessing the information ecosystem with wiki-based visualization dashboards', *IEEE Transactions on Visualization and Computer Graphics*, 15(6): 1081–1088.

Mell, P. and Grance, T. (2011) *The NIST Definition of Cloud Computing: Recommendations of the National Institute of Standards and Technology*.Special Publication 800-145. Retrieved from: https://nvlpubs.nist.gov/nistpubs/Legacy/SP/nistspecialpublication800-145.pdf (accessed 27 April 2020).

Nilsson, N.J. (1980) *Principles of Artificial Intelligence*. San Francisco, CA: Morgan Kaufmann.

Rudman, R. and Bruwer, R. (2016) 'Defining Web 3.0: Opportunities and challenges', *The Electronic Library*, 34(1): 132–154.

Soni, D. (2018) 'Introduction to Bayesian networks'. Retrieved from: https://towards-datascience.com/introduction-to-bayesian-networks-81031eeed94e (accessed 27 April 2020).

Xin, Y., Kong, L., Liu, Z., Chen, Y., Li, Y., Zhu, H., Gao, M, Hou, H. and Wang, C. (2018) 'Machine learning and deep learning methods for cybersecurity', *IEEE Access*, 6: 35365–35381.

FURTHER READING

CHAPTER 1

Suggested readings complement the material from the chapter by providing further details about managers and the management of technology and information systems, as well as emerging challenges and prospects.

Antoniou, P.H. and Ansoff, H.I. (2004) 'Strategic management of technology', *Technology Analysis & Strategic Management*, 16(2): 275–291.

This article provides additional information about strategic management of technology. It complements the chapter focusing on the role of technology in strategy design. The role of managers in managing technology and integrating technology with strategy is also explained.

Drake, R. and Lake, P. (2014) 'Style', in *Information Systems Management in the Big Data Era*. Cham, Switzerland: Springer. pp. 81–101.

A useful source discussing information systems and management of information systems within the new era of big data. Various organizational factors such as structure, strategy, style, staff, sources, etc. of this era of big data are discussed broadly in the book.

Koc, E. (2018) 'Is there really a skills gap?', *NACE Journal*, 1 February. Retrieved from: www.naceweb.org/talent-acquisition/trends-and-predictions/is-there-really-a-skills-gap/ (accessed 18 April 2020).

This reading discusses whether there is a skills gap in today's business world. Interesting statistical data about job openings and wages are presented. The role of education in relation to the skills is explained.

Kolding, M., Sundblad, M., Alexa, J., Stone, M., Aravopoulou, E. and Evans, G. (2018) 'Information management – a skills gap?', *The Bottom Line*, (31)3/4: 170–190.

This article discusses the skills gap in the current era where big data has been changing many aspects of organizations. The article provides complementary views from an academic perspective. More specifically, the article explains information management and provides useful quotes from various experts that represent the main views about the topic.

McAfee, A. and Brynjolfsson, E. (2012) 'Big data: The management revolution', *Harvard Business Review*, 90(10): 60–66.

This article, written by two very well-known scholars, explains the changes big data brings to management. The authors introduce the topic of data-driven companies, discussed later in the book.

Ogrean, C. (2018) 'Relevance of big data for business and management: Exploratory insights (Part I)', *Studies in Business and Economics*, 13(2): 153–163.

This article provides complementary information about big data and its role and relevance in management. Interesting statistical information is provided for the reader.

Power, D.J. (2016) 'Data science: Supporting decision-making', *Journal of Decision Systems*, 25(4): 345–356.

This article explains the new roles emerging with big data and analytics. The data scientist role is discussed in detail.

CHAPTER 2

Suggested readings provide further details about barriers and prospects of big data. In addition to detailed academic and technical information, various cases provide real-life examples.

Alharthi, A., Krotov, V. and Bowman, M. (2017) 'Addressing barriers to big data', *Business Horizons*, 60(3): 285–292.

This article examines big data implementations in organizations, mainly focusing on the barriers they face. It provides a holistic view about barriers to big data, a resource that is considered strategic to organizations. Barriers are explained from technological, human and organizational perspectives.

Laskowski, N. (2013) 'Ten big data case studies in a nutshell'. Retrieved from: https://searchcio.techtarget.com/opinion/Ten-big-data-case-studies-in-a-nutshell (accessed 18 April 2020).

The article discusses the advantages, prospects, challenges and disadvantages of big data. The main characteristics of big data (3Vs) are expanded (10Vs) and discussed along with the relevant technologies.

Moorthy, J., Lahiri, R., Biswas, N., Sanyal, D., Ranjan, J., Nanath, K. and Ghosh, P. (2015) 'Big data: Prospects and challenges', *Vikalpa*, 40(1): 74–96. doi: 10.1177/0256090915575450.

The reading provides examples of real-world big data cases. Several examples from industry and well-known organizations are provided.

Zeng, J. and Glaister, K.W. (2018) 'Value creation from big data: Looking inside the black box', *Strategic Organization*, 16(2): 105–140. DOI: 10.1177/1476127017697510.

This article provides information on how organizations use and benefit from big data. The value creation from big data is explained from the academic perspective. Interesting quotes from experts provide valuable and practical information about the topic.

CHAPTER 3

Suggested readings provide academic articles for the students interested in more detailed and technical information. Also provided are case studies and business-oriented articles with real-life cases for more practitioner and management-oriented students.

Barton, D. and Court, D. (2012) 'Making advanced analytics work for you', *Harvard Business Review*, 90(10): 78–83.

This article explains how organizations can use and benefit from big data and analytics in simple and practical language for the reader.

Brynjolfsson, E. and McAfee, A. (2017) 'The business of artificial intelligence', *Harvard Business Review*.

Another article from two well-known scholars, simply explaining how AI and machine learning work. The authors provide useful information on how AI can be used by organizations.

Davenport, T.H. (2018) 'From analytics to artificial intelligence', *Journal of Business Analytics*, 1–8.

This article explains the relationship between analytics and artificial intelligence. Different eras of analytics, from Analytics 1.0 to Analytics 4.0, along with analytics capabilities are discussed.

Duarte, N. (2014) 'The quick and dirty on data visualization'. Retrieved from: https://hbr.org/2014/04/the-quick-and-dirty-on-data-visualization (accessed 20 April 2020).

An HBR reading explaining different ways of data visualization that managers greatly rely on for decision-making. This is a useful complementary reading for students to see one of the final stages of analytics that are presented to managers.

Frick, W. (2014) 'An introduction to data-driven decisions for managers who don't like math'. Retrieved from: https://hbr.org/2014/05/an-introduction-to-data-driven-decisions-for-managers-who-dont-like-math (accessed 20 April 2020).

This reading introduces analytics and data-driven decision-making using non-technical terminology.

Gallo, A. (2018) '4 analytics concepts every manager should understand'. Retrieved from: https://hbr.org/2018/10/4-analytics-concepts-every-manager-should-understand (accessed 20 April 2020).

Another HBR article introducing basic and very common analytics concepts in a non-technical way. This article can help non-technical readers to have a better understanding of some of the popular analytics concepts.

Porter, M.E., Davenport, T.H., Daugherty, P. and Wilson, J. (2018) *HBR's 10 Must Reads on AI, Analytics, and the New Machine Age*. Cambridge, MA: Harvard Business Review Press.

A collection of popular readings from HBR explaining the analytics and AI concepts from managerial and non-technical perspectives.

Tim, Y., Hallikainen, P., Pan, S.L. and Tamm, T. (2020) 'Actualizing business analytics for organizational transformation: A case study of Rovio Entertainment', *European Journal of Operational Research*, 281(3): 642–655.

The article discusses business analytics and how successfully adopting analytics transforms organizations. A case study is discussed to provide a real-world example of the topic.

CHAPTER 4

Suggested readings offer students more in-depth academic and theoretical knowledge about the main points of the chapter. A case study from industry contributes to the knowledge of students by providing real-life examples of decision-making.

Chongwatpol, J. (2016) 'Data analysis and decision-making: A case study of re-accommodating passengers for an airline company', *Journal of Information Technology Teaching Cases*, 6(1): 23–35. doi:10.1057/jittc.2015.16.

This article discusses decision-making using business intelligence and data analytics. Decision-making is explained through analysis and real-world examples/cases that provide practical information for the reader.

Intezari, A. and Pauleen, D. (2019) *Wisdom, Analytics and Wicked Problems: Integral Decision-making in the Data Age*. Routledge: London

This book provides detailed information about analytics and related concepts. While the concepts are discussed, connection with managerial decision-making makes the book a very useful complementary source for various chapters.

Jarrahi, M.H. (2018) 'Artificial intelligence and the future of work: Human–AI symbiosis in organizational decision-making', *Business Horizons*, 61(4): 577–586.

This article builds on other suggested readings, as well as the chapter, providing information about decision-making using AI. The implications and impact of AI on humans and work in an organizational context are discussed. It provides a good introduction to different types of decision-making, such as intuitive decision-making, covered in subsequent chapters of this book.

Michel, L. (2007) 'Understanding decision-making in organizations to focus its practices where it matters', *Measuring Business Excellence*, 11(1): 33–45.

The article explains decision-making and good decision-making practices in organizations. An example using a specific tool is demonstrated.

Mintzberg, H. and Westley, F. (2001) 'It's not what you think', *MIT Sloan Management Review*, 42(3): 89–93.

The article, from one of the well-known management experts, explains what decision-making is in the organizational context. It explains how a decision-making approach can be actualized.

CHAPTER 5

Suggested readings bring additional material to complement the information on management decision-making using analytics. They offer interesting perspectives on theoretical and practical aspects of data-driven decision-making.

Akter, S., Bandara, R., Hani, U., Wamba, S.F., Foropon, C. and Papadopoulos, T. (2019) 'Analytics-based decision-making for service systems: A qualitative study and agenda for future research', *International Journal of Information Management*, 48: 85–95.

The article explains analytics-based decision-making.

Anadiotis, G. (2018) 'Business analytics: The essentials of data-driven decision-making'. Retrieved from: www.zdnet.com/article/business-analytics-the-essentials-of-data-driven-decision-making/ (accessed 21 April 2020).

The reading provides information about some analytics tools, types of analytics, data-analytics-related technologies, and recent statistics about the use of data and analytics in organizations. While practical information is explained in non-technical language, predictions about analytics are also made.

Harvard Business Review Analytics Services (2012) *The Evolution of Decision-Making: How Leading Organizations Are Adopting a Data-driven Culture*. Harvard Business Review analytics services report, 2012. Harvard Business School.

A popular report from an industry leader analytics company. Decision-making as well as benefits from using analytics for decision-making are explained and supported with data.

Hopkins, M.S. and Brokaw, L. (2011) 'Matchmaking with math: How analytics beats intuition to win customers', *MIT Sloan Management Review*, 52(2): 35–41. Retrieved from: https://sloanreview.mit.edu/article/matchmaking-with-math-how-analytics-beats-intuition-to-win-customers/ (accessed 21 April 2020).

This article explains data-driven and intuitive decision-making. The authors discuss the argument that analytics might be better than intuition when making decisions about customers.

Kowalczyk, M. and Buxmann, P. (2015) 'An ambidextrous perspective on business intelligence and analytics support in decision processes: Insights from a multiple case study', *Decision Support Systems*, 80: 1–13.

This academic article discusses how business intelligence and analytics are used in decision-making. The impact of use of analytics and intuition on decision quality is discussed. Findings from multiple case studies conducted in various industries are presented to provide rich insights about decision processes.

Salas, E., Rosen, M.A. and DiazGranados, D. (2010) 'Expertise-based intuition and decision-making in organizations', *Journal of Management*, 36(4): 941–973. doi: 10.1177/0149206309350084.

This article provides detailed explanations about intuitive decision-making, the other side of decision-making. It also introduces the main theory, dual process theory, the founding theory adopted in this book.

CHAPTER 6

Suggested readings provide additional sources to better understand the type of managers in organizations. Furthermore, some of the readings provide alternative tools allowing individuals to assess themselves on management types and skills.

'CliftonStrengths'. Retrieved from: www.gallup.com/cliftonstrengths/en/home. aspx (accessed 21 April 2020).

In order to provide more information about the tool presented in the chapter, popular tools from reputable organizations are provided as suggested readings. The online tool from CliftonStrengths is a very popular one helping individuals find out their strengths and potential areas to improve for being better leaders while providing a detailed explanation about the type of manager/leader they are.

Harvard Business Review Analytics Services (2012) *The Evolution of Decision-Making: How Leading Organizations Are Adopting a Data-Driven Culture*. Harvard Business Review analytics services report. Boston, MA: Harvard Business School.

Previously introduced as suggested reading in Chapter 5 as well. A popular report from an industry leader analytics company. Decision-making as well as benefits from using analytics for decision-making are explained and supported with data. The importance of integrating analytics into organizational culture is discussed.

Kiron, D., Prentice, P.K. and Ferguson, R.B. (2014) 'The analytics mandate', *MIT Sloan Management Review*, 55(4): 1–25.

This report, although it can fit into the previous chapter, is recommended in this chapter to refresh the knowledge about using analytics in decision-making. As a report, the reading provides varied practical and descriptive information about the use of analytics as part of decision-making. Then the report explains the importance of embedding analytics into organizational culture, and creating an analytics culture. This should be remembered as a final objective when using the tool given in the chapter.

'What is your management style?' Retrieved from: www.switchmybusiness.com/resources/quiz-whats-your-management-style/ (accessed 21 April 2020).

In order to provide more information about the tool presented in the chapter, popular tools from the reputable organizations are provided as suggested readings. This is another tool that can help managers to identify their management style.

'What type of manager are you?' Retrieved from: www.workfront.com/blog/what-type-of-manager-are-you-find-out-with-this-quiz (accessed 21 April 2020).

In order to provide more information about the tool presented in the chapter, popular tools from the reputable organizations are provided as suggested readings. This tool from Workfront helps managers to identify what type of manager they are.

CHAPTER 7

Suggested readings provide in-depth theoretical and practical information about analytics maturity while presenting different maturity models. They also offer a detailed examination of different levels as shown in the ecological framework, affecting organizational analytics maturity and its impact on management decision-making.

Chen, L. and Nath, R. (2018) 'Business analytics maturity of firms: an examination of the relationships between managerial perception of IT, business analytics maturity and success', *Information Systems Management*, 35(1): 62–77.

A supplementary, very academic-oriented reading about analytics maturity of the firms. The article presents various maturity items that can be used by the readers in their organizations to find out the level of analytics maturity of their organizations.

Comuzzi, M. and Patel, A. (2016) 'How organisations leverage big data: A maturity model', *Industrial Management & Data Systems*, 116(8): 1468–1492.

This article discusses maturity of organizations about big data and big data-enabled analytics. Various maturity models from the literature are explained. This reading develops and presents a maturity model that can be used by the readers in their organizations.

Dremel, C., Overhage, S., Schlauderer, S. and Wulf, J. (2017) 'Towards a capability model for big data analytics'. Paper presented at 13th International Conference on Wirtschaftsinformatik, St. Gallen, Switzerland.

This article complements the other suggested readings and the chapter by presenting a capability model about big data and analytics. The authors present various capability groups and capabilities that readers can familiarize themselves with towards creating an organizational culture where analytics is a natural part of decision-making.

Halper, F. (2017) *TDWI Self-Service Analytics Maturity Model Guide*. Retrieved from: www. microstrategy.com/getmedia/77370952-e99e-4093-b607-76c3204f2c4e/TDWI-Self-Service-Maturity-Model-Guide.pdf (accessed 27 April 2020).

A popular analytics maturity model discussed in detail with all stages, examples and evaluation methods.

Lismont, J., Vanthienen, J., Baesens, B. and Lemahieu, W. (2017) 'Defining analytics maturity indicators: A survey approach', *International Journal of Information Management*, 37(3): 114–124.

Another analytics maturity study using a different approach. This article uses a survey approach for their analytics maturity model. This reading is useful to provide an alternative view for building and interpreting maturity models.

Perera, R. (2017) *The PESTLE Analysis*. Avissawella, LK: Nerdynaut.

This book provides detailed information about PESTLE analysis from various perspectives.

Popovič, A., Hackney, R., Tassabehji, R. and Castelli, M. (2018) 'The impact of big data analytics on firms' high value business performance', *Information Systems Frontiers*, 20(2): 209–222.

This article explains the impact of big data and analytics implementation on organizational performance. Decision-making performance from various perspectives is also explained and compared for before and after analytics implementation.

Unicef (n.d.) 'SWOT and PESTEL'. Retrieved from: www.unicef.org/knowledge-exchange/files/SWOT_and_PESTEL_production.pdf (accessed 27 April 2020).

Practical information by UNICEF about SWOT (Strengths, Weaknesses, Opportunities and Threat) and PESTEL (Political, Economic, Social, Technological, Environmental and Legal) analysis. The reading provides useful information about how these two techniques can be used in a complementary way and also applied in a business context. Various factors of PESTEL are discussed.

Warrick, D.D. (2017) 'What leaders need to know about organizational culture', *Business Horizons*, 60(3): 395–404.

This article talks about organizational culture. As discussed in the chapter, organizations need to make analytics part of their organizational culture. This article is a useful reading since it covers the important aspects of organizational culture and the role of leaders in forming the culture.

CHAPTER 8

Suggested readings provide in depth and complementary information from academic, philosophical and practical points. Readings from different perspectives like these are useful for understanding complex and multidimensional topics like the ones presented in this chapter.

Amankwah-Amoah, J. and Adomako, S. (2019) 'Big data analytics and business failures in data-rich environments: An organizing framework', *Computers in Industry*, 105: 204–212.

This article develops a framework explaining big data analytics capabilities in data-rich environments. Unlike many other articles, this one explains situations where analytics leads to business failure. In that sense, the article provides an interesting perspective about data analytics.

Baesens, B., Bapna, R., Marsden, J.R., Vanthienen, J. and Zhao, J.L. (2016) 'Transformational issues of big data and analytics in networked business', *MIS Quarterly*, 40(4): 807–818.

This article explains organizational transformation from technical and managerial perspectives. The role of data science, and therefore big data and analytics, is discussed in business transformation.

Bürger, O. (2019) 'How to structure a company-wide adoption of big data analytics'. Retrieved from: www.fim-rc.de/Paperbibliothek/Veroeffentlicht/781/wi-781.pdf (accessed 23 April 2020).

This article explains and provides a roadmap for structuring a company-wide adoption of big data analytics to improve innovativeness and decision-making. A case study provides a real-world example of the adoption.

Head, B.W. and Alford, J. (2015) 'Wicked problems: Implications for public policy and management', *Administration & Society*, 47(6): 711–739. doi: 10.1177/0095399713481601.

This article provides a general overview about wicked problems with some common dimensions. Although the article focuses on the policy and management about wicked problems (and strategies for dealing with them), it provides useful insight into solving difficult problems. The article provides complementary information to decision-making from a different perspective for readers interested in the policy side of decision-making.

Nelson, J.R. and Grubesic, T.H. (2019) 'Oil spill modeling: Computational tools, analytical frameworks, and emerging technologies', *Progress in Physical Geography: Earth and Environment*, 43(1): 129–143. doi: 10.1177/0309133318804977.

This article explains oil spill modelling based on the Deepwater Horizon incident. While there is some discussion about tools and analytical frameworks used in this case, discussion about the technologies provides a connection to Chapter 10, where emerging technologies are discussed.

Turnbull, N. and Hoppe, R. (2019) 'Problematizing "wickedness": A critique of the wicked problems concept, from philosophy to practice', *Policy and Society*, 38(2): 315–337.

This article provides supplementary information about wicked problems. This concept is explained from both philosophical and practical perspectives for the curious readers.

van Leent, R. (2020) 'Solving wicked problems with predictive analytics'. Retrieved from: www.digitalistmag.com/improving-lives/2018/06/07/solving-wicked-problems-with-predictive-analytics-06171703 (accessed 23 April 2020).

This reading explains wicked problems and how analytics can be used to solve wicked problems. It is an interesting complementary reading about a data-driven approach for tackling wicked problems.

Wright, G., Cairns, G., O'Brien, F.A. and Goodwin, P. (2019) 'Scenario analysis to support decision-making in addressing wicked problems: Pitfalls and potential', *European Journal of Operational Research*, 278(1): 3–19.

The article explains strategic decision-making and wicked problems. It provides details of a technical approach for tackling wicked problems.

CHAPTER 9

Suggested readings provide additional material on this very popular and dynamic topic about ethics, cybersecurity, and privacy. While some readings discuss the topic from academic perspectives, some discuss social and policy issues about the topic. Additional web sources to provide up-to-date information from practitioners are also included in the list of readings.

Barlow, C. (2016) 'Who are the hackers?', TED Talk. Retrieved from: www.ted.com/playlists/10/who_are_the_hackers (accessed 24 April 2020).

Famous TED talks explaining hackers and various other topics.

Computer World, for latest news on issues dealing with security issues and computer issues in general – www.computerworld.com (accessed 24 April 2020).

Various readings on computer and security issues.

Culnan, M.J. (2019) 'Policy to avoid a privacy disaster', *Journal of the Association for Information Systems*, 20(6): 854–862.

This article contributes to the chapter by providing a deeper academic view about privacy. While the reading provides information on how to avoid privacy problems, it discusses the new challenges to privacy with the emergence of big data. A case study provides a real-world example of privacy issues.

Electronic Frontier Foundation – www.eff.org (accessed 24 April 2020).

A good source of recent readings about digital privacy and security.

Ethical Hacker Network – www.ethicalhacker.net/ (accessed 24 April 2020).

A link to various readings and a learning environment about ethical hacking.

Hacker Community – www.hackerone.com/start-hacking (accessed 24 April 2020).

A practical link about hacking. The link provides training material for hacking. Readers can get detailed information about hacking and learn various techniques.

Martin, K. and Murphy, P. (2017) 'The role of data privacy in marketing', *Journal of the Academy of Marketing Science*, 45(2): 135–155.

This article explains the role of data and information privacy in the domain of marketing. Specific discussions about the global perspective on privacy, ethics, psychology and economics of privacy in the age of big data provide deeper discussion on the topic.

Matthews, J. and Goerzen, M. (2019) 'Black hat trolling, white hat trolling, and hacking the attention landscape', in Companion Proceedings of the 2019 World Wide Web Conference. New York: Association for Computing Machinery. pp. 523–528.

This article provides complementary information about different types of hackers and techniques they use for hacking. In particular, the definitions provided in the paper will be useful to the readers.

Parenty, T.J. and Domet, J.J. (2019) 'Sizing up your cyberrisks', *Harvard Business Review*, 97(6): 102–109.

This article discusses cyber risk as well as organization-wide solutions to cyber threats. Supplementary information about how cyber attacks occur, and consequences of attacks, is provided.

Yampolskiy, R.V. (2017) 'AI is the future of cybersecurity, for better and for worse', *Harvard Business Review*, 8 May.

This article explains cybersecurity with the focus on AI. The authors discuss the role of AI in cybersecurity from different perspectives.

CHAPTER 10

Suggested readings below provide detailed explanations on selected emerging technologies mentioned in the chapter. Some articles explain the impact of AI on decision-making in organizations. Both academic and practitioner sides of the technologies are covered by examples in these readings.

Davenport, T.H. and Kirby, J. (2015) 'Beyond automation', *Harvard Business Review*, 93(6): 58–65.

This article discusses an emerging technology, augmentation, in detail. Context-wise, this reading revisits Chapter 1 material about the mindset, roles and skills and integrates it with an emerging technology.

Davenport, T.H. and Ronanki, R. (2018) 'Artificial intelligence for the real world', *Harvard Business Review*, 96(1): 108–116.

This reading provides supplementary material about AI, an emerging technology. Davenport and Ronanki explain different types of AI and how businesses can benefit from AI.

Gans, J.S. and Christensen, K. (2019) 'Exploring the impact of artificial intelligence: Prediction versus judgment', *Rotman Management Magazine*, 1 January, 7–11.

An interesting article discussing the role of AI and judgment in decision-making. A discussion on judgment provides complementary information to intuitive decision-making discussed in earlier chapters of the book.

Haenlein, M. and Kaplan, A. (2019) 'A brief history of artificial intelligence: On the past, present, and future of artificial intelligence', *California Management Review*, 61(4): 5–14. doi: 10.1177/0008125619864925.

A detailed look into AI. The past, present and future of AI are discussed in the article. Students can read this article to gain sufficient background on the topic.

Kaplan, A. and Haenlein, M. (2019) 'Siri, Siri, in my hand: who's the fairest in the land? On the interpretations, illustrations, and implications of artificial intelligence', *Business Horizons*, 62(1): 15–25.

This article provides information about AI and different types of AI in a complementary way to the chapter. Potential as well as risks associated with AI are discussed through some cases.

Metcalf, L., Askay, D.A. and Rosenberg, L.B. (2019) 'Keeping humans in the loop: Pooling knowledge through artificial swarm intelligence to improve business decision-making', *California Management Review*, 61(4): 84–109. doi: 10.1177/0008125619862256.

This article discusses AI and its role and use in decision-making. It provides information about the role of humans along with the developments of AI for decision-making. Therefore, it provides an interesting angle to the discussion about decision-making in the future when AI is more advanced, along with the role of humans.

Power, B. (2017) 'How Harley-Davidson used artificial intelligence to increase New York sales leads by 2,930%', *Harvard Business Review*, 30 May.

This article demonstrates use of AI by a company. The impact of using AI on the company, which all of us are probably familiar with, is discussed.

Ransbotham, S., Kiron, D., Gerbert, P. and Reeves, M. (2017) 'Reshaping business with artificial intelligence: Closing the gap between ambition and action', Research Report, *MIT Sloan Management Review* and the Boston Consulting Group, September: 1–18.

This report discusses and compares information from executives, managers, analysts as well as information technologist about expectations. This is an interesting complementary reading showing the gap between the perception about, understanding, and expectation from AI and what organizations really do with AI.

Saarikko, T., Westergren, U.H. and Blomquist, T. (2017) 'The Internet of Things: Are you ready for what's coming?', *Business Horizons*, 60(5): 667–676.

This article provides detailed information about IoT, an emerging technology. Several issues about IoT (i.e. technology, business applications, data ownership, etc.) as well as solutions to IoT issues are explained through a case.

Shrestha, Y.R., Ben-Menahem, S.M. and Von Krogh, G. (2019) 'Organizational decision-making structures in the age of artificial intelligence', *California Management Review*, 61(4): 66–83. doi: 10.1177/0008125619862257.

This article complements the discussion about decision-making using AI. Interaction of humans and AI are discussed regarding decision-making.

Tambe, P., Cappelli, P. and Yakubovich, V. (2019) 'Artificial intelligence in human resources management: Challenges and a path forward', *California Management Review*, 61(4): 15–42. doi: 10.1177/0008125619867910.

The role of AI in the HR domain is explained. Potential challenges as well as HR operations using AI are discussed.

Wilson, H.J. and Daugherty, P.R. (2018) 'Collaborative intelligence: Humans and AI are joining forces', *Harvard Business Review*, 96(4): 114–123.

An interesting reading explaining human–machine collaboration in organizations. The impact of AI and its collaboration with human on various aspects is discussed.

INDEX

Page numbers in *italics* refer to figures; page numbers in **bold** refer to tables.

9 781526 492005